LUTHER AND THE DAWN
OF THE
MODERN ERA

STUDIES IN THE HISTORY
OF
CHRISTIAN THOUGHT

EDITED BY

HEIKO A. OBERMAN, Tübingen

IN COOPERATION WITH

HENRY CHADWICK, Oxford
EDWARD A. DOWEY, Princeton, N.J.
JAROSLAV PELIKAN, New Haven, Conn.
BRIAN TIERNEY, Ithaca, N.Y.
E. DAVID WILLIS, San Anselmo, Cal.

VOLUME VIII

LUTHER AND THE DAWN
OF
THE MODERN ERA

LEIDEN
E. J. BRILL
1974

LUTHER AND THE DAWN
OF
THE MODERN ERA

PAPERS FOR
THE FOURTH INTERNATIONAL CONGRESS
FOR LUTHER RESEARCH

EDITED BY

HEIKO A. OBERMAN

LEIDEN
E. J. BRILL
1974

ISBN 90 04 03947 3

CARL MEYER †

WILLEM F. KOOIMAN †

EDITOR'S PREFACE

Carl S. Meyer, scholar and editor, is especially remembered by many as the personification of the Concordia Seminary welcome extended to the international company of Luther scholars who gathered in St. Louis in the late summer of 1971. Unfortunately, his untimely death prevented his taking responsibility for the complex task of supervising, according to the standards envisioned by him, the publication of the papers presented at the Fourth International Congress for Luther Research.

In order to avoid a further loss of time which threatened to bring the date of this publication too close to the next Congress in 1977, I preferred to proceed as speedily as possible and thus to have only the most disturbing inconsistencies removed. Furthermore, in this way the flavor of oral delivery present in each paper is maintained.

Within these limits, Miss Marilyn Harran, candidate for the Ph.D. degree in the Department of Religious Studies at Stanford University, undertook the taxing task of seeing this manuscript through the press.

Without the support of the Lutheran World Federation, this edition in the series "Studies in the History of Christian Thought" would have been financially impossible.

This volume is dedicated to the memory of two men : Carl Meyer, American Luther scholar and Congress host in St. Louis, and Willem F. Kooiman, Dutch Luther scholar and *spiritus rector* of the three preceding Congresses.

Tübingen, Easter 1974   Heiko A. OBERMAN

CONTENTS

FOREWORD

The Fourth International Congress for Luther Research, held in Saint Louis, Missouri, August 22-27, 1971, was an event both in the history of Reformation scholarship and in the history of American intellectual life. It brought together scholars from many countries for mutual exchange and discussion, and it provided a forum for co-operative inquiry by theologians of various confessional traditions. Thus it represented the continuing development of Luther research as a field of historical and theological investigation in its own right, as well as the broader enterprise of critical analysis and reflection upon the persistent issues raised by the faith and thought of Martin Luther.

The theme of the Congress, "Luther and the Dawn of the Modern Era (Luther und die Neuzeit)," united these several concerns. From this theme came several major areas of study, the results of which are set forth in this volume. The essays and lectures printed here may each be read independently, as a learned interpretation by a scholar of international standing who has summarized here the results of ongoing research; as such, they provide a useful *Forschungsbericht* on the present state of our knowledge about the several historical questions involved. They are also, however, part of a larger whole. Believing as most of them do that the only way to a trustworthy synthesis is through precise analysis, the authors of these lectures have combined a careful and even a meticulous *explication de texte* with a consideration of the larger—and perforce more speculative—issues of how the Reformation does (and does not) bring about the rise of the modern epoch of Western history.

In one very important sense, the reader of this volume will be unable to share in the educational experience of the Congress. A large part of the time during the crowded days of our meeting was devoted to seminars on a variety of topics related to the general theme. Here the members of the Congress examined pertinent texts from Luther himself and from other authors (Augustine, Aquinas, Karlstadt, to name only a few) whose thought is pertinent to an assessment of Luther's place in intellectual history. The literary deposit of these seminars cannot be presented in such a volume as this, for it will become evident only in the individual productions of the members of the several groups, many of whom have testified that their publications in the future will be different for their having been participants in the Congress and in its seminars.

As the fourth of the Congresses for Luther Research, the meeting in Saint Louis followed earlier ones in Aarhus, Denmark; Münster, Germany, and Järvenpää, Finland. Those of us who have been members of the Congresses from the beginning can document the account of their evolution from 1956 to the present. At our first meeting, a decade after the end of World War II, "Bücher wurden Menschen," as names previously known to us only from our bibliographies now became acquaintances and even friends. By now the Congress has acquired an identity of its own, more international and certainly more ecumenical than it had originally been, but also more committed than ever to the scholarly study of Luther.

The Congress in Saint Louis would not have gone as it did had it not been for the dedication and energy of Carl S. Meyer. As Executive Director of the Foundation for Reformation Research, which acted as host for the Congress, Professor Meyer spent many hours in preparing for the Congress and helping to make it a success. His belief in historical scholarship and his integrity as a Christian gentleman were in evidence, quietly and unobtrusively, throughout the Congress. It was a loss for his many friends and for the scholarly cause when Carl Meyer died on December 17, 1972. Thus the appearance of this volume is also a tribute to his memory.

JAROSLAV PELIKAN, President
Fourth International
Congress of Luther Research

ABBREVIATIONS

ARG   *Archiv für Reformationsgeschichte.*

CR   *Corpus Reformatorum* (Halle, 1834ff.).

LW   *Luther's Works* (American edition; Philadelphia and St. Louis, 1955ff.).

NZST   *Neue Zeitschrift für Systematische Theologie und Religionsphilosophie.*

RGG   *Religion in Geschichte und Gegenwart* (3rd ed.; Tübingen, 1957).

WA   *D. Martin Luthers Werke : Kritische Gesamtausgabe* (Weimar, 1883ff.).

WA, Br   *D. Martin Luthers Briefwechsel* (Weimar, 1930ff.).

WA, Tr   *D. Martin Luthers Werke: Tischreden* (Weimar, 1912ff.).

LUTHER COMES TO THE NEW WORLD

Jaroslav Pelikan

Four hundred fifty years ago, in April 1521, Martin Luther stood
before the assembled authorities at the Diet of Worms, including Emperor Charles V, and declared (whatever his exact words may have been)
that, with the help of God, he could not do otherwise, since it was
neither safe nor honest to act against conscience. In that same month,
halfway around the world in the Philippine Islands, a violent death
came to Ferdinand Magellan, the Portuguese navigator who had, under
the sponsorship of Emperor Charles V, carried out what Samuel Eliot
Morison has recently called "the greatest recorded voyage of all time"
to discover the Pacific. The historical coincidence of these two events
prompts the question : Which of these was the real discoverer of the
New World, Luther or Magellan ?

That all depends, of course, on what one means by the equivocal
phrase, "the New World." We use the phrase, it seems to me, in at
least two distinct senses. *The Random House Dictionary of the English
Language,* [1] under the entry "New World" simply lists the cross-
reference : "See Western Hemisphere." But "New World" is also
sometimes used to identify what we in this Congress are calling "the
modern era", *die Neuzeit,* which refers to the complex of attitudes and
ideas associated with science, technology, secularity, and democracy.
Because much of this complex, though by no means all of it, has developed here in America, we sometimes identify (or confuse) the two
meanings of "New World," with rather distressing consequences. Now
Luther's relation to the New World defined as "the modern era" is the
master theme of this Fourth International Congress for Luther
Research, on which, beginning with Professor Ebeling's opening
lecture of yesterday afternoon, colleagues from several countries have
been and will be addressing us. In this lecture I propose to discuss
Luther's relation to the New World defined as the Western Hemisphere, more specifically as the United States.

Luther was, of course, aware, as were most of his informed European

---

[1] *The Random House Dictionary of the English Language* (1st ed. ; New York, 1966),
p. 964.

1

contemporaries, that the New World was being discovered during his time. He mentioned it several times in his writings, usually in rather vague terms. Thus a reference in 1522 to the "islands" which had recently been discovered became the occasion for one of his relatively infrequent comments on the program of Christian missions. Yet, although he knew of the discoveries, Luther continued to consult one or another of the recensions of the maps of "Ptolemy" all his life as an authority in matters geographical and, more importantly, to look upon the rest of the world from a European perspective. Nevertheless, Luther and the New World were intertwined in their fates almost from the beginning. Various Catholic monarchs and church leaders regarded the opening up of the New World as a providential means to recoup, through discovery, conquest, conversion, and colonization, the losses brought about by Luther and the Reformation. For their part, Protestant spokesmen invoked the same Providence to account for the chronological simultaneity of discovery and Reformation : God had made this new and unspoiled land available as a place for the old and unspoiled truth of the gospel to take root.

Luther came to this New World quite early, presumably in the bookcases of New England clergy during the first part of the seventeenth century. For many of his works had been translated into English by this time; and the Puritan divines—some of whom could, to be sure, read him in Latin if not also in German—quoted him in writings and addresses. For example, an early president of Harvard University, Urian Oakes, invoked Luther's authority in a Latin address of 1675 to prove the close relation between theology and the liberal arts. During the eighteenth century Luther came to the New World in another way, when the Henkel Press in Newmarket, Virginia, published some of his works. A century later it was here in Saint Louis that, beginning at the same time as the monumental Weimar Edition of Luther in Germany, the first attempt at a comprehensive American edition of Luther's collected writings was launched, a thoroughly revised version of the old edition of Walch. Early in the twentieth century J.N. Lenker published thirteen volumes of Luther in English, and a few years later came the Philadelphia (or Holman) Edition. And then in 1955 there was begun the American Edition of *Luther's Works*, which has, I believe, already put more of Luther into English than had ever been translated before into any language other than his own.

In one sense, then, Luther may be said to have been coming to the New World for a long time. Yet this international conclave of scholars must surely represent a new chapter in the history of Luther's coming to the New World, and one whose implications for the understanding both of Luther and of the New World must not be neglected. Two generations ago there was published a fanciful book entitled *Little Journeys with Martin Luther*,[1] in which the American replica of the Worms statue of Luther from 14th Street and Massachusetts Avenue in Washington came to life and Martin Luther stalked the United States in search of a place where his teaching was still alive—and, predictably, found none. Not even Saint Louis qualified; for here there was a theologian who "was so overanxious to walk erect that he leaned backward—an attitude which all the Missouri ckergymen assume in the realm of doctrine, for these good people make such a gigantic effort to be truly orthodox that most of them lean the wrong way." Although the satire is a trifle heavy-footed and the moral of the story rather obvious, the idea behir d *Little Journeys with Martin Luther* bears further consideration as Luther comes to the New World in this Congress. Having had something to do both with the Congress and with the American Edition of his *Works*, I may perhaps claim the right to ponder out loud over the possible contributions that Luther's coming can bring to the New World, but also over those that the New World can bring to Luther and his heritage.

What can Luther's coming mean to the New World? "Much every way," as Luther's favorite apostle said. It can, in the first place, contribute to a recovery of the meaning and mystery of the creation. This crisis of the American physical environment has vividly shown us, and the critiques of the American student generation have stridently reminded us, that there is something fundamentally askew in the attitude Americans take toward the created world of nature. They regard it as an enemy to be vanquished rather than as a fellow creature to be cherished and cooperated with. Whatever the other ideological sources of this attitude may be, American religion cannot escape responsibility for helping to bring it about, or at any rate for helping to provide it with a rationale. The evangelical Christianity in which America has been reared stressed the centrality of salvation in a manner which my late colleague, H. Richard Niebuhr, used to call a unitarianism of the Second Person, with the result that a "commitment to Christ" did not change one's relation to the world of plants and animals, rivers and lakes, seedtime and harvest. At the same time, the advancement of

---

[1] Brother John [W. N. Harley], *Little Journeys with Martin Luther* (Columbus, Ohio, 1916), p. 227.

man's understanding of the creation had to contend, at almost every step, with the resistance of the theologians, who claimed to know from the sources of revelation what the nature and the origins of the universe are. And now the blasphemous separation between the realm of nature and the realm of grace has begun to take its revenge.

If the insights of Luther could be brought into this issue, both the cosmological and theological perspectives would look different. As one of the founding fathers of this Congress put it :

> Luther's religious faith also embraced a picture of the world, the picture found in the Bible.... But in the clumsier hands of his successors and fused by Melanchthon with the Aristotelian system of science, this picture became the antithesis of the new picture of nature.

And therefore, continues this same scholar :

> Until far into modern times an uncertainty and indecision devoid of the magnificent freedom once displayed by Luther prevailed in Protestant thinking on questions of nature. His rich bequest to posterity has been dissipated. And when the modern view of nature insistently rapped at the church's and at theology's door for admittance, there was no one who ventured to reach for the treasure that lay at hand in Luther's views for a true approach to the modern concept.[1]

At the heart of this "treasure" is the art which Luther learned and practiced, that of acknowledging the centrality of Christ in such a way that thanksgiving for the mystery and power of creation is not excluded, but hallowed. In the Psalms he found "a kind of liturgy for such thanksgiving, where the sun, the moon, the stars, the fish, and the dragons are commanded to praise the Lord." In these words "Luther catches the vision of man at worship surrounded not only by the saints and the angels, but by all his fellow creatures. They share his glory." Only by the recovery of such a vision can the Christian doctrine of God be addressed to the contemporary understanding of the world, and only by such a vision can the zeal for nature among the young be rescued from the sentimentality and subsequent cynicism that will so easily beset it.

When Luther comes to the New World, he brings with him a definition of the corporate character of human existence which nevertheless respects the human person. Both within the churches and in our society as a whole, the antithesis of individual and collective has assumed imposing proportions. Entire political campaigns have been mounted on

---

[1] Heinrich Bornkamm, *Luthers geistige Welt* (2nd ed.; Gütersloh, 1953), p. 200, p. 217 (English translation by Martin H. Bertram, *Luther's World of Thought* [Saint Louis, 1958], p. 177, p. 194).

the basis of this antithesis, with the American way of life usually being
identified as one of concern for the individual (or at least for some individuals). In Christian denominations, too, the once proud title "evangelical" has come to mean "individualistic", so that the salvation of
the individual, usually only of his soul, has been taken to be the
responsibility of the church and the object of the gospel, while the collective entities of human society have been thought of as nothing more
than an assemblage of individuals. If, therefore, one can transform the
hearts of the individuals, one can transform the world. Men are to be
saved one at a time, and neither racial injustice nor economic deprivation nor international disorder should be the concern of the church
except when and insofar as it is related to the moral inwardness of the
individual. Such an attitude is, to be sure, easy to caricature, but the
worst caricatures of it have, alas, come from its advocates, and they
still do. If recent polls are any indication, an impressive percentage
of those who identify themselves with the name and heritage of Martin
Luther would take this to be a fair application of his teachings to contemporary life.

Now there is in Luther a profoundly "individualistic" perspective.
As he never tired of saying, a man must do his own believing as he
does his own dying. In his own experience as a believer, as a doubter,
and as a Reformer, he had known the solitariness of one upon whom
the call of God had fallen. About the Diet of Worms, whose anniversary
we commemorate, he said that there he was the church. Above all,
in his moments of *Anfechtung*, of attack and temptation, he knew what
it meant to be cut off from all help in earth or heaven and to stand alone
in the presence of the Holy. He knew also that each man must be held
to account for his life, and that no effort to pass the buck to other cul-
prits would exonerate a man of his accountability. Perhaps no Western
theologian between St. Augustine and Søren Kierkegaard spoke as profoundly about the individual before God as did Martin Luther.

But he always embedded his understanding of the individual in an
even more comprehensive understanding of the corporate. A man must
do his own believing as he must do his own dying; but when he believes,
as when he dies, he is surrounded by a cloud of witnesses. Although it is
often maintained by Protestant and by American historians that the
Reformation rescued the individual from the church, Luther's boast was
the opposite : that, as a result of his reformatory teaching, "thank God,
a seven-year-old child knows what the church is, namely, holy believers
and sheep who hear the voice of their Shepherd." The Reformation

brought about a recovery of the sense of the corporate, not only in the Christian life, but in life as such. Luther insisted that his work had made possible a new view of the corporate, accompanied by a profound respect for the human person. Luther managed to transcend the conventional antithesis between individual and collective, asserting simultaneously that a person had no merit in the sight of God but must have respect in the sight of men. If my reading of contemporary American life is at all accurate, we need ways of achieving a similar insight. It is my hope and earnest prayer that it will come soon, that it will come at least in part from the churches, and that Luther's arrival in the New World may help to bring it about.

When Luther comes to the New World, he brings to it an affirmation of the will of the Creator for the common life that nevertheless admits its ambiguity and avoids the snares of "the rule of the saints". More perhaps than any other thinker of our time, Reinhold Niebuhr recognized "the irony of American history" in its constant espousal of a moralistic position, combined with its persistent resort to tactics of oppression as a way of achieving the kingdom of God on earth. George Kennan has applied Niebuhr's insights to the complexities of American foreign affairs in a devastating critique of the incurable American propensity for identifying its international and national purpose with the will of God. In private matters, too, American moralism has sought to regulate conduct with a precision about right and wrong that has prescribed the details of personal morality in various areas of human existence—most of all in sex, least of all in economics—with a consummate assurance. The tragicomic history of the prohibition of alcohol by law, indeed by constitutional amendment, is perhaps the most flagrant recent instance of this moralism. And in many ways the current repudiation of bourgeois morality by a supposedly liberated generation participates in the very rigidity it claims to reject.

What both sides of the generation gap need is what Luther's doctrine of justification was intended to supply. Among the various of Luther's works which it has been my privilege not only to edit, but to translate, for the American Edition have been his "Commentary on the Sermon on the Mount" of 1530-1532, his "Lectures on Galatians" of 1535, and his "Notes on Ecclesiastes" of 1526. Each of these articulated the meaning of justification over against the false alternatives of his time—and of ours. In opposition to the choice usually drawn between objectivity and subjectivity, Luther asserted in the Lectures on Galatians :

> This is the reason why our theology is certain: it snatches us away from ourselves and places us outside ourselves, so that we do not depend on our own strength, conscience, experience, person, or works but depend on that which is outside ourselves, that is on the promise and truth of God, which cannot deceive.[1]

The fixed point of man's life, therefore, was not his own moral achievement, or lack of it, but the utterly reliable mercy of a God who does not lie. In man's own conduct, meanwhile, the best that was attainable was not a "mathematical point" of moral precision, but a "physical point" at which one approximated, amid the ambiguities of our history, the true meaning of obedience to the will of God under the unsymmetrical cross of Christ. "The rule of the saints" could not be trusted to bring about such obedience, as Luther remembered all too well from his monastic days. Even in the civil realm, the true saints—viz., those who lived by the jagged mercy of forgiveness rather than by their own moral pretensions—were not necessarily the best equipped to regulate the affairs of men. In some ways the best government in Europe was that of the Turk, with its speedy justice and its sense of equity. Not the law of the Bible in either Testament, but the rule of reason and the application of common sense and collective experience could be relied upon to achieve a just social order. Thus, as Luther learned and as America must soon discover, the road to morality is not the road of moralism. To the contrary, only when man's ultimate destiny does not depend on his moral rectitude can he be free to make mistakes, to pursue and to achieve justice—or, at any rate, as much justice as can be reached under the conditions of human existence.

Thus a sober reading of the cleavages within American thought and life today would lead to the conclusion that Luther's coming to the New World can bring enormous benefits. But the benefits are not all in one direction. There is also much in this situation that could deepen, improve, and even (if I may be permitted to say so to this audience) correct Luther's teaching. Let me mention only three areas where this seems both necessary and possible. The first is the understanding and appreciation of other Christian traditions. When Luther comes to the New World, one result is the discovery that the left wing of the Reformation, *Schwärmer* for whom he had such contempt, have done much to preserve and to advance the Christian gospel. To cite merely one area among many, it was not primarily the theological descendants of

---

[1] Jaroslav Pelikan, "Luther and the Liturgy" in Jaroslav Pelikan, Regin Prenter and Herman A. Preus, *More about Luther* (Decorah, Iowa, 1958), pp. 21-22.

Luther, but those of the "heavenly prophets," as well as of Zwingli,
Bucer, and Calvin, who took upon themselves the responsibility of
preaching the gospel to all mankind. It was not the defenders of the
Lutheran doctrine of the inspiration of the Bible, but the *Schwärmer*,
who had the Bible translated into the tongues of the nations and dis-
tributed to the ends of the earth. Luther would, I suspect, be surprised
to discover the profound Christian vigor of those whom he tended to
dismiss in so condescending a way.

Nor is the left wing of the Reformation the only version of Christianity
whose American experience would be a corrective to Luther. The
United States is one place where representatives of each of the major
Reformation groups have the opportunity today for continuing and
furthering significant exchange with one another and with spokesmen
for large communities of both the Roman Catholic and the Eastern
Orthodox traditions—as well as with interpreters of Judaism (of which
more in a moment). What Roman Catholicism has learned and is learning in America has helped to revise its views on religious liberty in a way
that stands as a corrective not only on the Middle Ages but also on the
Reformation. Moreover, as the coming of our Roman Catholic colleagues
into this Congress has served to remind us, a confrontation between
Luther and Thomas Aquinas can help to correct the almost incurable
tendency of Luther's theological descendants in America to minimize
the place of the critical intellect in the service of God. From his nominalist heritage Luther did bring, it seems to me, a well-founded suspicion
of the pretensions of the reason to understand the mysteries of God;
but this suspicion could easily degenerate into a hostility to the life of
the mind.

As for Eastern theology, I may begin by quoting Luther's own rather
overenthusiastic words of 1520 : "The Muscovites, the White Russians,
the Greeks, the Bohemians...—all of them believe like us, baptize
like us, preach like us, live like us." Whatever validity these words may
have as an effort at confessional cartography, they do express an intui-
tion that has reappeared from time : that some of the solutions for the
debates between Luther and Roman Catholicism must come from
beyond Western Latin Christendom altogether. Protestantism and
Lutheranism, also in the United States, have manifested a continuing
inclination to isolate the authority and the interpretation of the Bible
from the tradition of the teaching and worship of the church, either by
absolutizing the Bible as somehow suspended from the historical process
or by losing it in the cultural-religious history of the Near East. Beyond

both of these, Eastern Christianity has located the authority of the
Bible in the context of the teaching and praying church, thus enabling
the theologian simultaneously to define its uniqueness and to affirm its
participation in history. And it is only here in the New World that
Luther's theology can meet all of these Christian options simultaneously
in a vigorous and challenging form.

Even more apparent is this need if one adds to the partners of such
a discussion the ancient people of God. I have read—and, indeed, I have
sometimes repeated—most of the conventional defenses of Luther's
harsh language about the Jews: his disappointment that they did not
accept the gospel now that it had been brought to light, his recognition
of the difference between the believers of the Old Testament and the
Jews after Christ, his indignation at the distortions of the Bible by rab-
binical interpreters, and the like. Without minimizing the seriousness
of any of these considerations, I cannot escape the conviction that the
time has come for those who study Luther and admire him to acknowledge, more unequivocally and less pugnaciously than they have, that
on this issue Luther's thought and language are simply beyond defense.
But any such acknowledgement must be based, theologically, on a much
more fundamental conviction, namely, that Judaism is not, as Luther
and the centuries before him maintained, a "shadow" destined to dis-
appear with the coming of Christianity even though it stubbornly held
on to its existence, but a permanent part of the wondrous dispensation
of God in human history. I do not pretend to know with any finality
what this implies for the Christian view of revelation, or for the Christian
doctrine of Jesus Christ. But I am sure that this generation of Christians and Jews is obliged to look again at the issues that divide them.
Christians cannot evade the problem of the continuing validity and
unique witness of Israel, and Jews cannot continue to treat as a mere
upstart a movement that embodies some of the central insights of the
Hebrew Bible. And if this is so, then today it will have to be here in the
New World that the two confront each other : a new Judaism, chastened
by the holocaust and revived by a new entry into the promised land ;
and a Christianity, hopefully also chastened and revived by these enormous historical realities, a Christianity in which the voice of Luther is
both compelled and privileged to speak with special fervor.

There is at least one more benefit that Luther can derive from the
New World : a greater trust in the people. Here again the apologies
for Luther's stand in the Peasants' War of 1525 make a lot of sense—at
least on one level. He did stand for justice to the common people, and he

did believe that the legal and political structures of the time could be used as an expression for the grievances of the people. With Edmund Burke and with many of us, he did believe that revolution often brings on greater evils than it abolishes : Stalin was worse than the Czars. Having said all of this, however, one must go on to say that Luther would have been able to learn something from the modern experiment in government by the people, both here in America and in many other lands, including some of the lands that stand most closely in his own spiritual succession. The fear of anarchy is valid, but it must be counterbalanced by the fear of tyranny and by the recognition that the people can do something about abolishing tyranny without necessarily relapsing into either anarchy or an even more oppressive tyranny. All of this we have begun to learn in the ninetheenth and twentieth centuries, thanks in part and quite indirectly to Luther; and all of this Luther and his tradition can learn by coming to a New World in which, despite all the political and moral ambiguities of which Luther spoke so profoundly, the people have nevertheless learned some of the art of ruling themselves and are learning more of it even now.

Thus it is not to bury Luther, nor to praise him, that we gather here at this Congress. It is to understand him and, if possible, to confront him with the New World, and the New World with Martin Luther. A generation ago, during the Nazi time, a German Luther scholar said it very well :

> Will a book about Luther still find some interest ? I hope so, for I believe that in Luther's theology there are hidden those dynamics which can make even the religious crisis of the present fruitful in a positive way. One must only give up the stylized Luther and learn to see the real Luther. Even then we cannot and should not repristinate him, but we want his power and blood to flow from him into our life of faith. We do not want any "Luther renaissance." What we need is a Luther revolution !

We still do.

LUTHER AND THE BEGINNING OF THE MODERN AGE *

GERHARD EBELING

I. Towards the History of the Problem

1. *Interpretation in the Manner of Salvation History*

In his lectures on the philosophy of history Hegel calls the Reformation "the all-illuminating sun, which follows that day-break at the end of the Middle Ages." [1] This metaphor of the dawning day to which the night gives way has a long history as an expression for a decided break in history.[2] Here the picture is recalled only as an allusion and only in so far as it affects an understanding of the Reformation.

In the age of the Reformation and of Orthodoxy an ever recurring theme of the Protestant understanding of the Reformation event is that after a time of Egyptian darkness the light of the gospel arose again through Luther's word and deed.[3] For that matter, this picture can also

---

* Published in : *Zeitschrift für Theologie und Kirche* 69, 1972, 185-213 ("Luther und der Anbruch der Neuzeit").

[1] I quote Hegel, unless otherwise indicated, according to H. Glockner, ed., *Georg Wilhelm Friedrich Hegel, Sämtliche Werke, Jubiläumsausgabe in zwanzig Bänden* (Stuttgart-Bad Canstatt, 1956-1965) ; here, XI, 519. Cited as *Werke*.

[2] Compare the eschatological use in Rom. 13 :12.

[3] Evident already in Melanchthon's funeral oration on 22 February 1546, CR, XI, 728 : "Lutherus veram et necessariam doctrinam patefecit. Fuisse enim tenebras in Doctrina de poenitentia densissimas, manifestum est." Translated into German in E.W. Zeeden, *Martin Luther und die Reformation im Urteil des deutschen Luthertums*(Freiburg, 1952),II,3.

See also especially Matthias Flacius Illyricus, *Ecclesiastica historia, Cent. II, Praef.*, as given with translation in Zeeden, II, 46 : "………tempora quidem Germanici prophetae MARTINI LUTHERI, cuius voce ac ministerio lux Evangelii quasi e tenebris Aegyptiacis revocata est, propemodum Apostolorum aetati respondent."

J.F. von der Strass (Sub Presidio J.C. Dannhaueri), *Memoria Thaumasiandri Lutheri* (Strasbourg, 1661), pp. 1-2, as given with translation in Zeeden, II, 125-26 : "Lux haec preciosissima, post Christi in coelos ascensionem (………) ministerio Apostolorum et Apostolicorum virorum ore et calamo per totum mundum clarissime diffusa fuit. Sed dormientibus hominibus sub Antichristi tyrannide (heu quanta miseria) obscurata est (………) Obducto itaque his rebus pessimis Ecclesiae coelo, tenebrae erant crassae, non quidem penitus lux Evangelii interierat, nec tamen etiam ita fulsit, ut diem quis dicere posset et non nisi raro tenues emisit radios. (………) Misertus igitur est Deus Ecclesiae suae, Papali tyrannide pressae, et votis et gemitibus piorum exoratus Heroem Chris-

be applied to the inner illumination which Luther experienced, instead
of to the general spread of the gospel.[1] These phrases give expression to
an ecclesiastical and salvation-historical interpretation of Luther's appearance.

In Hegel's statement, however, Luther and the Reformation are
integrated in the history of thought. To this we must immediately add
a twofold explanation. First, for Hegel, history as such is the history
of thought. Hence here "history of thought" (*geistesgeschichtlich* [2])
does not have its usual sense, only *one* aspect of history among others.
Furthermore, in the process of the spirit that reaches an awareness of
itself, Luther and the Reformation are assigned a niche which in a
sense also has a salvation-historical, yes, an eschatological dignity.
It is a matter of "the new, the last banner..., around which the nations
gather, the flag of the free spirit." [3] By the use of the same metaphor
the word "Enlightenment" likewise connotes such a pathos of salvation. The way in which the Enlightenment appealed to the Reformation and integrated it into its self-understanding [4] indeed seems by

---

tianum (.........) excitavit, qui doctrinam Evangelii a variis corruptelis ita repurgavit, ut
piis novam lucem exoriri videretur. Heros ille fuit MARTINUS LUTHERUS, ...
cf. Zeeden, II, 43, 66; also *ibid.*, II, 15, 20, 24.

[1] Johannes Müller, *Lutherus defensus* : *Das ist Gründliche Widerlegung dessen was
die Bäpstler D. Lutheri Person fürwerffen* (Arnstadt, 1645), pp. 250-51, in Zeeden, II,
113-14 : "Also sehen wir am Tage / dass es Liecht worden sey [gemeint ist die Luther
widerfahrene Erleuchtung] / ob wir gleich die Minut nicht wissen / wann das Liecht
vollkommen worden sey. Also thut auch nicht vonnöthen / dass wir genaw müssen
wissen / welch Jahr und Tag Lutherus vollkommen sey erleuchtet worden..." This was
written in 1634.

[2] In contrast to the much discussed concept *Geisteswissenschaften* the history of the
word *Geistesgeschichte* with its derivative *geistesgeschichtlich* has not been investigated, so
far as I know. Hegel does not use the word, it seems. Evidently we are dealing here with
an inner scientific method resulting from a narrowing to a particular aspect of history.
For instance, compare H. Rickert's critical delimitation in opposition to this "that
someone orientates himself unilaterally to the so-called *Geistesgeschichte* in contrast to
political or economic history." *Die Grenzen der naturwissenschaftlichen Begriffsbildung* :
Eine logische Einleitung in die historischen Wissenschaften (5th ed. ; Tübingen and Leipzig,
1929), p. 591. Compare also the frequent distinctions between Church History or History
of Theology and (general) *Geistesgeschichte*.

[3] *Werke*, XI, 524.

[4] See Zeeden, II, 269-300 (J.S. Semler); *ibid.*, II, 300-25 (G.E. Lessing); *ibid.*, II,
328-40 (Fredrick the Great). G. Hornig, *Die Anfänge der historisch-kritischen Theologie* :
Johann Salomo Semlers Schriftverständnis und seine Stellung zu Luther (Göttingen, 1961),
especially ch. V, "Semlers Lutherkritik," ch. VI, "Semlers Luthernachfolge." H. Bornkamm, *Luther im Spiegel der deutschen Geistesgeschichte* : *Mit ausgewählten Texten von*

comparison to Hegel as superficial. On a higher level of reflection Hegel was intent on maintaining the connection with the innermost theological concerns of the Reformation. [1]

Yet even the sharply negative assessment of the Reformation by such men as Jacob Burckhardt [2] and Friedrich Nietzsche [3] and their followers insists on qualifying soteriologically the beginning of the modern age as a transition from night to day. Of course the role of the Reformation receives a diametrically different evaluation. Nietzsche is of the opinion, "If Luther had been burned like Huss, the dawn of the Enlightenment might perhaps have come a little earlier and more brilliantly than we can now imagine. " [4] Alexander Ruestow thinks that the Reformation, together with the Counter Reformation, for which Luther and Calvin also are said to be responsible, ushered in a new period of darkness, a relapse into extreme medievalism, and this after the onset of a new era was already well on the way in the late Middle Ages and in the Renaissance.[5]

The concept of dawning implies not only the sharp contrast between darkness and light but permits also shadings in the transition from one extreme to the other. Dawn proclaims the end of the night, the aurora, the sunrise. This, in turn, is only the beginning of the day in which the all-illuminating sun runs its course and performs its task. As far as I can see, the obvious thought of the ultimately returning sunset does not overshadow the application of that history-interpreting metaphor to the Reformation and the modern age. The light of the gospel may be threatened by ever recurring periods of darkness; nevertheless, it has the

---

Lessing bis zur Gegenwart (2nd ed.; Heidelberg, 1970), pp. 16-21. There further literature about Lessing's relations to Luther. W. von Loewenich, *Luther und der Neuprotestantismus* (Witten, 1963), pp. 16-22.

[1] E. Hirsch, *Fichtes, Schleiermachers und Hegels Verhältnis zur Reformation* (Göttingen, 1930). H. Bornkamm, pp. 31-36. W. von Loewenich, pp. 28-33. E.-W. Kohls, *Das Bild der Reformation in der Geisteswissenschaft des 19. Jahrhunderts (G.W.F. Hegel, L. von Ranke, J. Burckhardt)*, NZSTh, IX (1967), 229-46.

[2] Bornkamm, pp. 91-92, 266-74. W. von Loewenich, *Jacob Burckhardt und die Kirchengeschichte*, in: W. von Loewenich, *Humanitas-Christianitas* (Witten, 1968), pp. 103-29. Kohls, pp. 242-45.

[3] Bornkamm, pp. 92-94 (see for additional bibliography), pp. 305-14.

[4] Fr. Nietzsche, "Menschliches, Allzumenschliches: Ein Buch für freie Geister," 1878, no. 237, in: *Nietzsches Werke* (Leipzig, 1899-1904), I, ii, 224-25. See also Bornkamm, pp. 306-7.

[5] A. Rüstow, *Ortsbestimmung der Gegenwart: Eine universalgeschichtliche Kulturkritik*, vol. II, *Weg der Freiheit* (Erlenbach-Zürich, 1952), 303.

character of finality, even as the conviction that a definitive source of
light has risen is combined with the light of reason.

It is true, in that original salvation-historical interpretation of the
Reformation only very limited use is made of the possibility of differentiation. There is indeed an awareness of certain omens and antecedents
of Reformation insights.[1] As far as Luther's Reformation breakthrough
is concerned, in his autobiographical remarks he makes much of the
fact that he was held captive for a long time in his papistical bias from
which he extricated himself only with great difficulty.[2] Farthest from
the mind of the reformatory self-understanding and the orthodox understanding of the Reformation, at least within Lutheranism, was the
thought of an evolving development. The left wing of the Reformation
had indeed raised the complaint early that the Reformation had gone
only half-way, yes, had retrogressed in a reactionary way, and was
therefore still awaiting its consummation.[3] Very early the need was felt
to distinguish between the lights and shadows of Luther's personality.[4]
Not until the age of Pietism did the idea arise also in Lutheranism that
the Reformation had remained unfinished and needed to be continued.[5]
All of these differentiations with reference to the prehistory and progress
of the Reformation, as well as with reference to the evaluation of Luther's
person, were extraordinarily intensified later, during and since the
Enlightenment, because of an increasing awareness of historical con-
ditionalities and changes.[6]

---

[1] The references to prophesies which are said to have been fulfilled in Luther (cf., e.g.,
Zeeden, II, 12, 63-66, 98), imply the direct opposite from the historical, genetic questions
which were far removed in that time. Luther made some allusions, granted very sub-
jectively colored, in this respect to Tauler, Hus, von Staupitz, and others.

[2] Especially in the preface to vol. I of the *Opera Latina* of the 1545 Wittenberg edition.
WA, LIV, 179 : 22ff., 183 : 21 ff.

[3] For example, Thomas Müntzer, "Hochverursachte Schutzrede..." (1524), in *Thomas
Müntzer : Politische Schriften mit Kommentar*, ed. C. Hinrichs, (Halle [Saale], 1950),
p. 101 : 545-46. Cf. p. 97 : 479-81; Thomas Müntzer, *Schriften und Briefe : Krit. Gesamtausgabe*, ed. G. Franz (Gütersloh, 1968), pp. 342-43:27-28; cf. p. 340:14-16). I am indebted
to Reinhard Schwarz for the references.

[4] See Zeeden, II, 4 (Melanchthon); *ibid.*, II, 104 (E. Willich); *ibid.*, II, 129-30 (J. M. A.
Musäus); *ibid.*, II, 157-58 (V.L. Frhr. von Seckendorf); *ibid.*, II, 186, 188-89, 191 (Ph. J.
Spener); *ibid.*, II, 218-22 (G. Arnold).

[5] Zeeden, II, 198-200 (Ph. J. Spener).

[6] Historical preparation : see Zeeden II, 270 (J.S. Semler); *ibid.*, II, 352-53 (I. Iselin).
Continuing Reformation : *ibid.*, II, 278-79 (J.S. Semler). Luther's person : *ibid.*, II, 275,
281 (J.S. Semler); *ibid.*, II, 303-4 (G.E. Lessing).

2. *Hegel*

Strictly speaking, it was Hegel who first assumed the task of integrating the Reformation into the history of thought. Its precondition is a view of history which does not stop with external symptoms, such as incidental abuses in the Middle Ages, but takes note of the inner movement of the event and for that reason encompasses everything in its dialectical necessity and in its comprehensive context.[1] With Hegel this assumes the character of a universal teleological view of history, that sees the changes as evolving aspects of a single basic theme, progress in the consciousness of freedom.[2] This constitutes the grandeur but also the problematics of his understanding of history. Therefore the predominant impression is that here, because of a dogmatic prejudice, Luther's Reformation is understood as turned toward the modern age without a break, and the integration into the history of thought is not at all regarded as a problem. Nevertheless, Hegel's historical judgment of Luther and the Reformation is more carefully differentiated than seems to be the case.

From Luther to the Middle Ages on the one hand and to the modern era on the other, there are intimately intertwined positive and negative relationships. Hegel indeed knows that the principle of subjectivity did not simply arise because of the Reformation.[3] All of the well-known phenomena, which demonstrate that man had recovered confidence in himself and enjoyment of the earth, are part of the day-break at the close of the Middle Ages that preceded the all-illuminating sun.[4] However, it is only in relationship to God that freedom authenticates itself, loses its particularity, and thus its nearness to the barbaric, and is recognized not only as permitted but simply as necessary.[5] Thus, according to Hegel, the reformatory faith provides the

---

[1] *Werke*, XI, 519-20.

[2] G.W.F. Hegel, *Die Vernunft in der Geschichte*, ed. G. Lasson, Ph. Bibl. 171a, 40.

[3] *Werke*, XIX, 255; see p. 253: "Die Haupt-Revolution ist in der lutherischen Reformation eingetreten..."

[4] *Werke*, XI, 518; *ibid.*, XIX, 266-67.

[5] *Werke*, XIX, 255: "Diess Gelten des Subjektiven hat nun jetzt einer höheren Bewährung und der höchsten Bewährung bedurft, um vollkommen legitimiert zu seyn, und sogar zur absoluten Pflicht zu werden; und um diese Bewährung erhalten zu können, hat es aufgefasst werden müssen in seiner reinsten Gestalt. Die höchste Bewährung des Princips ist nun die religiöse Bewährung: so dass diess Princip der eigenen Geistigkeit, der eigenen Selbständigkeit erkannt wird in der Beziehung auf Gott und zu Gott; dann ist es durch die Religion geheiligt. Die blosse Subjektivität, blosse Freiheit des

true legitimation, but with that also the critical norm for that movement from the Middle Ages to the modern age, a movement that is in
progress *per se* apart from the Reformation but is not on the right track
without the Reformation.

True, the main accent is on the antithesis to the Middle Ages. According to Hegel, their corruption arises from the fact that the presence
of the Eternal in the world, the linking of the finite with the infinite—the
"this," as he expresses it in an enigmatic formula [1] — has been exter-
nalized.[2] Superstition, external authority, asceticism, and the material-
ization of the means of salvation are the symptoms.[3] As the most pregnant phenomena he names the adoration of the host and the yearning
for the possession of the Holy Land, especially the Holy Sepulcher,
which then, however, as a conquered empty grave elicited an experience
of disappointment and therewith brought about the crisis of the Middle
Ages.[4] But Hegel would be completely misunderstood, if he is understood as trying to dissolve the connection between the secular and the
eternal. On the contrary, he is concerned precisely about the right place
and the correct manner of this connection.[5] In this point, as an advo-
cate of the Christian faith in the modern age, Hegel is in agreement with
Luther :

> Luther's simple teaching is this, that the "this," the infinite subjectivity,
> that is, the true spirituality [*Geistigkeit*], Christ, in no respect is present and

---

Menschen, dass er einen Willen hat, und damit diess oder jenes treibt, berechtigt
noch nicht; der barbarische Wille, der sich nur mit subjectiven Zwecken erfüllt, die
nicht vor der Vernunft Bestand haben, ist nicht berechtigt." *Werke*, XIX, 256 : "So
ist hier das Princip der Subjecktivität, der reinen Beziehung auf mich, die Freiheit,
nicht nur anerkannt: sondern es ist schlechthin gefordert, dass es nur darauf ankomme
im Kultus, in der Religion. Diess ist die höchste Bewährung des Princips, dass dasselbe
nur vor Gott gelte, nur der Glaube des eigenen Herzens, die Überwindung des eigenen
Herzens nöthig sey; damit ist denn diess Princip der christlichen Freiheit erst aufge-
stellt, und zum Bewusstseyn, zum wahrhaften Bewusstseyn gebracht worden."

[1] About *dieses* as the concrete content of the direct assurance of the *jetzt* and *hier*,
see *Werke*, II, 81-92; in religious respect, *Werke*, II, 494-99, 520-23.

[2] *Werke*, XIX, 265.

[3] *Werke*, XI, 520-21.

[4] *Werke*, XI, 494-99.

[5] *Werke*, XIX, 266 : "Das Princip der inneren Versöhnung des Geistes war an sich
die Idee des Christenthums, aber selbst wieder entfernt, nur äusserlich, als Zerrissenheit,
unversöhnt. Wir sehen die Langsamkeit des Weltgeistes, diese Äusserlichkeit zu über-
winden. Er höhlt das Innere aus, — der Schein, die äussere Gestalt, bleibt noch; aber
zuletzt ist sie eine leere Hülse, die neue Gestalt bricht hervor."

real in an external manner, but is attained as spiritual at all only in the reconciliation with God, in faith and in partaking [that is, *in usu*, not *extra usum*]. [1]

Hence, according to him, the essence of the Lutheran faith consists in

> that man is in a right relationship to God and... his piety requires... that his
> heart, his innermost being, is involved.... The individual himself must repent,
> himself be contrite in his heart, and his heart must be filled with the Holy
> Spirit. [2]

piety

This is what Hegel has in view in reducing the essential content of
the Reformation to the formula : "Man is destined through himself to be
free." [3]

Nevertheless, the relationship of the Reformation to the modern age
is ambivalent. The spirit does not at once appear in the full consummation. [4] Just as the church's doctrine was only gradually developed
after the beginnings of Christianity, so correspondingly here. The
freedom of the spirit began with Luther, only embryonically, and
therefore required subsequent explication. [5] At first it was restricted
to the religious sphere. [6] But this principle had then also to be brought
into the world and above all to penetrate the political realm. [7] Both
aspects must be emphasized : What is already present in the Reformation and what is not yet there ; that the modern age rightly goes beyond

---

[1] *Werke*, XI, 522; *ibid.*, XIX, 257 : "Nur im Genuss und Glauben stehe ich in Beziehung zu Gott."

[2] *Werke*, XIX, 256; *ibid.*, XIX, 253 : "Aus dem Jenseitigen wurde so der Mensch zur
Präsenz des Geistes gerufen ; und die Erde und ihre Körper, menschliche Tugenden und
Sittlichkeit, das eigene Herz und das eigene Gewissen fingen an, ihm Etwas zu gelten."
Ibid., XI, 523: "[Der Glaube] ist überhaupt nicht Glauben an Abwesendes, Geschehenes
und Vergangenes ; sondern die subjektive Gewissheit des Ewigen, der an und für sich
seyenden Wahrheit, der Wahrheit von Gott. Von dieser Gewissheit sagt die lutherische
Kirche, dass sie nur der heilige Geist bewirkt, d.h. eine Gewissheit, die nicht dem Individuum nach seiner particularen Besonderheit, sondern nach seinem Wesen zukommt."

[3] *Werke*, XI, 524.

[4] *Werke*, XI, 532.

[5] *Werke*, XIX, 254-55.

[6] *Werke*, XIX, 258 : "Diess Princip nun ist zuerst aufgefasst innerhalb der Religion,
dadurch hat es seine absolute Berechtigung erhalten, ist aber zunächst nur in Beziehung
auf religiöse Gegenstände gesetzt erschienen ; es ist noch nicht ausgedehnt auf die
weitere Entwicklung des subjektiven Princips selbst."
Ibid., XI, 532 : "Die Versöhnung Gottes mit der Welt war zunächst noch in abstracter
Form, noch nicht zu einem Systeme der sittlichen Welt entwickelt."

[7] *Werke*, XI, 524; *ibid.*, XI, 526 : "Doch war zu einer politischen Umgestaltung, als
Consequenz der kirchlichen Reformation, die Welt damals noch nicht reif."

the Reformation and yet, correctly understood, can be nothing else than an actualization of the legacy of the Reformation.

Here indeed is the cause of conflicts between the modern age and the empirical shape of Protestantism. The religious content was conserved as something historically given and remained something external and foreign to faith, instead of being speculatively tested as to its truth. As a result the germ of an unspiritual mode of comprehension entered the freedom of the spirit.[1] Consequently the subjective religious principle was separated from philosophy. This constitutes a step backward even in relation to medieval scholasticism.[2] Either a bad subjectivity, emptied of the objective, remains, abandoned to the torture of religious self-contemplation,[3] or the biblical texts are surrendered to a purely historico-philological exegesis which strangles the spirit in the text[4]. Both phenomena, pietism and rational biblical scholarship, which are generally regarded as marks of transition from Old Protestantism to Neo-Protestantism, Hegel regards as degeneracy. The reason for this state of affairs is that there has been no self-critical reshaping of the Reformation for modern time.

3. *Troeltsch*

The terms, Old and Neo-Protestantism, are not in Hegel's vocabulary, but were coined by Troeltsch. Therefore they come from that late phase in which the thought-historical treatment of Luther and the Reformation was expanded into the cultural-historical method of study.[5] It was only at this point, though not without preparation by

---

[1] *Werke*, XIX, 258.

[2] *Werke*, XIX, 259.

[3] *Werke*, XI, 532-33.

[4] *Werke*, XIX, 261 : "Ein anderes und unrichtiges Verhalten zu dem Inhalt ist, demselben äusserlich zu nehmen, z. B. nach dem grossen neuen Princip der Exegese, dass die Schriften des neuen Testaments behandelt werden sollen, wie ein griechischer oder lateinischer und anderer Schriftsteller, kritisch, philologisch, historisch. Das wesentliche Verhalten des Geistes ist nur für den Geist. Und es ist ein verkehrtes Beginnen einer störrischen Exegese, auf solche äusserliche philologische Weise die Wahrheit der christlichen Religion zu erweisen, wie diess die Orthodoxie gethan hat; der Inhalt wird so geistlos."

[5] With this designation I indicate how in historical questions, especially by taking up sociological aspects, Troeltsch maintains a (real or supposed) narrow approach to considerations in the history of thought. However, I am conscious that he wants to use

Dilthey [1] and Harnack,[2] that the self-evident manner in which the predominant opinion, that assigned Luther and the Reformation to the
modern age, was subjected to so startling a critique that for the first
time the historical classification became a controverted problem, and
indeed a problem, and of extraordinary range. For the position one
takes with regard to this problem manifestly determines the significance
that one assigns to Luther for the present and the future.

As Hegel's conception was simplified to mean that Luther was the
standard bearer of the modern age, so Troeltsch's thesis caused a stir
in its exaggerated form that Luther was a representative of the Middle

---

the concept *Kulturwissenschaften* as little as *Geisteswissenschaften*. See *Gesammelte
Schriften* (Tübingen, 1912ff.), III, 84 : "Die Bezeichnung historisch-ethische Wissenschaften für die Zusammenfassung von entwickelnder Geschichtsdarstellung, soziologisch ver-
gleichender Systematik, systematischen Geisteswissenschaften und Ethik ziehe ich den
gangbaren Bezeichnungen 'Geisteswissenschaften' (Mill und Dilthey) vor, die bald psycho-
logistisch, bald spiritualistisch verstanden werden und den Anteil der Natur an der
Geschichte ausser Augen lassen und 'Kulturwissenschaften' (Hermann Paul und Rickert),
die bald soziologistisch, bald werttheoretisch aufgefasst werden. Die Doppelbezeichnung
weist zugleich auf den engen Zusammenhang von Sein, Werden und Sollen auf diesem
Gebiete hin. Auch der Unterschied gegenüber der gar nicht zu leugnenden, aber anders-
artigen Naturgeschichte und-entwicklung ist damit ausgesagt."

[1] E.g., in W. Dilthey, "Auffassung und Analyse des Menschen im 15. und 16. Jahrhundert" (1891-92), *Gesammelte Schriften* (5th ed.; Stuttgart, 1957), II, 56-57 : "...dieser
mit der grossen Tradition der Kirche einige Glaubensinhalt gab den Reformatoren die
heroische Kraft, Apparat und Disziplin der Kurie abzuschütteln und kirchenbildend zu
wirken. Aber zugleich muss es doch dabei bleiben : dieser Zusammenhang religiöser
Begriffe ist nicht der Ausgang des Dogma, das 'Ende des alten dogmatischen Christen-
tums'..., sondern hat dieses überall zu seiner notwendigen Voraussetzung. Er steht und
fällt selbst mit dem Dogma. Ja sogar das mönchische, franziskanische religiöse Ideal
muss als die Voraussetzung für die Lehre von der Sünde und von dem Unvermögen zum
Guten angesehen werden. In dem Masse, in welchem die Erbsündenlehre von dieser
dualistisch motivierten Unterlage losgelöst wurde, musste sie zu einer ganz unhaltbaren
Darstellung der Erfahrungen über die Menschennatur greifen." See H. Bornkamm,
pp. 100-3, 314-23 ; W. von Loewenich, pp. 48-55 ; E.-W. Kohls, "Das Bild der Reformation
bei Wilhelm Dilthey, Adolf von Harnack und Ernst Troeltsch," *NZSTh*, XI (1969), 269-91.

[2] *Lehrbuch der Dogmengeschichte* (5th ed.; Leipzig, 1932), III, 809 : "Die Reformation,
wie sie sich in dem Christenthum Luther's darstellt, ist... in vieler Hinsicht eine altkatho-
lische, resp. auch eine mittelalterliche Erscheinung, dagegen auf ihren religiösen Kern
beurtheilt, ist sie es nicht, vielmehr Wiederherstellung des paulinischen Christenthums
im Geiste einer neuen Zeit." 810f : "Es ist eine ganz einseitige, ja sträflich abstracte
Betrachtung Luther's, die in ihm den Mann der neuen Zeit, den Helden eines herauf-
steigenden Zeitalters oder den Schöpfer des modernen Geistes feiert." See H. Bornkamm,
pp. 83-84, 290-97 ; W. von Loewenich, pp. 118-29 ; W. Pauck, *Harnack and Troeltsch :
Two Historical Theologians* (New York, 1968) ; E.-W. Kohls, pp. 278-85.

Ages. However, if the nuances in both are observed, they approach each other more closely. Already with Hegel the outlines of the problem are delineated. They are met with again in Troeltsch, filled with a far richer historical perception and therefore essentially differentiated better, but also accentuated differently. Both thinkers are agreed on a passionate affirmation of the turn from the Middle Ages to the modern age, and both feel themselves obligated to Luther's innermost intention. Both are opposed to a superficial derivation of the modern age from Luther and the Reformation, since before, contemporaneously, and afterwards, radically different forces promoted the modern age. The new religious impulses and their roles in the upheaval of the times must be carefully distinguished from these. Finally, both Hegel and Troeltsch are aware also of the ambivalence of the Reformation and its historical effects, the twilight zone of the already and the not yet, the contradictory trends of further development and retrogressive encasement.

Nevertheless, with Troeltsch [1] there is an unmistakable change in perspective. Although he ultimately agrees with Hegel in the premise of an integration of religion and philosophy;[2] nevertheless, in contrast to him (Hegel), he does not claim to outline the necessary explanation of the idea. Rather, he confines himself in a purely experiential-imminent way to clarifying the extremely complicated relationship of the cultural types that succeed and overlap each other.[3] For that reason his

---

[1] From E. Troeltsch's writings I cite the following : "Protestantisches Christentum und Kirche in der Neuzeit," in *Kultur der Gegenwart* (2nd ed.; Berlin and Leipzig, 1909), I, iv, 1 (1906), 431-755; "Luther, der Protestantismus und die moderne Welt," in *Ges. Schr.*, IV, 202-54 (to this two previous essays provided by the compilation of the editor, H. Baron, "Luther und die moderne Welt," 1908, and "Luther und der Protestantismus," 1917—see *ibid.*, IV, xi-xiv); "Die Bedeutung des Protestantismus für die Enstehung der modernen Welt," *Historische Zeitschrift*, XCVII (1906), 1-66, or "Beiheft" 2 of the *Historische Zeitschrift* (cited as "Die Bedeutung"). For Troeltsch's concept of Luther and the Reformation : H. Bornkamm, pp. 107-10, 373-83; H. Fischer, "Luther und seine Reformation in der Sicht E. Troeltschs," *NZSTh*, V (1963), 132-72; W. von Loewenich, 130-40; W. Pauck; E.-W. Kohls, 285-91.

[2] *Ges. Schr.*, IV, 253 : "Die religionslose Philosophie und die unphilosophische Religion müssen schwinden, wenn es wieder Gesundung und geistigen Zusammenhang geben soll, und wer die Dinge in diesem Lichte sieht, der beobachtet auch in dem Werden des modernen Geistes überall die Arbeit an jenem Gedanken der coincidentia oppositorum, dem weder Theologie noch Philosophie der alten Zeit gewachsen waren. Hegel hat das Problem des Cusaners wieder aufgenommen, und das moderne Denken sucht im Grunde neue Mittel zur Lösung der Hegelschen Probleme."

[3] "Die Bedeutung," p. 7.

way of reflecting and presenting oscillates sharply and changes the accent and emphasis from one sketch to another.[1] As he himself knows, in this procedure empirical orientation and construction wrestle with each other,[2] knowledge of historical details and an instinct for historical relationships that often are not matched by a corresponding knowledge, a combination which again is not unlike what is found in Hegel, eliciting at once admiration and criticism. But what allows Troeltsch's understanding of history to diverge from Hegel's not only in method but also in content is the fact that Troeltsch, born about a century later, is conditioned by a more advanced experience with the modern age.

For Hegel the antithetical relationship between modern times and the Middle Ages was still a necessary aspect within the realization of the Christian principle which coincides with the goal of the movement of the world spirit itself. For Troeltsch, on the contrary, the essential aspects of the modern age are throughout independent of what is Christian. Therefore he contrasts the modern age with the churchly culture of the Middle Ages in a way that immediately creates the impression of being anti-Christian:[3] over against theology, rationalism; over against authority, autonomy; over against the infallible truth of revelation, relativism; over against an ascetic orientation toward the life to come, thisworldliness; over against the pessimism of sin, the optimism of progress.[4] In short, the individualism of the human person and the imminence of the divine are the two chief principles of the

---

[1] An exact, chronological, comprehensive investigation of the problem how Troeltsch changed his accents and nuances in the historical arrangement of the Reformation and under what influences this happened, in consideration of the revision of individual writings from edition to edition as well as with reference to the interdependent circumstances would be a very difficult, but perhaps a rewarding task.

[2] "Die Bedeutung," pp. 6-7.

[3] *Ibid.*, p. 12 : "An diesem Gegensatze erhellt nun das Wesen der modernen Kultur. Sie ist überall die Bekämpfung der kirchlichen Kultur und deren Ersetzung durch autonom erzeugte Kulturideen, deren Geltung aus ihrer überzeugenden Kraft, aus ihrer immanenten und unmittelbar wirkenden Eindrucksfähigkeit folgt. Die wie immer begründete Autonomie im Gegensatz gegen die kirchliche Autorität, gegen rein äussere und unmittelbare göttliche Normen, beherrscht alles. Auch wo man neue Authoritäten prinzipiell aufrichtet oder tatsächlich befolgt, wird doch deren Geltung selbst auf rein autonome und rationale Überzeugung begründet; und auch, wo die älteren religiösen Überzeugungen bestehen bleiben, wird doch ihre Wahrheit und verpflichtende Kraft, wenigstens bei den Protestanten, in erster Linie auf eine innere persönliche Überzeugung und nicht auf die herrschende Autorität als solche begründet."

[4] *Ibid.*, pp. 8-16. See also the essay, "Das Wesen des modernen Geistes" (1907) in *Ges. Schr.*, IV, 297-338.

modern age.[1] Not that Troeltsch saw the modern age moving irresistibly toward a complete lack of religion. But he is profoundly obsessed by the thought that the configuration of religious life in the modern world presents an extremely dark problem.[2] Thus in one sense the antithesis between the Middle Ages and modern times became more acute; but in another respect it indeed was relativized, because the direct connection with internal Christian controversies was dissolved. From the viewpoint of the history of culture Catholicism and Protestantism are moving into a continually closer relationship. In spite of the break between the Middle Ages and the modern age, the Middle Ages can nevertheless be valued now as "the mighty maternal lap of all West European life."[3]

Hegel already restricted the positive participation of Luther and the Reformation in the rise of the modern age to the religious aspect. But since it seemed to him that the modern age was inseparably connected with the idea of Christianity, the religious factor in the genesis of the modern age had a different value for him than for Troeltsch. On the one hand, Hegel could unequivocally equate the Protestant principle, as it is relevant for the modern age, with the essence of Luther's reformatory teachings. On the other hand, he expected of this Protestant principle an immediate impact on culture as a whole. For Troeltsch, however, the direct impact of Protestantism in its original form on modern culture did not come into consideration at all.[4] For the Refor-

---

[1] *Ges. Schr.*, IV, 230.

[2] "Protestantisches Christentum und Kirche," p. 433.

[3] *Ibid.*

[4] "Die Bedeutung," p. 16 : "Es ist damit nicht gesagt, dass alle israelitisch-christlichen Kräfte des religiösen Lebens wurzellos geworden seien. Aber so, wie sie die Erlösungsanstalt der autoritativen, für das Jenseits erziehenden und disziplinierenden Kirche zu begründen vermochten, sind sie allerdings ausserordentlich matt und schwach geworden. Sie können keine kirchliche Kultur mehr erzeugen und tragen."

Ibid., p. 30 : "... von einer Wirkung des Protestantismus zur Herbeiführung der modernen Kultur kann nur in bezug auf die verschiedenen Gruppen des Altprotestantismus die Rede sein, während der Neuprotestantismus selbst ein Bestandteil der modernen Kultur und von ihr tiefgreifend beeinflusst ist."

Ges. Schr., IV, 215 : "In Wahrheit ist die neue Religion der Gnade, des Glaubens und der Erwählung eine ungeheure Vereinfachung der Religion, eine gründliche Verinnerlichung und Verpersönlichung, eine Wiedereinsaugung des Moralismus in die religiöse Idee; es bedurfte nur der Ablösung von dem scholastischen Weltbild, von den christologisch-trinitarischen Dogmen, von der übernatürlichen Offenbartheit der Schrift und von der anthropomorphen Gottesidee, um daraus die ganze Welt heutiger religiöser Inner-

mation was still embedded in the churchly culture of the Middle Ages as
a religious renewal, and historically constituted itself in an analogous
form. For that reason Troeltsch can formulate his well-known provoca-
tive judgments. Protestantism appears, first of all, "as a completely medievalistic reaction, which swallows up the already achieved
beginnings of a free and secular culture."[1] Protestantism "similar to,
or even more than the Counter-Reformation, is a second blossoming of
the Middle Ages... which deprives the already formed sprouts and buds
of a secular culture of their sap."[2] The Reformation was "a reformation of the urban class of the Late Middle Ages."[3] Of course, "by shat-
tering the sole authority of the Catholic church Protestantism has broken the power of ecclesiastical culture in general, in spite of its transitory revival"[4] and participated in this way negatively in the rise of
the modern era. Troeltsch also concedes that modern individualism and
rationalism, autonomy and faith in progress have their deepest roots
in the religious personalism which has its origins in the Old Testament
prophets and in Christianity.[5] But these are only subconscious and

---

lichkeit und persönlicher Glaubensüberzeugung hervorzubringen. In Wahrheit ist Christ-
liches und Weltliches, Staat und Kirche, Kultur und religiöse Innerlichkeit doch scharf
getrennt und nur nachträglich und mühsam wieder zu einer Analogie der mittelalterlichen Lebenseinheit zusammengebogen ..."

[1] "Die Bedeutung," p. 44; ibid., pp. 44-45 : "... so erlebte Europa trotz gleichzeitiger
Verbreitung der Ideen und Lebensformen der Renaissance wieder zwei Jahrhunderte
mittelalterlichen Geistes. Wer freilich von der Geschichte des Staatsleben oder der Wirt-
schaft herkommt, wird diesen Eindruck nicht haben, da hier die Ansätze des Spätmittelalters sich ungebrochen weiterentwickeln, ja den Protestantismus zum guten Teil in
ihren Dienst nehmen. Aber wer von der Geschichte der Religion, des Ethos und der
Wissenschaft herkommt, wird sich dem Eindruck nicht entziehen können, dass erst der
grosse Befreiungskampf des endenden 17. und 18. Jahrhunderts das Mittelalter grundsätz-
lich beendet."

[2] Ges. Schr., IV, 214.

[2] Ges. Schr., IV, 215 : "Wie im Frühmittelalter Ritter und Mönch die Brennpunkte
einer Ellipse bildeten, so wird jetzt die Verschmelzung von Bürger und Christ der Mittel-
punkt eines geschlossenen Lebenskreises. Ein verinnerlichtes, verpersönlichtes und ver-
bürgerlichtes, in seiner religiösen Tiefe bis zum höchsten Glauben und bis zum Fanatismus
neu erregtes Spätmittelalter steht hier vor uns."

[4] "Die Bedeutung," p. 46; ibid., "Dazu kommt weiter, dass die innere kirchliche
Struktur der protestantischen Kirche, vor allem des Luthertums, doch bedeutend schwä-
cher ist als die des Katholizismus und daher gegenüber der modernen Ideenwelt weniger
dauernde Widerstandskraft besass als der Katholizismus."

[5] Ibid., pp. 22-23 : "Indem der Protestantismus gerade an der Herausbildung dieses
religiösen Individualismus und an seiner Überleitung in die Breite des allgemeinen Lebens

hidden, indirect and secularized influences in which Protestantism also participates to the extent that it has elevated this religious personalism to a principle. However, the area in which Protestantism actually became creative for the modern world is that area in which the modern age itself is deficient, namely the religious life.[1] Under this aspect, Troeltsch gives the question a shift in direction. He moves from that which constitutes the new age, to that which it lacks; from the impact of Protestantism on the modern age, to the impact of the modern age on Protestantism. The first, because according to Troeltsch the modern era cannot be sufficient unto itself, but is in need of a religious-metaphysical tie.[2] The second, because Protestantism of itself cannot provide

---

seine Bedeutung hat, ist von vornherein klar, dass er an der Hervorbringung der modernen Welt erheblich mitbeteiligt ist."

See also within the context of the citation in the previous note *ibid.*, p. 47 : "Die geringere Widerstandskraft allein hat es nicht getan. Der Protestantismus besass vielmehr allerhand der modernen Welt entgegenkommende Strebungen, die ihn befähigten, im Konflikt nicht bloss zu unterliegen, sondern sich mit dem neuen zu amalgamieren, und zwar viel stärker zu amalgamieren, als das auf seine Weise auch der Katholizismus in der Kultur der Gegenreformation und in seiner modernen Entwicklung gekonnt hat."

[1] *Ibid.*, p. 88 : "Die eigentliche und letzte Frage, wenn es sich um die Bedeutung des Protestanismus für die moderne Welt handelt, ist daher die, in welcher Beziehung gerade seine religiöse Kraft und Grundidee zu dem religiösen Wesen des modernen Geistes steht, ob dieses, wie es auch in der Gegenwart seine relative Unabhängigkeit von den einzelnen Kulturgestaltungen besitzt, in ihm wesentlich wurzelt und von ihm bestimmt ist. Die Frage nach seiner Bedeutung für die Entstehung der modernen Welt fällt nicht zusammen mit der nach seiner Bedeutung für die der modernen Kultur. Denn diese ist nicht identisch mit dem in ihr sich aufringenden religiösen Leben. Es bleibt die letzte Frage die nach dem Verhältnis der protestantischen Religiosität zur modernen Religion, zu der mit der modernen Kulturwelt zusammenhängenden, aber in ihr nicht erschöpften Religion."

Ges. Schr., VI, 206-7 : "In England haben Locke und der Deismus, in Frankreich Rousseaus Menschenrechte und Gefühlsreligion, in Deutschland die mit Leibniz, Lessing und Kant eröffnete deutsche Religionsphilosophie eine neue Religiosität nicht aus sich begründet, aber von sich aus bedingt und zur Einfügung in ein neues Bild der Dinge und in ein neues Ideal der Gesellschaft und Kultur genötigt. Alles das ist nicht ohne den Protestantismus geschehen, negativ überhaupt durch Zerbrechung des Kirchentums ermöglicht und positiv aus vielen Lebenssäften des Protestantismus genährt, aber nach andern Seiten hin von den Nachwirkungen der Renaissance und des Humanismus und von dem konfessionell gänzlich unberührten Geiste der neuen Philosophie aufgebaut. So gesehen erscheint der Protestantismus als Vorbedingung und Anreger einer neuen, spezifisch modernen, jedenfalls von dem Kirchenwunder und altchristlichen Dogma gelösten Religiosität."

[2] Troeltsch, "Die Bedeutung," p. 92, posits it for a *geschichtlicher Erfahrungssatz* "dass ohne religiöse Grundlage, ohne Metaphysik und Ethik, ein einheitlicher und starker Kulturgeist unmöglich ist." "So wird man auch rein tatsächlich sagen dürfen, dass die

the modern era with a religion appropriate to it, without itself experiencing a profound transformation under the influence of the modern age.[1] Therefore the service which Protestantism is rendering to the modern era is not really one of shaping the culture—according to Troeltsch Christianity can no longer do this—rather, if I may say so, it is one of providing therapy for the culture.

Therefore, too, according to Troeltsch, the relationship between the Middle Ages and the modern age appears in Protestantism itself as the relationship between Old and Neo-Protestantism. From this process of change, and only from it, the ideas that were already concealed in Luther and the Reformation are disclosed, ideas that point forward to the modern age but remained bound to the Middle Ages in their historical form. For the central teachings of the Reformation are still under the spell of medieval questions, a spell which they do not break even as newly formed answers.[2] Hence a definition of Protestantism is possible after all only as a reflection on its relationship to the Middle Ages and to the modern age.[3] In its historical form it is a phenomenon of transition

---

Religion der modernen Welt wesentlich vom Protestantismus bestimmt ist und dass hierin seine stärkste historische Bedeutung liegt. Freilich ist es kein einheitlicher Protestantismus. Es ist ein tief und innerlich gewandelter ..."

Compare also Troeltsch's judgment about the historical dependence of the three new forces (the modern natural sciences, the new philosophy which is related to them, and the new political system of national superstates) on the old forces (antiquity, Christianity, and the Roman-Germanic spirit of the Middle Ages) and his judgment of the enduring references to these. *Ges. Schr.*, IV, 203 : "Dieses Neue hängt nun aber mit den alten Urgewalten nicht bloss überall näher oder enger entwicklungsgeschichtlich zusammen und trägt sie dadurch sozusagen in seiner Tiefe mit sich, sondern ist überdies so wenig befähigt, den ganzen Lebenswillen auszufüllen und zu formen, dass daneben eine selbständige, ununterbrochene Mitwirkung jener drei alten Urgewalten stattfindet, die nun nicht mehr bloss unter sich ihre Gegensätze, Verwandtschaften, Berührungen und Fortentwicklungen auszuwirken fortfahren, sondern auch mit den neuen modernen Elementen die verschiedenartigsten Verbindungen eingehen und Gegensätze hervorrufen."

[1] "Die Bedeutung," p. 30 : "... von einer Wirkung des Protestantismus zur Herbeiführung der modernen Kultur kann nur in bezug auf die verschiedenen Gruppen des Altprotestantismus die Rede sein, während der Neuprotestantismus selbst ein Bestandteil der modernen Kultur und von ihr tiefgreifend beeinflusst ist."

[2] "Protestantisches Christentum und Kirche," pp. 438-39; "Die Bedeutung," p. 32; *Ges. Schr.*, IV, 212, 214.

[3] Cf. Hanns Rückert, "Die geistesgeschichtliche Einordnung der Reformation," *Zeitschrift für Kirche und Theologie*, LII (1955), 48 where he cites correctly as a masterful formulation Troeltsch's statement from "Protestantisches Christentum und Kirche," p. 436 : Der Protestantismus "ist *zunächst* in seinen wesentlichen Grundzügen und Aus-

composed of inner contradictions.[1] Only the dissolution of its classical
form permits the comprehension of its true kernel. It is true, in one
sense Troeltsch exempts Luther himself from this judgment. Although
with him too the new and the medieval are intertwined, he juts out into
the arena of the timeless and universal-human.[2] The catchword,
"religious individualism," which is intended to fix the congruence
between the "exploding new spirit" in Luther and the spirit of the
modern era,[3] calls to mind the principle of subjectivity which according
to Hegel was brought to its decisive breakthrough by Luther. According
to Troeltsch, however, Hegel would say that the emptying of all
dogmatic content results in a bad subjectivity, in an individualism
which emancipates itself from the power of the universal.[4] In the end
Troeltsch seems to draw Luther more forcibly to the side of the modern
age than Hegel did.

4. *The Development of the Question after Troeltsch*

The attempts to integrate Luther and the Reformation into the
history of thought are themselves conditioned by the history of thought.
On their part they document an increasingly sharpened wrestling with

---

prägungen eine Umformung der mittelalterlichen Idee, und das Unmittelalterliche,
Moderne, das in ihm unleugbar bedeutsam enthalten ist, kommt als Modernes erst voll,
in Betracht, nachdem die erste und klassische Form des Protestantismus zerbrochen
oder zerfallen war."

[1] *Ges. Schr.*, IV, 205 : "[Die Reformation und der Protestantismus bilden] eine gross-
artige und mächtige Übergangserscheinung, nicht in dem Sinne, wie alle geschichtlichen
Schöpfungen aufblühen und abwelken und neuen Platz machen, sondern in dem Sinne,
dass ihr ganzes inneres Wesen sich aus dieser Zwischenstellung erklärt und das Alte und
Neue eigentümlich und unwiederholbar verbunden in sich trägt. Nicht ihre Vergäng-
lichkeit, von der ja bis jetzt gar nicht die Rede sein kann, sondern ihre widerspruchsvolle
innere Zusammengesetztheit bedeutet also der Ausdruck 'Übergangserscheinung'."
Also *Ges. Schr.*, IV, 231.

[2] *Ges. Schr.*, IV, 231 : "... diese Charakterisierung als Übergangsgebilde gilt nur vom
protestantischen Kirchentum, genauer gesagt vom orthodoxen Altprotestantismus. Sie
gilt nicht von dem Manne, der den Ausgangspunkt und Sammelpunkt aller dieser Kräfte
bildet, von Luther selbst. Wenigstens kann sie von ihm nur sehr viel eingeschränkter
gelten. Er ragt ... in die Region des Zeitlosen und Allgemein-Menschlichen hinein,
... durch die Ursprünglichkeit und Kraft seines religiösen Erlebnisses."

[3] "Die Bedeutung," pp. 20ff; *Ges. Schr.*, IV, 220.

[4] "Die Bedeutung," pp. 12-13 : "Eine absolut überindividuelle Bindung bringt nur
eine so ungeheure Macht wie der Glaube an eine unmittelbare supranaturale göttliche
Offenbarung hervor, wie sie der Katholizismus besass ..." Here one must ask, of course,
how Troeltsch relates individualism to "the region of the timeless and common
humanness". See note 2 above.

the relationship between theological and thought-historical ways of thinking. Hegel's claim of the philosophical perfection of theology was transformed by Troeltsch into a mere administration of the theological legacy, in so far as this legacy after its historical decline could still be made use of at all in the philosophy of religion. It is understandable that a tendency to mutual repulsion increased. Dialectical theology believed it could derive a theological profit from the thought-historical antithesis between the modern age and the Reformation. But on the other hand the philosophical concern for the "legitimacy of the modern age" [1] went beyond Troeltsch and identified theology thoroughly with the Middle Ages. For the change from one age to the other Luther and the Reformation are now worthy only of marginal comment. Driven to extremes, theological absolutism is said to reveal completely its human unbearableness and involuntarily to legitimize man's self-assertion,[2] this basic trait of the spirit of the new age. Alongside that, the efforts within theology continued to bring the theological and thought-historical view into a relationship fruitful for both. Together with the systematicians Paul Tillich, Emanuel Hirsch, and Friedrich Gogarten, grateful mention should be made of historians and Luther researchers like Heinrich Bornkamm, Walter von Loewenich, Wilhelm Pauck, and Hanns Rückert. This task requires further work.

II. Fundamental Considerations to Luther's Thought-historical Significance

If I add some further considerations to these analyses, it will seem doubly presumptuous in view of how much thought has already been given to this matter and how much still needs to be considered to make some essential progress. But we would not be doing justice to our assignment, if we should want to spare ourselves the exertion of further consideration.

The nature of the theme and its destiny require very general reflections to discover where and how the detailed work on the texts— the really rewarding business in dealing with history—must begin anew to expedite the solution of our problem.

---

[1] H. Blumenberg, *Die Legitimität der Neuzeit* (Frankfurt-M., 1966).

[2] *Ibid.*, pp. 143-44, 59. The interpretation of Luther as the radical epitome of Nominalism is likely the weakest passage in this volume, which in many respects is stimulating.

1. *The Defects in Classifying Luther in respect to the Middle Ages and the Modern Era.*

I begin with the following observation: The more we move toward the center of Luther's theology, the stronger the impression becomes that his way of thinking is in contrast both to the spirit of the Middle Ages and to the spirit of the modern age, and to both at the same points. Luther's understanding of sin would be an example. Others could be adduced with equal justification. And all of them together probably constitute a single state of affairs.

This surmise draws explicit support from the well-known fact that Luther reduced to a common denominator the dissimilar opponents on his two battle fronts, the so-called papists and the so-called Enthusiasts, the scholastics and the humanistic theologian Erasmus. Thus he had to stress the same points in both directions.[1] Even though one does not unreservedly accept the wide-spread thesis that spiritualists and humanists of all shades were farther removed from the Middle Ages and closer to the modern age than Luther, one must still admit : In the fermenting sixteenth century they represented a stance that evokes the sympathy of modern times, already because of the contrast to Luther and the Catholic tradition. What differentiates Luther's position among his contemporaries, it seems to me, has a much greater significance for his position between the Middle Ages and the modern era.

We do not deny a relative right to the customary thought-historical form of questioning as Troeltsch in general has handled it brilliantly and impressively, though individual details may be challenged. Without doubt it is profitable heuristic procedure which in the historical studies opens one's eyes and sharpens the awareness of the problem, when we assign the historical phenomena as a whole either to the Middle Ages or to the modern era, indeed in most cases more appropriately, in part thus, in part so, in respect to the many factors and the complexity of their interrelationships. For this Luther provides inexhaustible material: from starkly medieval conceptions of the devil to critical expressions regarding the Bible; from the most daring acts of breaking with tradition to a cautious conservation of the status quo, "an infinitely conservative revolutionary," as Troeltsch once put it.[2] Even in such historical

---

[1] Cf. e.g., the well-known statement of the Smalcald Articles. *WA*, L, 245: 1-247: 4; *Die Bekenntnisschriften der evangelisch-lutherischen Kirche* (6th ed.; Göttingen, 1967), pp. 453 : 16-456: 18.

[2] *Ges. Schr.*, IV, 236.

confrontations, that more readily lead us to expect a heightening of his characteristic medieval features, certain aspects provoke in us astonishing claims for his modernity. Karl Marx regards him as the oldest German national economist;[1] Erik H. Erikson sees him as the forerunner of Sigmund Freud.[2]

Even when this way of interpretation is employed with a high degree of sensitivity and one perceives the modern already under the medieval and the medieval still under the modern, since both do not stand side by side but interpenetrate each other, this is hardly the way to get at the essential in Luther. What is appropriate is not a coordination with regard to the Middle Ages and the modern era according to the scheme either-or, or both-and, but here evidently neither-nor is valid.

With this consideration we would be on the wrong road if we wanted to withdraw the theological question from contact with the history of thought and pit it dogmatically against the latter. Even the distinction between shell and kernel, form and content must be regarded as unsatisfactory—this peaceful seperation which has served since the rise of historical consciousness as a formula for the co-existence of the variable and the constant, the transitory and the permanent. The intention would indeed be understandable, but the difficulty of the problem would not be pondered sufficiently, if the thought-historical consideration were concerned only with elements of form : forms of thought, of style, of society, etc., of which the theologically relevant would be untouched, so that one could be isolated from the other as formal and material aspects. The study of history is necessarily compartmentalized into a large number of aspects and questions. But precisely this makes the sharp twofold division into history of thought and history of theology questionable. One would even have to say that in the final analysis they become one, if history in its theological aspects is interpreted correctly. To obtain clarity on this point both are necessary : To interrogate theology about its relation to history, and the thought-historical interpretation about its ultimate presuppositions.

Self-evidently, problems of this sort are encountered not only in connection with Luther. Yet his stature in its historical context and its future historical effect—one would almost like to say—compels in a unique way and in exemplary acuteness the question about the thought-

---

[1] See H. Bornkamm, p. 75.

[2] E. H. Erikson, *Der junge Mann Luther : Eine psychoanalytische und historische Studie* (Hamburg, 1958), pp. 9, 53, 236, 238, 278-79.

historical classification and at the same time makes the relationship of thought-historical and theological patterns a problem. That is a symptom of the historical rank of Luther's person and of the objective relevance of his work. And it provides the explanation why a treatment of the theme, "Luther and the Beginning of the Modern Age," cannot withdraw from the onslaught of the general problem of the understanding of history.

2. *The Essence of Historical Relationship*

To a certain degree historical relationship may perhaps be grasped by means of physical causality or biological evolution. But these means for comprehending history miss the essential, the specifically human. All action and suffering, all experience and expression, all contemplation and planning, all destruction and construction, societal processes and individual control of life, insensibility and communication, enmity and friendship, hatred and love, despair and hope, unbelief and faith— all of this is actualized by the medium of language and is condensed therein to thought and conversation, to understanding and analysis. History as the context of language in a sense is actualized on two planes. First, in the immediate controversy of the time event and, correspondingly, the immediate influence on history so that word becomes deed and deed becomes word; but language also becomes institutionalized and institutions become means of regulating language. Secondly, in the transmission of fixed language and in its understanding across long distances of time, so that what was once thought and spoken, experienced, and decided asserts itself anew in a different situation and thus influences history mediately.

Therefore historical interest tends in two directions. On the one hand, it asks about the historical genesis of specific phenomena; on the other, about their present significance. The center of gravity of historical interest lies in the first, to recognize how something came to be. Naturally this includes also the question about its further development as the genesis of its change in form. Aspects of the history of transmission and effect are also included in so far as they likewise contribute to the clarification of its historical genesis. At the same time they form the bridge to the interest in the present. Consciously or unconsciously this interest in the present time is involved in all historical interest. But it gains the upper hand when the transmitted material is studied with a hungry heart because history promises to meet something the present needs. Only then, when the historical distance is taken seriously, can a gift for the present grow out of the dialogue with history.

"Luther and the Beginning of the Modern Age"—according to this theme Luther can be investigated in his historical dimension, the growth and development of his personality, and especially his theology. To what extent do essential features of modern thought assert themselves among all of the influences which impinged on Luther and the way in which he utilized them ? The ties with the Middle Ages, which received little attention formerly, are being noted more and more today, but have not yet been interpreted adequately. In contrast, as I see it, the influences on Luther of the dawning modern age, influences which can be grasped only with great difficulty, have been neglected by research, because especially here we cannot be satisfied with mere literary references but very subtle problems will have to be dealt with. Such problems are : What germs of the modern age are contained in Occamism or in late medieval mysticism and were transmitted from them to Luther ? Or, to say it somewhat crudely, what is the relationship of the modernity of the *via moderna* and the *devotio moderna* to modern day modernity ? Or, how much of the humanistic climate, beyond Luther's known modest relationship to humanism, made an impact on him and at least elicited some reactions ? To what extent did the Renaissance-consciousness of life and the times influence him, perhaps in the development of his historical self-consciousness and his picturesque literary style ?

But the theme can also be considered in the opposite direction, with regard to the contribution which Luther made to the beginning and the continuation of the modern age ; through the acceleration—or retardation—of developments that were already on the way, through new insights that were translated into historical forces pregnant with the future, or through thought forms which did not affect history until much later, perhaps still awaiting adequate consideration. This line of questions therefore necessarily points beyond the genesis of the modern age to its continuity to the present. We simply cannot examine Luther's impact on the beginning of the modern age without being swept out onto the open sea of the modern age. This has implications for our treatment of Luther here. We must transcend the very necessary concentration on the biographical and, the historical in the narrow sense, in his appearance. Therefore, we were forced again and again to mention Luther and the Reformation in one breath, not to make them identical, but to indicate the historical forces which continue in the history of

Luther's influence to the present. But now also the previously indicated
shift to the dominance of interest in the present arrives on the scene, a
shift no longer merely to the question about what Luther contributed
to the rise of the modern age once upon a time, but what Luther con-
tributes to the continuation of the modern age to the present.

If in this way our theme comprehensively brings into play all aspects
of the interest in history, then critical reflection on the thought-historical method of treatment up to this point suggests the question whether
this method was handled openly and broadly enough. I cannot enter
further into the most obvious criticism of the concept of the history of
thought today. If one has in mind the restriction to an absolutized
partial aspect, because of which the reference to other aspects is impro-
perly neglected, then already Troeltsch's expansion into the history of
culture and society indicates both that corrections must be made and
how they are to be made meaningfully. However, if one is offended by
the conception of the spirit as historical *movens*, a conception which,
diluted in comparison with Hegel, stands behind the customary usage
of the term *Geistesgeschichte*, then the following must be borne in mind :
The concept of the history of thought (*Geistesgeschichte*) is inseparably
connected with the task of determining far-ranging periods of history
according to the norm of their characteristic facial features, hence
physiognomically. The spirit of the times, in the sense of what finds
expression in the face of a period, may serve as interpretation of the
controverted concept of the history of thought (*Geistesgeschichte*) until
further notice.

3. *Toward Designating Epochs and Periods*

It is incontestably proper to examine history in terms of epochs,
outstanding moments of history in which time, as it were, holds its
breath and a pause in the movement of time occurs ; or, to use Hegel's
picture which in an opposite way expresses the same thing, epochs in
which the spirit seems to have donned seven-league boots after a long
snail's pace.[1] In this sense, beyond doubt the appearance of Luther is
eminently epochal. Even if it is remembered that his appearance occurs
in the broader phenomenon of the onset of an epoch, its epochal character is hardly diminished, but, if anything, enhanced. Also incontestable
is the necessity to proceed from such epochs and delimit periods in both

---

[1] *Werke*, XIX, 266.

directions, contracted, or stretched out, depending on the dominant point of view, and provided with correspondingly smaller or larger transitional phases. The more universally the many strata of life and strains of events in a given time are embraced, the farther the beginnings of the epochs are separated from each other and the more complex they become.

To take a century as a period is a practical procedure which has the advantage of completely neutral labeling. If it is handled with chronological breadth, it is less mechanical than it seems. But this is not adequate. The continued, very problematical, labeling of the overlapping periods of Western history as Ancient History, the Middle Ages, and the Modern Era, whose original humanistic interpretation has long been rejected, betrays a corresponding need and at the same time an embarrassment. It is obvious that we are dealing with profoundly different ages. But to give them names oriented to their content, names universally acknowledged, appears impossible in view of the complexity of the state of affairs. For that reason those customary formal designations have the advantage of ciphers which permit free play to the constantly new search for historical knowledge. Moreover, the humanistic evaluation of at least the relationship between the Middle Ages and the Modern Era is quite compatible with the predominant modern evaluation of history.

If now the understanding of Luther has been derived from his place between the two periods, the way in which their essence is determined will be decisive. It is evident that the so-called Middle Ages, as a Christianized era, constitute a cohesive period of history, even though the chronological boundaries are disputed, and the way in which Christianity and culture were fused requires critical interpretation. It is much more difficult to define the Modern Era. As an open-ended period its total picture is constantly subject to changes in perspective. This is all the more so, since in contrast to the strong continuity of the Middle Ages, revolution has entered into the essence of the modern age, in one sense, as a principle. Yet even from this perspective the so-called Modern Era is sharply differentiated from the Middle Ages through all of its changes, and is clearly recognizable as an historical period with its own stamp by its progressive emancipation from the sacral structure of order in the medieval world as well as by the rapidly advancing scientific-technical conquest of the world.

By this yardstick Luther undoubtedly occupies a highly complicated intermediate position. Closely bound to the Middle Ages according to

his origin, he was, because of his own transformation, more deeply involved in conflict with this age than any one else; and for that very
reason, because he was on such intimate terms with the heart of the
Middle Ages, he moved into opposition to the Middle Ages just at this
point, rather than at merely peripheral issues. As for the dawn of the
Modern Era, however, as far as it already appeared, Luther himself was
not so much inspired by it, but only illumined by it from the outside.
And that all the more, the more visibly he stood at the focus of his time;
and yet, the more deeply he touched, also in this direction, the innermost part of what constitutes an age, he was in one sense far ahead of
the course of the modern age, precisely because he was in opposition to
its principal trend.

That here a both-and is affirmed, and yet is transferred into a neither-
nor, appears as a contradiction. So as not to fall prey to this impression
prematurely, we must go behind the acknowledged periodization of
history and ask what, in the last analysis, constitutes a period of
history. What is the nature of its unifying force? According to the
common understanding a historical period is to some extent a closed
monad—to borrow this metaphysical concept from Leibniz in a hack-
neyed expression[1] and apply it to the problem of history—, a monad
which is determined by principle. Even though the idealistic tracing
back of complex historical movements to principles which are realized
in them has long since yielded to a more modest pragmatic view, yet
the converse with historical periods and the attempt to reduce them to
formulas betray the over-simplifying tendency to conceive of them as
ultimately pure monads. But already the observation that the peculiarity of a period can be determined only by comparison with another
and by its delimitation against another opposes such an approach.
Yet the following is more important.

What is constitutive for an age is the constellation of a series of long-
lasting data of the most diverse character, factors having to do with
geography, population, tradition, etc. But what is characteristic about
it is not simply a status of one kind or another, but the constellation of
a task, the creation of elbow room or a restricted arena, within which
the problematics of an age come to a final decision. To point it up paradoxically, one could say : What unifies an age is that about which there
is conflict. Especially also the matters, which are self-evident for an age

---

[1] See E. Heintel, *Die beiden Labyrinthe der Philosophie* : *Systemtheoretische Betrach-
tungen zur Fundamentalphilosophie des abendländischen Denkens* (Munich, 1968), I, 59.

and which are so characteristic for its image, contribute to its profile
primarily by determining the playing field and the rules of the game,
and within these boundaries the great discussions of an age are carried
on. For the Middle Ages this can be illustrated by the persistent struggle
for Christendom's diversified unity, while for the modern age this can
be done by the struggle for world change. The fact that every age is
dominated by the discussion about its true image is not the least indication of how much an age's assigned struggle belongs to its essence.
Since this constantly also involves ideas of the goal which pertain to
humanity and the state of the world, one can say that an age is characterized by its soteriological situation.

Intimately connected with this is the fact that no age is sufficient to
itself. Every age transcends its boundaries in a threefold respect. First,
into the past: It is dependent on what is transmitted, what it has not
produced itself and with which it must come to terms in order to gain
spiritual nourishment which is again transformed into new traditions.
Hence every age is characterized by where outside itself it has its
sources of life and what it does with them. Secondly, into the future :
Since it is never at the goal and never completely satisfied with itself,
every age is occupied with its change, strives beyond itself for better
times, and, not only through revolutionary means but also through conservative endeavors, consciously or unconsciously prepares changes
which will finally consolidate into the onset of a new epoch. Finally,
every age transcends its own concrete time and becomes a part of history as such. At all times mankind is confronted by the problematics of be-
coming and passing away, of living and dying, of time lost and fulfilled,
hence basic questions of humanness. These questions by no means
always remain timelessly the same as to their explication, yet in all ages
they are kindled at the same neuralgic points, because they are evoked
by the temporality of existence.

These three directions, in which an age has, as it were, open windows,
belong together as dimensions of a single state of affairs. The task which
arises from the specific constellation of an age—its soteriological situation, as I formulated it—, calls for a sovereign word which is suitable
for the time and able to cope with its problems. But this requires that
those three directions are given attention in the same measure : the
source of the great historical traditions, the goals of historical responsibility, and the basic questions of historical existence. A contemplation
of history that is open to the breadth and depth of the dialogue of an
age will therefore have to take note of the controversial correlation of

situation and word. With this catchword I refer to the distinction which Troeltsch employed for our problem, between medieval questions to which Luther is said to have given unmedieval answers; and furthermore, to Arnold Toynbee's historical categories of challenge and response, as well as to Paul Tillich's theological method of correlation [1] by means of which he relates to each other the questions from the situation and the answers from the message. It must be said by way of criticism that the new answer also changes the way the question is to be put, or already presupposes a change in the questions. For in the understanding of the situation, there is already an intimation of what is needed to master it.

4. Correction of the Treatment of Luther's Classification in the History of Thought

The net gain of this far-ranging excursion into basic problems of the understanding of history may be summed up in the following observation: The traditional handling of Luther's integration in the history of thought made a one-sided, and therefore false, use of opposing viewpoints. It affirmed a comprehensively exclusive opposition between the Middle Ages and the Modern Era, so that the question about the classification was simply posed disjunctively. Consequently this approach reduced the belonging to an age to a conformity free of contradiction and reckoned the remaining antitheses to the succeeding ages. For that reason, this historical method was not capable of doing adequate justice to the theological aspects and brought about a sham opposition to the theological concepts. So as not to surrender this criticism to the misunderstanding that the valid aspects in the thought-historical questioning were being denied, the three critical viewpoints shall be elucidated further.

First : The experience of liberation, which is so characteristic of the transition from the Middles Ages to the Modern Era, understandably produced the fascination of a purely antithetical reference of the periods to each other. The implications given by the labels to the periods have confirmed this impression. In spite of everything that is correct here, an age presents a far more complex state of affairs, when one extricates oneself from the notion of a windowless monad. The contrast between the Middle Ages and the Modern Era becomes alive and differentiated

---

[1] P. Tillich, *Systematische Theologie* (Chicago, 1951ff.), I, 74ff.

only in the context of what they have in common : the abiding factors, the overlapping problems, and a dialogical confrontation of the ages which does not really begin until one age has succeeded another. As much as belonging to the Modern Era demands its affirmation and excludes the medieval world as a possibility, so, on the other hand, this No can be as little a simple disparaging as the Yes can do without criticism.

Secondly : By its position in the transition from Middle Ages to the Modern Era a historical figure seems to be surrendered to the contraries of the old and the new, and so in a special measure to the transitory. Yet the opposite is the case with Luther, because heterogeneous elements were not accidentally mixed in him. Rather, in him a process of upheaval was accomplished, the poles of which simply were not only Late Middle Ages and Early Modern Era, but, on the one hand, the fountain of Christian faith which precedes even the Middle Ages, and, on the other hand, the future of the Modern Era into which the reformatory understanding of the Gospel makes its way without restriction. Thus Luther was occupied with a state of affairs that transcends Middle Ages and Modern Era. Precisely this qualified him to criticize in both directions. He broached anew the essentially Christian and discovered that this had been distorted just in the Christianized age. In this way he assisted in the demise of the Christianized age to a high degree and, at the same time, prevented the beginning of the modern age from continuing and completing itself in the same way in which it had started, namely as an immediate issuing from the Middle Ages. Because a new consideration of what is essentially Christian was injected, the detachment of the Modern Era from the Middle Ages took place under greatly changed conditions. Because of the Reformation, the Christian faith could approach the dialogue with the problems of the Modern Era in a form different from the medieval. Because the Christian faith was not identical with the age that was passing away, it was capable of a confrontation with the new age such as the medieval form of Christianity could not have achieved. To use Hegel's beautiful phrase, it was the "infinite elasticity of Christianity" [1] which created the possibility of going into the new age without falling prey to it. However, the history of Old and Neo-Protestantism shows how much this possibility was endangered and in how many ways it failed to be realized.

---

[1] *Werke*, XI, 514.

Thirdly : If the thought-historical approach is corrected in the sense
of that opening and differentiation, which I could only indicate, the
foolish rivalry with the theological interest falls away. Room is provided
for the appropriate grasp of the theologically relevant aspect in historical research, as far as this research in a self-critical way, resists its
contraction. That this really does justice to the theological questioning
is clear from the insight that the reference to time is essential for the
Christian faith. The Word, to which it must cling and which it must
transmit, is not a rigid formula that ostensibly would be removed from
time. All the more for that very reason it is subjected to it, but it is a
living word event which always demonstrates its superiority to time
in a superior manner by entering into time. Hence it becomes concrete
only when it confronts the temporal situation and only in that way does
it demonstrate its power. For that reason the Christian faith is not
definitively bound up with a specific period of culture, even though it
can integrate itself so thoroughly with an age that in its expressions of
life it seems to be identical with it. Although the Christian faith is not
dependent for its existence on a Christianized culture, it constantly
knows itself responsible for the total life of an age, as long as it itself is
alive. Thus it is to the advantage of the theological questioning if, by an
appropriate inclusion of the culture-historical aspects, it is preserved
from a pseudo-theological restriction, while by an inappropriate intrusion of these aspects it is indeed perverted into the pseudo-theological. It
would be the task of a fundamental theology to explicate this further.

III. Prospect of a Corresponding Future Task of Interpretation

Not without reason will my treatment of the theme, "Luther and the
Beginning of the Modern Age," appear as too rambling and too ambitious. As far as I am concerned, a different impression has imposed
itself on me more strongly, namely, that I have remained too much and
too exclusively with the perhaps necessary job of tidying up. The detail
work on the texts, which I claimed to be the really rewarding business
in the study of history, should now begin, to demonstrate by example
the problem structure that we have worked out. It was my intention to
do this with Luther's understanding of sin, because on the one hand, a
chief argument by Troeltsch would have to be invalidated at this point,
and on the other hand, the peculiarly controversial correlation between

the modern situation and Luther's thinking would be set forth.[1] Troeltsch was wrong in simply placing Luther's understanding of sin on the side of the Augustinian-medieval mode of thought, since it is considerably different not only from the scholastic, but also from the Augustinian understanding. What is new in the reformatory insight is inseparably linked with this difference. At the same place, indeed in a much more perceptible way, the deep chasm opens which separates Luther's understanding of sin from the modern age. In its main currents this age not only makes a trifle of sin but also seems to have lost every perception of what it means at all. But it would now have to be shown that Luther's understanding of sin could attack this situation far more sharply than the scholastic conception, because he could deal with the causes of sin in a most pertinent way. The modern in Luther shows itself here especially in the ability to enter the discussion about the Modern Era. Isolated from the understanding of sin, Luther's reference to the modern age loses its specific character, whether one sees the modern in Luther as rooted in the idea of personality or in the idea of freedom. In any case, without Luther's understanding of sin, theology deteriorates into moralism. A bad accommodation to the modern age in the Enlightenment arrived at that result and is doing so again today. But this means not only a betrayal of Luther but also a betrayal of the Modern Era.

Translated by the Rev. Prof. HERBERT J.A. BOUMAN, D.D.

---

[1] Cf. the essay *Theologie zwischen reformatorischem Sündenverständnis und heutiger Einstellung zum Bösen* in : Gerhard Ebeling, *Wort und Glaube* vol. III (Tübingen, 1975).

HEADWATERS OF THE REFORMATION

Initia Lutheri — Initia Reformationis

HEIKO A. OBERMAN

I. DISTINCTIO REALIS — DISTINCTIO RATIONIS

The "Reformation" whose origins or headwaters we seek to chart is
confined here to a much abbreviated phase, focusing as it does upon
Martin Luther. To be sure, the Lutheran Reformation would not have
been able to profit from the protective political and military shield
around its homelands without the other multiple origins in Zurich and
Geneva and without their rapid developments in the middle of the sixteenth century. The additional importance of a long enduring paral-
ysis of France—as a matter of fact until the eve of the opening of the
Council of Trent—cannot be easily overestimated as a factor in the
survival of Luther's heritage.

But even so, when taken in its restricted sense, reformation means
more than the life and thought of Martin Luther; it carries the connotation of a movement and evokes the image of a tidal wave sweeping
along not only theological but also political and social currents. It is
questionable, however, whether a shift of our attention from Luther to
the reception of his thought by his contemporaries can provide us with
a grasp of the shape and texture of the inner structures of this movement, since at its height it swept along many elements which were to
be separated out in the years to come. As symbols of such eliminated
persons, groups and ideas, the names of Staupitz, Karlstadt, Sickingen,
the Müntzerites, and the Erasmians can be mentioned.

Some scholars may be inclined to regard these eliminations as clarification and purification of the currents so darkened in the maelstrom
of the turbulent beginnings of the Reformation movement; particularly
during this last stage of the Middle Ages, academic critique, national
pathos, and social unrest could not but have added interpretations and
expectations alien to Luther's message. Others find instead a multiform
tradition with the young Luther himself wherein the Reformation discovery was prepared, engendered, and born—in, with, and underneath
nominalistic, humanistic, mystical, and Augustinian layers. In this view

Luther's later opponents were early temporary allies on the common platform of genuine Lutheran elements, subsequently deemphasized by Luther himself or even cast off like snakeskins.

To return to the original water imagery : the element of truth in the latter position seems to me to be that Luther's development can be described as a series of successive waves, one tumbling over the other. Hence the perplexing difficulty of establishing the point at which we may locate the Reformation breakthrough. Too often reduced to a single idea in Luther's mind or to an event in his study, this breakthrough has not been viewed sufficiently in relation to his public reception, which was soon to become a movement in its own right. Although we shall argue for the importance of a distinction between the *initia Lutheri* and the *initia reformationis*, the two paths for a time coincide. To express this intimate relationship between an idea and its reception, we are well-advised to think in terms of sound waves, each one reaching past an ever-widening and qualitatively different audience.

1. The first period is richly documented by the *Dictata super Psalterium* and the lectures on Romans which prove from the very beginning [1] to challenge Luther's colleagues and to appeal to the theological students. Johann Lang reports from the Augustinian monastery in Wittenberg on 10 March, 1516 to Spalatin that the students *en masse* are dropping out of the courses on scholasticism. While he does not mention Luther by name, it is obvious that he reports on the new excitement emanating from the Augustinian monk holding the chair for biblical studies. Yet he does go on to explain the rebirth (*reviviscere*) of biblical studies and the vivid interest in the *antiqui scriptores* by pointing to the learning and integrity of Reuchlin and Erasmus, "erudite and honest beyond words." [2]

---

[1] See Kenneth Hagen, "An Addition to the Letters of John Lang : Introduction and Translation", *ARG*, LX (1969), 27-32. In this letter of Lang to Spalatin from the Augustinian monastery at Wittenberg dated 10 March 1516, we have now the earliest documentation of Luther's impact. This also settles the question of dating Luther's letter to Lang in Erfurt : with *WA Br*, I, 88 against the Gotha Ms., letter no. 34, it is to be dated in 1517 (8 February). Without mentioning Luther's name explicitly Lang writes: "... sacram bibliam antiquosque scriptores complures et anhelant et laetanter audiunt, dum scholastici doctores (quod appellant) vix aut duos aut treis [sic] habent auditores", Hagen, 30.

[2] "Quod ut fiat maximo sunt adiutorio Ioannes Reuchlinus, vir doctissimus pariter et integerrimus, et Erasmus Roterodamus ultra quem [quam ?] dicere possum et eruditus et frugi", Hagen, pp. 30-31. Lang refers to Mutian as "Rufum nostrum, non tantum amicum sed et patrem". *Ibid.*

A few weeks later Luther makes a crucial strategic move when he enlarges the Wittenberg sphere of influence by appointing Lang as prior of the Erfurt house of the Reformed Augustinians. Whereas Lang looks at Luther from the perspective of the Erfurt humanist circle around Mutianus Rufus, [1]Luther in informing Mutian of his decision indicates explicitly that Lang is indeed well-versed in his Greek and Latin, but what is more—"quod maius est"—he is an upright man—"syncerioris cordis." [2] It is important for us to note that in contrast to the humanist's ideal man who is equally (*pariter*) learned and upright—expressed time and again in letters and dedications— Luther indicates that for him no such balance holds : a *cor syncerum* is more important than classical learning. And that in a letter to Mutian! In Lang we meet a representative of a whole group of first adherents who, inspired as they are by humanist ideals and expectations, are bound to interpret Luther in such categories.[3] In Lang's letter to Spalatin we have the earliest reflection of Luther's emerging image; at the same time it is the earliest proof of the bewildering complexity of the question of Luther's relation to the temper and forces of his day.

2. The public disputation *Contra scholasticam theologiam* before the forum of the whole University of Wittenberg is formally a call for a reform of theological studies. Its content reveals both the deep gulf separating Luther from the tradition in which he himself was reared and the extent to which he participates in the broader Wittenberger platform *contra omnes*, against the joint medieval tradition. Hence this disputation is to be understood in conjunction with Karlstadt's earlier 151 theses of 26 April 1517, in which the later "Brother Andrew" is ahead of Luther on a number of central points.

3. Whereas the Ninety-five Theses are addressed to theologians—"docendi sunt christiani"—and are eagerly handed around by the enlightened few, the *Sermon von dem Ablass und Gnade* carries the attack on indulgences "far and wide into circles untouched by the Ninety-five

---

[1] Cf. *WA Br*, I, 40-41, note 2.

[2] *WA Br*, I, 40:22; 29 May 1516, Luther to Mutian.

[3] Johannes Geiling also belongs to this group. Oswald Bayer and Martin Brecht called attention to him in connection with their important discovery : "Unbekannte Texte des frühen Luther aus dem Besitz des Wittenberger Studenten Iohannes Geiling", *ZKG*, LXXXII (1971), 229-258, 254 ff.

Theses," [1] establishing Luther as pastor to the nation.[2] His opting for the German language is based on the conscious decision to serve the common folk rather than the sodalities of *eruditi*. We should not too eagerly interpret this decision as an expression of "social protest." Primarily it is related to the discovery of the dimension of *experientia*, *Erfahrung*, which is to become thematic in Luther's tracts and sermons of the coming years, the experience of God and death which does not know social boundaries.

4. The Heidelberg Disputation on 26 April, 1518 provides Luther with the opportunity to present his theology to the Order to which he owed more, as we shall see, than to any other single influencing factor, and where he received more than a profound respect for the "Founding Father" of Hippo. In Heidelberg he pits what he self-consciously calls *mea theologia* (and a moment later *vera theologia*) against the dialectics of his Erfurt teacher, Trutvetter. It is also here that he provokes the historically loaded comment of the youngest Heidelberg Doctor Georg Niger, received at that time with hearty laughter : "If the peasants heard this, they would certainly stone you to death." [3] With foresight Niger related the swelling peasant protest to the new *theologia crucis*, particularly to the *XXI. conclusio* of Luther, where the enemies of the cross of Christ are characterized as those who "hate their cross and sufferings." [4] Whereas this warning is an effort of an opponent to ridicule him, Luther can report [5] that he has won over many among the younger generation. However, if Bucer may function as a test case, the *theologia crucis* has not come through clearly and the Wittenberger is once

---

[1] Robert Herndon Fife, *The Revolt of Martin Luther* (New York, 1957), p. 263. Cf. note 77 referring to Knaake's list, *WA*, I, 240ff.

[2] "Es gibt in jenen ersten Jahren noch keine eigentliche lutherische Bewegung im Volk ... Luther ist hier noch nicht als Parteiführer, sondern als Seelsorger bekannt." Bernd Moeller, "Die deutschen Humanisten und die Anfänge der Reformation", *ZKG*, LXX (1959), 46-61, 51.

[3] "Si rustici hec audirent, certe lapidibus vos obruerent & interficerent." *WA Br*, I, 173 28-29. Luther to Spalatin, Wittenberg, 18 May 1518.

[4] "Tales [sc. theologi gloriae] sunt quos Apostolus vocat Inimicos crucis Christi [Phil. 3 : 18]. Utique quia odiunt crucem et passiones, Amant vero opera et gloriam illorum, Ac si bonum crucis dicunt malum et malum operis dicunt bonum. At Deum non inveniri nisi in passionibus et cruce ..." *WA*, I, 362 26-29.

[5] "Ceterum adulescentulorum & totius Iuventutis animus per Bis diapason ab illis sentit. Et eximia spes mihi est, ut, sicut Christus ad gentes migravit reiectus a Iudeis, Ita & nunc quoque vera eius Theologia, quam reiiciunt opiniosi illi senes, ad Iuventutem sese transferat. Hec de me." *WA Br*, I, 174 44-47. Luther to Spalatin, Wittenberg, 18 May 1518.

again seen as an Erasmian, only more courageous than the cautious
scholar from Rotterdam. Among the first of the *jeunesse dorée* is Melanchthon who, a few weeks after his arrival in Wittenberg on 25 August 1518,
emphasizes Luther's singularity as the "elect servant of the indestruc-
table truth" and "expected messenger of God," even as $\Theta\epsilon\acute{o}\pi\epsilon\upsilon\sigma\tau\sigma$ [1]
—the unique mark of Holy Scripture (2 Tim. 3 : 16). In Luther's own
"history of the reformation" of 1545, he is to single out the arrival of
Melanchthon as a crucial event in the *initia reformationis*.[2] Even though
Luther responds in kind to Melanchthon's early accolade by designa-
ting him as a God-directed *organum*, yet their profound mutual respect
and *consensus* continue to be heavily tested. The severest challenge may
well have been the contested interpretation of St. Augustine, so differently understood by the learned man of letters and the monk from
the Order based on Augustine's Rule.[3]

5. The Leipzig Disputation in the summer of 1519 sets the defense
of the *vera theologia* against the charges of heresy and deviationism
before the theological world, generating reverberations among the *in-
telligentia*, political leaders and humanists. Here ecclesiological implications of the Ninety-five Theses are pursued, leading to the clarification that Luther's cause is not to be identified with the reemergence of
late medieval conciliarism.[4] As we shall see, there is a precedent in the

---

[1] *WA Br*, XII, 12 5-7.
[2] *WA*, LIV, 182 4-8.
[3] See p. 44, n. 2.
[4] Cf. Christa Tecklenburg-Johns, *Luthers Konzilsidee in ihrer historischen Bedingtheit
und ihrem reformatorischen Neuansatz* (Berlin, 1966), p. 160, n. 363, 192, 194. When Luther
scholars find the concept of the general fallibility of legitimate councils in the Luther of
1518-1519, they "universalize a particular" and thus argue in the same way that Luther
accused Eck of doing : "Credo autem, auditores meos forte dixisse, Concilium generale
saepius errasse et errare posse, tum quod rara sunt concilia illa legitime generalia quale
Nicenum fuit : hoc enim dicentes verissime dixerunt. At illi pro rusticitate sua ex parti-
culari mox intulerunt universalem, omne videlicet concilium reprobatum assumentes."
WA, II, 627 28-32. The same nominalistic (= scholarly !) interest appears in Luther's
defense of Hus against Eck's interpretation of Constance, as distorting the various
judgments "omnes in universum hereticos". *WA*, II, 288 19. The continuity with late
medieval conciliarism can be seen in art. 11 in the *Defensio* of 1519 : "Quod plus sit
credendum simplici laico scripturam alleganti quam Papae vel concilio scripturam non
alleganti." *WA*, II, 649 2-3. For Karlstadt's earlier application of this principle on the
basis of Gerson, see Ulrich Bubenheimer, *Consonantia Theologiae et Iurisprudentiae :
Andreas Bodenstein von Karlstadt als Theologe und Jurist auf dem Weg von der Scholastik
zur Reformation 1515-1522* (Diss., Tübingen, 1971), ch. III, pp. 3-7.

Augustinian Order for Luther's surprising association with the position of the abhorred heretic Jan Hus. At the council of Constance an Augustinian general had already highlighted the critical distance between the organizational Church and the elect *communio sanctorum*.

6. Finally the year 1520 with its widely read manifestoes calling for joint action, inner and outer reforms, climaxes in the public burning of "Exsurge Domine" and, even more important for daily life, the burning of books of canon law, a Wittenberg happening at the Elstergate in December which could be understood also by the illiterate. For all those who could read either Latin or German, the *De libertate christiana* presents without explicit polemics the platform of the new theology ranging from *iustificatio sola fide* to the priesthood of all believers and the distinction between law and gospel. The imperial Diet of Worms, *Reichsacht* and papal condemnations form no more than an epilogue to these *initia*. It is by no means obvious, however, that the designation of these early events as *initia reformationis* is appropriate. Franz Lau, for example, links the "Anbruch" and "Auslösung" of the Reformation with the decision of the Diet of Worms in May 1521.[1] As is indicated by the image of concentric sound waves, I fully agree with the emphasis upon public impact as implied in this use of the word Reformation. Yet we should be careful to integrate the *initia reformationis* with the *initia Lutheri* in the years before Worms, that is, before Luther has become both a potent political factor and a *fait accompli*.

Therefore when we try now to find a formula by which we can distinguish the *initia reformationis* from the *initia Lutheri*, with which it has too long been identified, we do so only after stressing that the two notions are intricately intertwined, particularly in the years 1516-1519. Luther is to be regarded not so much as a lonely prophet—let alone as the Hercules of the humanists—but as a leading member of the Wittenberg team which, in keeping with the motto of the university, initiated its program "in the name of St. Paul and St. Augustine."[2] In these years the difference should not be regarded as a *distinctio realis* but as a *distinctio rationis*; or to use the terminiology preferred by Melanchthon and Calvin, we should distinguish only *docendi causa*.

---

[1] Cf. Franz Lau, "Reformationsgeschichte bis 1532", § 2.1, "Die Auslösung der Reformation durch den Reichstag zu Worms ...," and § 1.9, "Reformatorische Anfänge unabhängig von Luther," *Die Kirche in ihrer Geschichte*, ed. K.D. Schmidt and E. Wolf (Göttingen, 1964), pp. 17, 13-14.

[2] Cf. my "Wittenbergs Zweifrontenkrieg gegen Prierias und Eck. Hintergrund und Entscheidungen des Jahres 1518", *ZKG*, LXXX (1969), 331-58; 334-5.

When Luther in his joyful letter to Lang of 18 May 1517 writes : "Theologia nostra et Sanctus Augustinus prospere procedunt... Aristoteles descendit paulatim...," [1] he describes with his own categories the same development which Lang had regarded a year before as a victory of humanism. Yet it is not Luther's own theological program to which the "theologia *nostra*" refers, but to that of a *team* of Wittenbergers. It may well be that the "nostra" includes also Lang, addressed now as Prior of the Augustinian house at Erfurt. In that case, the statement is related to Luther's later praise of Gregory of Rimini (d. 1358) as the sole medieval representative in the battle for Scripture and Augustine against the scholastic doctors.[2]

At the same time it is necessary to distinguish *docendi causa*, since the sources compel us to acknowledge that Luther "sui ipsius interpres," when viewed in the light of the much more ample documentation at our disposal today, understood the *vera theologia* differently from his interpreters, differently not only from his opponents but also from his early followers and allies. Several factors should be taken into account.

1. Methodical research into the reception of Luther's thought by his contemporaries is still in an early stage, due partly to its preference for studying single persons and hesitancy to move on to social groups in the Hanse and *Reichsstädte*.[3] One point is nevertheless clear and striking : the converging focus of interest for all, whether positively or negatively, is the newly preached Christian freedom thematically formulated in Luther's *De libertate christiana*. To point first to a negative confirmation of the centrality of this theme : Staupitz addresses his critique in his farewell to Luther, concerned as he is about the spreading abuse of liberty.[4] Albrecht Dürer on the other hand, in the Nuremberg

---

[1] "Theologia nostra et S. Augustinus prospere procedunt et regnant in nostra universitate Deo operante. Aristoteles descendit paulatim inclinatus ad ruinam prope futuram sempiternam. Mire fastidiuntur lectiones sententiariae, nec est, ut quis sibi auditores sperare possit, nisi theologiam hanc, id est bibliam aut S. Augustinum aliumve ecclesiasticae autoritatis doctorem velit profiteri." *WA Br*, I, 99 8-13. Luther to Lang, Wittenberg, 18 May 1517.

[2] *WA*, II, 303 12-15. See p. 39, n. 2.

[3] Apart from its helpful bibliography, the most recent publication in this area is paradigmatic for future investigations. Hans-Christoph Rublack, *Die Einführung der Reformation in Konstanz von den Anfängen bis zum Abschluß 1531* (Gütersloh, 1971).

[4] "... ad libertatem carnis video innumeros abuti euangelio." *WA Br*, III, 264 26. Salzburg, 1 April 1524. Cf. Th. Kolde, *Die Deutsche Augustiner-Congregation und Johann von Staupitz* (Gotha, 1879), pp. 446-47.

circle around Staupitz, the so-called *Sodalitas Staupitziana*, sees in Luther the prophet of liberty from the oppressive multitude of ecclesiastical laws.[1] And it is on this treatise of Luther's that the earlier prosecutor of Reuchlin, the Dominican Inquisitor van Hoogstraten (d. 1527), concentrates his perceptive and penetrating attack.[2] It is the freedom from man-made laws which motivates Karlstadt [3] and, temporarily, Melanchthon,[4] during the period of radical reform in Wittenberg before the return of Luther from the Wartburg. The same motif underlies the famous— and last— expression of appreciation on the part of Thomas Müntzer over against the new Wittenberg theology: "Theologi-

---

[1] "Offensichtlich ist Dürer vor allem an der von Luther neu erschlossenen Möglichkeit rechten christlichen Lebens und der Befreiung des Gewissens von dauernder Sünderfurcht ... interessiert." Gottfried Seebass, "Dürers Stellung in der reformatorischen Bewegung", *Albrecht Dürers Umwelt : Festschrift zum 500. Geburtstag* (Nürnberg, 1971), pp. 101-31, 107.

[2] "Fratris Iacobi Hoochstrati catholicae aliquot Disputationes contra Lutheranos", *Bibliotheca reformatoria Neerlandica*, ed. F. Pijper ('s-Gravenhage 1905), III, 609-10. Interpretation and English translation of the texts concerned with Steven E. Ozment, "Homo Viator : Luther and Late Medieval Theology", *Harvard Theological Review*, LVII (1969), 275-87; 285-86,

[3] "Nec scandali respectus est habendus in dispensandis humanis traditionibus, si cum iure divino observari non possint." Thesis 5 from "De scandalo et missa", Oct./Nov. 1521; Hermann Barge, *Andreas Bodenstein von Karlstadt I, Karlstadt und die Anfänge der Reformation* (Leipzig, 1905; Repr. Nieuwkoop, 1968), p. 491.

Cf. Melanchthon "De scandalo" in *Loci communes* (1521); *Melanchthons Werke*, ed. H. Engelland (Gütersloh, 1952), II, 1, 161-62, with the editions 1543 and 1559 where *ius divinum* is replaced by *mandata divina*; *ibid.*, II. 2, 752 ff. For Melanchthon's high regard and interpretation of *De Libertate* see *ibid.*, VII, 1, 106-8 (April/May 1521).

The point at which Melanchthon would differ from Karlstadt is the substitution of *fides* for *ius divinum* in the evaluation of the relation *libertas-scandalum* : "Leges humanae non obstringunt conscientiam, sed sunt servandae sine scandalo. Tum rursus abolendae sunt et non servandae quando per eas periclitatur fides." *Ibid.*, VII, 1, 108 45-48. Cf. Melanchthon's letter of 5 Feb. 1522, which went via Haugold of Einsiedel to the Elector : "... hab auch d. Carlstatt gebetten, das er sich wolde meßigen. Ich khan aber das wasser nicht halden, were von nodten, das man zu solchen sachen, so der seelen heyl betreffen, ernstlicher thette... Es ist eyn reformatio vorhanden, gott gebe, das sie zu seyner ehre reyche." For this letter in its context see Nikolaus Müller, *Die Wittenberger Bewegung 1521 und 1522 : Die Vorgänge in und um Wittenberg während Luthers Wartburgaufenthalt* (2nd. ed.; Leipzig, 1911), p. 181-82.

[4] In a letter to the Elector of 27 Dec. 1521, Melanchthon reports his impressions of the Zwickau prophets : "Nam esse in eis spiritus quosdam multis argumentis adparet, sed de quibus iudicare praeter Martinum nemo facile possit ... Cavendum enim est simul, ne spiritus dei extinguantur, simul, ne occupemur a Satana." *Werke*, VII, 1, 159 20-22, 27-29.

am vestram toto corde amplector, nam de funibus venantium animas electorum eripuit multas." [1]

2. As it appears, all followers assent to the first proposition of *De libertate*: "A Christian is a perfectly free lord of all, subject to none." But even those who call themselves *Martiniani* differ as regards the second proposition : "A Christian is a perfectly dutiful servant of all, subject to all." [2] In the interpretation of liberty as "freedom for service" referred to by Luther as the *officium charitatis*, the above-mentioned reformers step off the common platform to give this second proposition differing interpretations in Basel and Strasbourg, in Wittenberg and Bremen, in the *Reichsritter* revolt of Sickingen,[3] and in the more widely spread but equally abortive Peasant Revolt.[4]

So individually determined as each one is, there is a common characteristic. Freedom is understood as freedom *from* : from the liturgical *ceremoniae*, from the theological *opiniones* and from the *humanae traditiones*. A common characteristic is that *sola scriptura* is elevated to the same level of significance as Luther's *sola fide* and *sola gratia*. This *sola scriptura* is to form the guide, lawbook, or vision according to which the freedom *for* service, for renewal of the Church, for political action

---

[1] Thomas Müntzer, *Schriften und Briefe,* ed. G. Franz (Gütersloh, 1968), p. 380 3-4; letter to Melanchthon, 27 March 1522.

[2] *WA*, VII, 49 22-25; *LW*, XXXI, 344. For the designation 'Martiniani' see O. Clemen, "Georg Helts Briefwechsel", *ARG, Erg. Bd.* 2 (1907), 10-11, and Müller, 79, n. 2.

[3] See the significant advance made by Martin Brecht in showing the extent to which there is a common thrust of "Stadtreformation" as described by B. Moeller (*Reichsstadt und Reformation* (Gütersloh, 1962 [Schriften des Vereins für Reformationsgeschichte 180]) and the "Reichsritterrevolt" : "Wie alle gesellschaftlichen Schichten so ist auch die Ritterschaft von der Reformation stark beeinflußt worden. Daran wie dies geschah, läßt sich etwas erkennen von der weithin einheitlichen Wirkung der Reformation im sozialen Raum. Mehr als man bisher wohl erkannt hat, sind offenbar verschiedene Schichten der Gesellschaft von den gleichen Gedanken erfaßt worden, wie es das Phänomen der Ritterschaft neben den Städten beweist." "Die deutsche Ritterschaft und die Reformation", *Ebernburg-Hefte*, 3. Folge, 1969, 27-37, 32.

[4] Gordon Rupp observes quite rightly in the Peasant Revolt both the older appeal of "desperate conservatism" with "a concern not so much for abstractions—justice, liberty and the like—as for liberties ..." and a new element : "the subtle influence of Luther and the Reformation." This subtlety seems to me to exist in the reading together of liberty and justice. It is true that Luther and Melanchthon as mediators are suggested; but as Rupp observes "... there is an appeal to 'Divine Justice' (*Göttliches Recht*) which might owe something to the teaching of Ulrich Zwingli and sometimes to ancient Catholic doctrine." *Patterns of Reformation* (London, 1969), p. 232.

and social reform is shaped.[1] For Luther, liberty and justice *coram Deo* are established and guaranteed by faith in the promises of God, i.e., in the *verbum Dei* grasped in Scripture, so that the Christian conscience is set free to act in love, determined not by set precepts of Scripture nor in order to avoid the wrath of God but by the needs of the *proximus*, the fellow man.

It is on this threshold between the first and second proposition of *De libertate* that we may find one of the characteristic lines of demarcation between the *initia Lutheri* and the *initia reformationis*.

3. A new conception of the role of Scripture arises amid the *initia reformationis* with the issue of the *tertius usus legis*. With Luther and consonant with a never-forgotten medieval tradition, Scripture is read as the only convincing basis for settling theological questions. But among those involved in the *initia reformationis*, Scripture is elevated to the same rank as *sola gratia* and *sola fide* and used to determine the quest for reshaping public life, particularly in the cities. The *sola scriptura* articulated by Karlstadt before Luther (May 1518) is programmatically announced by Zwingli as the inspired reform charter for Zurich.[2]

As to the priority of Karlstadt, it should be pointed out that with all respect for the daring originalty of the Wittenberg representative of the *via antiqua*, he had literally to discover the authority of Scripture which

---

[1] Even when analyzing more precisely Luther's justification of armed intervention by the authorities against the peasants in revolt and also the extent to which he upholds their *gravamina*, the basic distinction is clear : the *libertas christiana* clearly warrants the "geystlich auffruhr", whereas the devil tries to compromise and suppress this threat to him by manipulating it into "ein leyplich auffruhr". *WA*, VIII, 683 30-31.

[2] Zwingli's underscored scriptural principle should not be seen in competition with the centrality of the doctrine of justification. See G.W. Locher, *Huldrych Zwingli in neuer Sicht : Zehn Beiträge zur Theologie der Zürcher Reformation* (Zürich-Stuttgart, 1969); B. Moeller, "Zwinglis Disputationen: Studien zu den Anfängen der Kirchenbildung und des Synodalwesens im Protestantismus", *Zeitschrift der Savigny-Stiftung für Rechtsgeschichte*, LXXXVII, Kantonische Abteilung, LVI, (1970), 275-324, 294. G.W. Locher, "Zwingli und Erasmus", *Zwingliana : 450 Jahre Zürcher Reformation*, XIII, (1969), 37-61, 58 : "Die Entwicklung Zwinglis ist ein prachtvolles Exempel für die Einheit von Formal- und Materialprinzip der Reformation; 'solus Christus' und 'sola scriptura' bedingen einander." The different function of the *sola scriptura* is rather to be seen in the vision of the gospel as the new law : "Wir stehen in der Freiheit vom Gesetz auf der Seite des Gesetzes. Deutlich gegen Luthers scharfe Antithetik heißt es : 'das gsatzt sye dem gotshulder (= pius) ein euangelium'. [*Huldreich Zwinglis Sämtliche Werke* (=*Z*), edd. Emil Egli, Georg Finsler, II, Leipzig, 1908, 232, 13 f.]". Locher, *Huldrych Zwingli in neuer Sicht*, pp. 234-35 with n. 255.

4

we see presupposed in the earliest notes of Luther, the Augustinian monk. As concerns the relation between Luther and Zwingli, neither the issue of the sole authority of Scripture, nor even of hermeneutics in the technical sense of the word is at stake, but rather Zwingli's concept of Scripture as the legislative charter for the Christian magistrate.[1] For Zwingli it is a half-truth or rather a half-error due to one of Luther's paradoxes to believe that the *regnum Christi* is not also a political, visible reign, "etiam externum,"[2] as he puts it. One does not need to have been an Augustinian monk to remember with fear and trembling to what extremes curialism, with its insistence upon the political dimension of the *regnum Christi*, had led. It had been advanced in just this way by the official doctor of the Augustinian Order, Giles of Rome, and issued in Boniface VIII's "Unam Sanctam."

This pervading application and emphasis on Scripture among the Reformers, who to a large extent hail from the *via antiqua*, can also be explained in terms of the large number of students of law who opted for the Reformation. At least initially, a striking number of leading men ranging from Karlstadt to Budé, Zasius, and Calvin were recruited, men who, almost without fail, stand in the tradition of the *mos gallicus* and its return *ad fontes iurisprudentiae*.[3] This is indeed one of the politically decisive points where humanism and the Reformation movement combine to perpetuate and transform the late medieval city-ideology of corporate holiness through the freedom of preaching and the firm establishment of schools replacing the monasteries.

4. Beyond or rather beneath these visible changes brought by the Reformation to an increasing number of cities, there lies a civic dream of the realization of the City of God, with explicit references, in the first

---

[1] *Zwinglis Briefwechsel: Die Briefe von 1527-1528* (Leipzig, 1925), ed. Walther Köhler, Z IX, 455,26-30(*CR*, XCVI): "... multo magis licet ei magistratui ... dum Christianus est, cum ecclesie consensu ... de externis istis, que aut servata oportet aut neglecta, statuere." Zwingli to Blarer, 4 May 1528.

[2] "... sed nos huc solum properamus, ut probemus Christi regnum etiam esse externum ... Vult ergo Christus, etiam in externis modum teneri, eumque imperat; non est igitur eius regnum non etiam externum." *Ibid.*, IX, 454 13-17. "... nobiscum videbis semierrorem istum, ex paradoxo Luteri ortum ..." *Ibid.*, IX, 454 21-22. Cf. Artur Rich, "Zwingli als sozialpolitischer Denker", *Zwingliana*, XIII (1969), 67-89, 71.

[3] See here particularly the works of Guido Kisch: *Humanismus und Jurisprudenz: Der Kampf zwischen mos italicus und mos gallicus und der Universität Basel* (Basel, 1955); *Bartolus und Basel* (Basel, 1960); *Gestalten und Probleme aus Humanismus uud Jurisprudenz. Neue Studien und Texte* (Berlin, 1969). See also Myron Gilmore, *Humanists and Jurists: Six Studies in the Renaissance* (Cambridge, Mass., 1963), pp. 85-86.

stages, to Plato's *Republic*.[1] Here the relation between *temporalia* and *aeterna* or between *externa* and *interna* is seen in terms of moral progress rather than of paradox. When Luther locates his *theologia crucis* exactly at the point where these two worlds meet in the believer, it is striking that Bucer, for example, in his enthusiastic report of the Heidelberg Disputation, relegates this aspect to the background. Bucer takes Luther's repeated reference to Augustine's *De spiritu et litera*[2] as the context of interpretation of Luther's intentions. The result is that he informs Rhenanus that in Luther's view we are justified through the *lex spiritus*.[3] Rather than giving a faithful report as it is usually understood, Bucer at the very moment that he is won for the Reformation introduces a far-reaching variant from "justification by faith" : justification through the lifegiving law of the Spirit in contrast to the killing letter of the law.[4] Lines can be drawn from here to his mediating position in the later eucharistic struggle and to the political pneumatology which would inspire his blueprint for a reformed commonwealth in England, the *De regno Christi*. Apparently there are limits to the extent to which Luther can be understood, even by his most dedicated adherents !

---

[1] See, e.g., the earliest description of Zwingli's theology by Beatus Rhenanus (d. 1547). He describes, in a letter of 6 December 1518, the content of Zwingli's preaching: "... propterea missum in terras a deo Christum ..., ut doceret nos pacem et concordiam ac pulchram rerum omnium communionen (nam nihil aliud est Christianissimus), qualem olim Plato magnis annumerandus prophetis utcunque in sua republica somniasse visus est ..." *Z*, VII, 115 19-20, 115 23-116 3.

[2] *WA*, I, 355 34-35; 356 1-4 : "Unde capite 8. [Rom. 8 : 2] appellat Legem legem mortis et legem peccati. Imo 2. Corinth. 3[: 6]. Litera occidit. Quod B. Augustinus per totum librum de spiritu et litera intelligit de qualibet etiam sanctissima lege Dei."

[3] Bucer bases his report not only on the public disputation but also on the *amica confabulatio* the next day : "postea ab ipso fui edoctus", *WA*, IX, 162 15. "... ut summatim iam complectamur haec omnia, est lex Spiritus divina quaedam 'ἐντελέχεια humanae menti deitus illapsa, irrequieta, perenni impulsu sursum ciens omnia, qua homo et animo prono iusta percipit et summa cum voluptate operatur. Hanc vero ita dari a Deo contendit, ut nulla prorsus mortalium opera emereri queat. Eam ipsam appellari quoque subinde gratiam, nonnunquam fidem, legem vitae, legem Spiritus ac etiam novam legem." *WA*, IX, 162 44-163, 5. Cf. *Briefwechsel des Beatus Rhenanus*, ed. A. Horawitz-K. Hartfelder (Leipzig, 1886; repr. Hildesheim, 1966), p. 108.

[4] "Haec ferme ille inter respondendum disseruit de Lege Spiritus, qua una excepta, quaecunque alia sit, nequaquam hominem possit ad iustitiam promovere sed obesse potius, libera voce pronunciabat." *WA*, IX, 163 21-23; *Briefwechsel des Beatus Rhenanus*, p. 109. In this 'libera voce' Bucer sees at this time the only difference between Erasmus and Luther : "... quae ille duntaxat insinuat, hic aperte docet et libere". *Ibid.*, p. 107; *WA*, IX, 162 9-10.

5. Significantly, these "deviations" from Luther are not a series of unrelated so-called "productive misunderstandings," nor is there reason to designate any one version as more "radical" than the others in any sense except that university reform, city reform, and reform of society may be regarded as progressive steps. They have in common, amid all other differences, a drive for political and pedagogical articulation of Christian ethics which can be regarded as one of the hallmarks of the *initia reformationis*, whether we look at Zwingli or Karlstadt, Müntzer or Melanchthon, Bucer or Calvin.

The theological key lies invariably in the understanding of the third Person of the Trinity. It is indeed not due to a *rabies theologorum* that the second generation saw the so-called *extra calvinisticum* as a major issue [1] which is directly related to Calvin's political testament.[2] Whereas for Luther faith is effectuated by the *verbum Dei*, the presence of Christ as the mode of the preached word, from Karlstadt, Zwingli, and Bucer to the most explicit statements with Calvin, faith as *operatio spiritus sancti* is a call to action. Faith is not, as Trent would put it, the *initium iustitiae* but it is the *initium regni*, the kingdom as the presence of Christ in the mode of the *ecclesio*-political community, implying the impatient reordering of creation, church and society.

It cannot be doubted that Melanchthon is respected by Luther until the very end of his life and that the *Praeceptor Germaniae* from his side regards himself as *explicator* of Luther : "Vestra collegi, et volui, quam possem simplicissime explicare." [3] Yet even in Melanchthon's case, a true *Epitome* of Luther's theology proves to transcend his gifts of interpretation.[4] Melanchthon's *Loci*, since the 1543 version, distinguish in the characterization of the *libertas evangelica* between the work of Christ in the forensic-synthetic imputation of righteousness and the work of the Holy Spirit which evokes acts in us in keeping with (*congruentes*) the law of God.[5] There is indeed ample reason to suggest that

---

[1] See the lucid analysis by E. David Willis, *Calvin's Catholic Christology. The Function of the So-called Extra Calvinisticum in Calvin's Theology* (Leiden, 1966), pp. 141-54.

[2] Heiko A. Oberman, "The 'Extra' Dimension in the Theology of Calvin", *JEH*, XXI (1970), 43-64 ; 46-47.

[3] *CR* III, 180 45-47.

[4] See the differentiated analysis of the "polare Einheit" by Martin Greschat, *Melanchthon neben Luther : Studien zur Gestalt der Rechtfertigungslehre zwischen 1528 und 1537* (Witten, 1965), pp. 248 ff.

[5] The conclusion can therefore be that through the *imputatio iustitia* "Abrogata est Lex, quod ad maledictionem attinet, non quod ad obedientiam attinet. Ideo et spiritus

Melanchthon implies more than the scholastic *distinctio rationis*, when he regards this distinction as made *docendi causa*.[1]

In looking from the historical to the theological distinction between the *initia Lutheri* and the *initia reformationis*, we come critically close to the suspenseful character of the Reformation movement. We sense this suspense prior to the establishment of *Landeskirchentum* and *Fürstenregime* in the constantly present tension between Luther's person-oriented rediscovery of the *solus Christus* and a community-oriented pneumatology in which, whenever *fides* is interpreted by *lex*, *spiritus* tends to issue in *Schwärmerei*, legalistic puritanism or both.

On the basis of our assessment we may come to the conclusion that even though a real distinction between the *initia Lutheri* and the *initia reformationis* as historical events may be dangerously artificial, we can note that the extent of the theological differences *in statu nascendi* are quite clear, notwithstanding the common share in the newly found Christian liberty. Since the professional inquisitiveness of the historian drives him to the very edge of the unknowable, we cannot avoid the temptation to join in the old quest for the forces which propelled Luther in his unique direction. These forces must, however, be measured by means of the double set of coordinates of a medieval-scholastic past and the ever-widening waves of the concurrent Reformation movement.

---

sanctus datur, ut deinde vere accendantur in cordibus nostris motus congruentes Legi Dei ..." *Melanchthons Werke*, II, 2, 771 22-26. The deviation from Luther's *De Libertate* with its *praesentia filii* expresses itself in the different evaluation of Augustine's doctrine of justification, implicitly here. *Ibid.*, II, 2, 765 32-766 7. It is explicit already in the disputation of 1536, *WA Br*, XII, 191 1-5; 193 88-94.

[1] Even more clearly than with Karlstadt and Müntzer we can see in the case of Melanchthon that he does not "distort" Luther, but rather relates to a particular phase in Luther's development, or combines—as in this case— elements from several stages of development. The conclusion of Sören Widmann is illuminating : "Bis zum Sommer 1520 liebte es Luther, das Zum-Glauben-Kommen mit der Eingiessung des Heiligen Geistes und der von ihm bewirkten Verwandlung in den Affekten zu identifizieren ... Ab Herbst 1520 glauben wir, neue Elemente in Luthers Reflexion über das Verhältnis von Wort und Glaube entdecken zu können. Diese Veränderung äussert sich darin, daß nun die Vermittlung des Heils vor allem christologisch und erst in zweiter Linie pneumatologisch begründet wird. Christus teilt sich durchs Wort dem Glaubenden mit allen seinen Gütern selbst zu." "Die Wartburgpostille : Untersuchungen zu ihrer Entstehung und zu Luthers Umgang mit dem Text", unpublished Ph. D. diss. U. of Tübingen, 1969, mimeographed, I, 241. See *Christus in verbo veniens*, *WA*, X, i. 1, 17 8; *WA*, VII, 58 38-59 2; Widmann, I, 303; II, 132.

II. Contra modernos

I regard it as a distinct advantage to speak not of "causes" of the Reformation with the loaded connotation of a deterministic philosophy of history, but to employ instead the more poetic, or if one prefers, the literally more fluid imagery of gathering tributaries to connote the contingency and complexity of the historical connection between impetus and movement.

Even so the traditional questions as to proto-reformation or contextual movements arise, though they are now to be answered in terms of the distinction between, as well as the perichoresis of, the *initia Lutheri* and the *initia reformationis*. We choose to pursue, or in this brief context rather to comment upon, three streams we have already encountered, namely nominalism, humanism, and Augustinianism, as currents within the history of the Reformation.

When we survey contemporary interpretations of Luther's incipient theology, we discern three basic tendencies :

1. Luther creatively rethought and reshaped traditional thought to such an extent that he must be seen as *sui generis*; Luther is his own man, at once a God-made and self-made man;

2. Luther is primarily to be seen as an Augustinian reared in a nominalistic climate of thought;

3. Luther is an Augustinian carried on the waves of the rising tide of humanism in Germany.

In all three positions, concepts are used which call for clarification, but the most resistent and ungraspable concept has hitherto proved to be "nominalism." As long ago as 1931, Paul Vignaux stated in his important article on Ockham in the *Dictionnaire de Théologie Catholique* that nominalism and the influence of Ockham seem to dominate the universities in the 14th and 15th centuries, but we cannot yet give to nominalism "une notion commune, ni mesurer avec quelque rigueur l'influence d'Occam." [1] Partly due to the very phenomenon itself, we have not yet reached an established consensus in sharpening the contours of nominalism; yet the achievements particularly of Philotheus Böhner are confirmed and elaborated by others who continue to work in this field. [2]

---

[1] *Dictionnaire de Théologie Catholique* (Paris, 1931), XI, 889. See also P. Vignaux, *Nominalisme au XIVe Siècle* (Montréal-Paris, 1948).

[2] See the survey and bibliography of Ph. Böhner by Helmar Junghans, *Ockham im Lichte der neueren Forschung* (Berlin, 1968), pp. 347-48. (Arbeiten zur Geschichte und Theologie des Luthertums, 21).

Two points are important for our further considerations. "Nominalism" is the more encompassing designation of the movement which transcends the limits of Ockham's work and hence is not to be identified with Occamism or Occamists as the adherents to the system of the *Venerabilis Inceptor*. Secondly, it proves a distorting reduction to limit the range of nominalism to logic or epistemology, even though in these areas the most original work was done. This is borne out by the fact that the "nominalistae" do not appear in our documents until the end of the 14th century,[1] later to give place to the even more general designation "via moderna," twice removed from the *ipsissima verba magistri*. Though Ritter [2] has convincingly challenged Benary's general thesis,[3] there is nevertheless some truth in the latter's observation that the *via moderna* at the turn of the sixteenth century is, in view of its documented attraction to Thomists and Scotists, often rather the designation of a research method than of clearly defined research results. There is apparently a need for a less ambiguous designation when the term *"via Marsiliana"* emerges in Heidelberg and "via Gregorii" in Wittenberg.

At any rate, Luther can use "Occamistae" and "moderni" synonymously when he argues against the condemnation by the theological faculty of Cologne (*via antiqua!*). He is not prepared to accept blind authority, even if it be that of his own school, the *secta* "Occamica seu Modernorum." [4]

---

[1] See Damasus Trapp : "The categories of realism and nominalism characterize the theology of the 15th century very well, because very historically. When these two categories are tacked upon the theology before the Schism, the two terms are less felicitous." It seems "that the term nominalista did not have currency, did not describe the philosophical dissenter, let alone the theologian of the 14th century as such". "Clm. 27034 : Unchristened Nominalism and Wycliffite Realism at Prague in 1381", *Recherches de théologie ancienne et médiévale*, XXIV (1957) 320-60, 321.

[2] "... dieser Parteistandpunkt [war] wesentlich nicht im Lehrstoff, sondern in der verschiedenen Beantwortung der Universalienfrage begründet ..." Gerhard Ritter, *Studien zur Spätscholastik : Via antiqua und via moderna auf den deutschen Universitäten des XV. Jahrhunderts* (Heidelberg, 1922), II 93; cf. pp. 15 ff. (Sitzungsberichte 13).

[3] F. Benary believes : "Der Unterschied liegt in der verschiedenen Methode,... nicht im Lehrstoff." *Zur Geschichte der Stadt und der Universität Erfurt am Ausgang des Mittelalters* III, *Via antiqua und via moderna auf den deutschen Hochschulen des Mittelalters mit besonderer Berücksichtigung der Universität Erfurt*, ed. A. Overmann (Gotha, 1919), p. 33. Cf. H.R. Abe, *Der Erfurter Humanismus und seine Zeit* (Jena, 1953), pp. 99-100.

[4] "Nec hoc quaesivi, ut me ad suos autores remitterent quasi mihi incognitos, sed ut scripturae autoritate aut ratione probabili sua vera et mea falsa esse convincerent. Quae est enim ista (etiam suo Aristotele prohibita) petitio principii, mihi responderi per haec

Late medieval nominalism is Ockham's sphere of influence; yet it constitutes a climate of thought which does allow for an independent attitude over against central teachings of Ockham or even for bypassing him in silence. Just as Ockham is at times called the "inceptor," so we find John Buridan referred to as the "inventor" of the *via moderna*.[1] Gerhard Ritter points to a list of representatives of the *via moderna* where Ockham is just one name among many : Marsilius, Buridan, Ockham, Burleigh, Holcot, Gregory of Rimini, d'Ailly, Gerson, Biel.[2] A similar enumeration is given by Marsilius of Inghen with mention of the common characteristic that all followed "nominalium viam et modernorum doctrinam." [3] The role of Ockham is thus not denied when we insist on "nominalism" as the appropriate designation of the whole movement encompassing such varied men and minds as Holcot, Rimini and d'Ailly along with Ockham. After all, John Wesel is known as a fervent defender of the *via moderna*, yet the name of Ockham does not appear in his work.[4]

Two basic points of the *via moderna* indicated as characteristic for the Erfurt tradition, including Jodocus Trutvetter and Bartholomäus von Usingen, may also be seen as the common features of the *via moderna* as such :

1. Rejection and pruning of all concepts which are not absolutely necessary, the so-called "razor;"[5]

---

ipsa, quae impugno. Non est quaestio, quid didicerint, audierint, legerint, senserint unquam, Sed quibus firmamentis ea muniant. Alioqui, cur et meae sectae resisterem, scilicet Occanicae seu Modernorum, quam penitus imbibitam teneo, si verbis voluissem aut vi compesci ?" *WA*, VI, 194 37-195 5. Cf. the two classifications in 1518 and 1520 : "Thomistae, Scotistae, Albertistae, Moderni" in *WA*, I, 509 13-14, and "Aristoteles [peperit] Scotistas, Thomistas, Occanistas" in *WA*, V, 371 36-37.

[1] "Buridanus, maximus Philosophus, qui invenit viam modernorum." *Rerum Familiarumque Belgicorum Chronicon Magnum*, coll. et ed. Joh. Pistorius (Frankfurt a.M., 1654), p. 293 25; quoted by Ruprecht Paqué, *Das Pariser Nominalistenstatut : Zur Entstehung des Realitätsbegriffs der neuzeitlichen Naturwissenschaft (Occam, Buridan und Petrus Hispanus, Nikolaus von Autrecourt und Gregor von Rimini)* (Berlin, 1970), p. 22, n. 13.

[2] *Studien zur Spätscholastik : Neue Quellenstücke zur Theologie des Johann von Wesel* (Heidelberg, 1926/1927), III, 49.

[3] Quoted by Paqué, p. 22, n. 13.

[4] Ritter, III, 9, n. 2.

[5] "Secundum namque viam modernam hoc habetur tamquam principium quod nullibi habetur pluralitas sine reali distinctione." Cod. Vat. Pal. 337, fol. 94va; quoted by Erich Kleineidam, *Universitas Studii Erffordensis. Überblick über die Geschichte der Universität Erfurt im Mittelalter 1392-1521* (Leipzig, 1969), II, 22.

2. The insistence on the <u>contextual interpretation</u>, the so-called *proprietas sermonis.*[1] For the application of this program Ockham was twice condemned in Paris, 1339 and 1340,[2] whereas the Augustinian Order realized immediately in 1345 the theological implications of these new hermeneutics.

Contentwise we find the characteristics of nominalism in an epistemology engendered by the <u>new logic which relates experience and experiment (the so-called *notitia intuitiva*)</u> in such a way that the individual — be it an inanimate object, a human being or an event—is understood in its own context as potentially new, original, and unique before it is identified by classification into *species.* This epistemological stance, which one may well characterize as born out of hunger for reality, is part of a more embracing revolt against the *meta*-world of heteronomous authority and canonized speculation obfuscating, overlaying and distorting reality. It is the revolt against *a priori meta*-physics in order to provide freedom for genuine *a posteriori* physics. Indeed, there are good reasons to claim that the <u>beginnings of modern science can be retraced to nominalism. In t</u>he same way it is the revolt against *meta*-theology to provide freedom for genuine theology. Conceived as a practical and not as a speculative "science," Ockham's razor proves to function by slicing away later crusts from more recent glosses,[3] not unlike the humanists' effort to return to the sources. Here lies as well the interest in the traditional antispeculative distinction between *potentia absoluta* and *potentia ordinata.* The description of the Church as *congregatio fidelium,* for instance, is preferred since this perception is closer to experienced reality than a "platonic" abstract universal "extra homines particulare," as Gabriel Biel put it.[4]

---

[1] "...secundum proprietatem sermonis, quam intendit via moderna ..." *Ibid.,* fol. 94vb; quoted by Kleineidam, II, 23.

[2] For the text of the statute of 1340 against Occam with the explicit mention of the *proprietas sermonis* see Paqué, p. 10. The statute of 1339 is more general : Paqué, pp. 306 ff. ; cf. Adolar Zumkeller, *Hugolin von Orvieto und seine theologische Erkenntnislehre* (Würzburg, 1941), p. 257, n. 4.

[3] In matters conciliar Ockham proves to be "conservative", as Brian Tierney terms it, "by preferring" to restate in detail the old arguments of Huguccio. Brian Tierney, "Ockham, the Conciliar Theory, and the Canonists", *Journal of the History of Ideas,* XV, 1 (Jan.-Mar. 1954), 40-70; Facet Books, Historical Series 19 (Philadelphia, 1971), p. 26.

[4] "... ecclesie meritum non est universale platonicum seu meritum abstractum extra homines particulares per se existens, sed est personarum et membrorum ecclesiam constituentium." Gabrielis Biel, *Canonis misse expositio* I, edd. H.A. Oberman-W.J. Courtenay (Wiesbaden, 1963), Lectio XXVI, I., p. 246.

Where such concerns express themselves theologically, it is appropriate to speak about "theological nominalism," but it is unwarranted
and confusing to designate such as "Occamism" when not expressly
related to the *Venerabilis Inceptor*.[1] When this relationship between
nominalism and Occamism is inverted by making Occamism the prior
category, we are forced either to confine nominalism to a movement in
the school of arts,[2] or to expand the concept of Occamism so far that the
umbilical cord between Ockham and the Occamists becomes stretched.[3]

These few comments about nominalism and its concerted action a-
gainst all *meta*-categories make it clear that the option for nominalism
meant more than the appropriation of a new system of logic. It meant
the involvement in a scientific revolution. This explains the increasing
concern of church and university for the continuity of doctrine, expressed in the Paris-Statutes of 1339 and 1349 and the succeeding censures
by the Augustinian Order in 1345 and 1348.[4] Thus it is possible for us
to grasp why Wessel Gansfort could repeatedly point to his shift in 1459
from the *via antiqua* to the *via moderna*,[5] referred to as "nominales", as

---

[1] Erich Hochstetter, "Nominalismus ?", *Franciscan Studies*, 9 (1949), 370-403; 372.

[2] In a review of E. Jane Dempsey Douglass, *Justification in Late Medieval Preaching*:
A study of John Geiler of Keisersberg (Leiden, 1966) Wilfried Werbeck implies such a view
when he rejects the thesis that Geiler is a nominalistic theologian : "Diese These ist in
dieser Formulierung um der begrifflichen Klarheit willen nicht haltbar. Vom Nominalismus kann man nur im Zusammenhang mit bestimmten philosophischen Anschauungen
sprechen, und eine nominalistische Theologie gibt es nur dort, wo solche philosophische
Position theologisch unmittelbar wirksam wird ... Frau D. meint natürlich mit 'nominalistischer Theologie' letztlich stets die ockhamistische Tradition." *ThLZ*, XCIII (1968),
759-61; 760.

[3] Thus Reinhard Schwarz can comment in connection with d'Ailly's "plagiarism"
from Gregory of Rimini : "Jedenfalls hat Luther bei d'Ailly—auch bei Biel—einen viel-
fältig gefärbten, keineswegs einen einfarbigen Ockhamismus kennengelernt !" *Fides,
Spes und Caritas beim jungen Luther unter besonderer Berücksichtigung der mittelalterlichen Tradition* (Berlin, 1962), p. 20, n. 44.

[4] "Item, quod nullus dicat propositionem nullam esse concedendam, si non sit
vera in ejus sensu proprio, quia hoc dicere ducit ad predictos errores, quia Biblia et
auctores non semper sermonibus utuntur secundum proprios sensus eorum. Magis igitur
oportet in affirmando vel negando sermones ad materiam subjectam attendere, quam ad
proprietatem sermonis, disputatio namque ad proprietatem sermonis attendens nullam
recipiens propositionem, preterquam in sensu proprio, non est nisi sophistica disputatio.
Disputationes dyalectice et doctrinales, que ad inquisitionem veritatis intendunt, modi-
cam habent de nominibus sollicitudinem." Paqué, p. 10. Text of the Augustinian condemnations of 1345 and 1348 in Adolar Zumkeller, *Hugolin von Orvieto*, p. 257, n. 4;
p. 258, n. 3.

[5] Cf. Maarten van Rhijn, *Wessel Gansfort* ('s-Gravenhage, 1917), pp. 78-83; 236. The

the newly won basis for clearer theological arguments.[1] Furthermore it
explains the tone of pride when Luther not only claims : "Occam solus
intellexit dialecticam," "Occam fuit prudentissimus et doctissimus,"
but also exclaims : "Occam, magister meus." [2] Finally it suggests why
one must concern oneself with the relationship nominalism-reformation
when dealing with the theme of Luther and the dawn of the modern era.

One cannot begin to answer this question without recalling the distinction made between the *initia reformationis* and the *initia Lutheri*.
As far as the Reformation in the broader sense of the word is concerned,
nominalism cannot be regarded as a factor in either a positive or a negative sense. By the beginning of the sixteenth century, nominalism had
been reduced in significance by two developments : first it suffered a
setback due to a rejuvenated Thomism through the work of Capreolus
(d. 1444) and Cajetan (d. 1534), in Germany concentrated in Cologne.
Simultaneously, the spread of religious humanism rapidly reduced the
magnetism of nominalism as the possibility of academic renewal from
within. Even though striking parallels can be observed between certain
trends in Italian humanism and nominalism, particularly as concerns
its anthropology, Paul Oskar Kristeller has done much to trace "the
partial continuity"[3] of Renaissance philosophy and the Aristotelian-

---

decisive agent was the crusading Hendrik van Zomeren. Cf. *Actuarium Chartularii
Universitatis Parisiensis*, edd. A.L. Gabriel-G.C. Boyce (Paris, 1964), VI, 235-36, n. 1.
See also Maarten van Rhijn, *Studien over Wessel Gansfort en zijn tijd* (Utrecht, 1933), p. 69.

[1] In his debate with Jacob Hoeck (*Actuarium* VI, 331 f. n. 11) on papal power to
promulgate plenary indulgences : "Nosti, schola nostra Nominalis talem verborum
dissidentiam et discohaerentiam non admittit." Wessel Gansfort, *Opera* (Groningen,
1614; Repr. Nieuwkoop, 1966), p. 890 (Monumenta Humanistica Belgica, 1). In his
'conversion report' Wessel makes quite clear that the *via moderna* cannot be a religious
authority for him : "... corrigi paratus mutavi sententiam, et Nominales adprehendi. In
quibus, ingenue fateor, si quid fidei contrarium putarem, hodie paratus remearem vel ad
Formales [= Scotisti], vel Reales [= Thomisti] ..." *Ibid.*, p. 877. "... quamdiu mihi
videtur quod Papa, vel Schola, vel quaecunque multitudo contra Scripturae veritatem
adserat, semper debeo Scripturae veritatem prima sollicitudinis parte amplecti, secundo
autem, quia non probabile tantos errare, debeo diligenter veritatem utriusque partis
pervestigare." *Ibid.*, p. 879. A monograph is being prepared by Sarah Reeves on the
relation of Wessel to nominalism.

[2] "Occam solus intellexit dialecticam, das es lige am definire et dividere vocabula, sed
non potuit eloqui." *WA Tr*, I, no. 193. "Occam fuit prudentissimus et doctissimus, sed
defuit ei rhetorica." *WA Tr*, I, no. 338. "Occam, magister meus, summus fuit dialec-
ticus, sed gratiam non habuit loquendi." *WA Tr*, II, no. 2544a.

[3] *Renaissance Philosophy and the Medieval Tradition* (Latrobe, 1966), p. 79. As to
Erasmus, however, we note the conclusion of John B. Payne : "Erasmus had considerable
knowledge of and appreciation for some of the scholastics, especially the late medieval

Thomistic tradition. Wessel Gansfort, one of the few and first Graecists
of his day, uniting in one person the ideals of nominalism and humanism,
could still be confident that the *via moderna* provides the means to by-
pass and abolish the *via antiqua* and thus to reach and read the true
antiqui, namely the Fathers.[1] When, however, Lefèvre d'Étaples and
Erasmus begin to publish the first patristic editions less than half a
century later, a more immediate access was provided for a return to the
sources.

After the Pfefferkorn affair and the literary and, what is more, ideological success of the "Letters of Obscure Men," the German intelligen-
tia in large numbers turns its back on all scholastic schools to place its
hopes in the study of the classics and the Fathers. In this way the
renewal movement issuing from *eloquentia* and *rhetorica* stole the glitter
of the *via moderna* which had raised its banner in the name of *logica* and
dialectica. Yet whereas humanism shaped the early modern era, it is
nominalism which determined the *Geist* and set the tone of the modern
era, notwithstanding the protest songs of the *via antiqua* surviving in
German idealism. As far as the theological world is concerned, it may
not be immaterial for those who see an inner connection between nominalism and the course of the Reformation to point first to the fact
that a number of nominalists belong to the earliest opponents of Luther,
among them such productive authors as Eck, Schatzgeyer, and Usingen.[2]

What is more, when we go on to recall some of the leading reformers
and their scholastic matrix, all evidence contradicts a more intimate
relationship between nominalist training and choosing the Reformation:
Karlstadt hails from the *via antiqua*, first more Thomistically, later
more Scotistically oriented.[3] Zwingli's marginals to the Sentences Com-

---

nominalistic tradition. He enlists the support especially of Gerson and Durandus, but
also of Biel." *Erasmus : His Theology of the Sacraments* (Richmond, Va., 1970), p. 229.

[1] "Ubicunque problematicum aliquod incideret [Buridanus] non secundum illorum
[Albertum, Thomam, vel Scotum, vel universae Realium aut Formalium scholae], sed
secundum Nominalium sententiam terminat. Alii sunt igitur antiqui illi, quorum sen-
tentiis, praesertim in *Moralibus* nunquam se confitetur deceptum." Wessel Gansfort,
Opera, p. 879.

[2] Cf. Otfried Müller, *Die Rechtfertigungslehre nominalistischer Reformationsgegner.
Bartholomäus Arnoldi von Usingen, O.E.S.A. und Kaspar Schatzgeyer, O.F.M. über Erb-
sünde, erste Rechtfertigung und Taufe* (Breslau, 1940).

[3] Karlstadt describes his own road to reformation in the revealing dedication to
Staupitz of his Commentary to Augustine's *De spiritu et litera*: "... quia sectam et capreo-

mentary of Scotus have not yet been published, but his having passed through the *via antiqua* cannot be contested.[1] Bucer received his theological training from the Dominicans.[2] Calvin may have been influenced by John Major but, whereas we have not yet succeeded in finding unambiguous parallels, similarities with Duns Scotus are firmly established.[3]

As far as the *initia Lutheri* are concerned, our question is more complex. Increasingly refined arguments are given for Luther's dependence on the system of Ockham, whether directly or as mediated by two of Ockham's disciples well known to Luther, Petrus d'Ailly and Gabriel Biel.[4] The wholesale identification of Ockham and nominalism with

---

linam et Scotisticam manifesta interpretatione successive profitebar." Ernst Kähler, *Karlstadt und Augustin : Der Kommentar des Andreas Bodenstein von Karlstadt zu Augustins Schrift De spiritu et litera* (Halle, 1952), p. 3 19-20.

[1] Walther Köhler, *Die Geisteswelt Ulrich Zwinglis. Christentum und Antike* (Gotha, 1920), pp. 14 ff. "Bei Luther wird mit Recht im Abendmahlsstreit der Rückgriff auf die scholastischen Lehrmeister betont. Bei Zwingli steht es nicht anders, nur daß er mit dem Material einer anderen Schule arbeitet." *Ibid.*, p. 19. For the marginals to Scotus see Walther Köhler, *Huldrych Zwingli* (2nd. ed.; Leipzig, 1954), p. 22.

[2] Cf. Heinrich Bornkamm : "... das Studium der thomistischen Theologie, dessen Spuren man später noch bei ihm findet ..." *Martin Bucers Bedeutung für die europäische Reformationsgeschichte* (Gütersloh, 1952), p. 8. Hastings Eells observes that Bucer "learned to detest" Aquinas, but draws on Bucer's later *Verantwortung* of 1523. *Martin Bucer* (New Haven, 1931), p. 3. He complains here that in the monastery his "Bücher, darauß man die latinisch sprach lernet", were taken away to be replaced by "sophistisch dautmären", children's tales; a quasi knowledge drawn from "den verfuerischen unchristlichen buechern ires Thomas von Wasserburg, den sye von Aquino nennen." *Martin Bucers Deutsche Schriften, Frühschriften 1520-1524*, ed. Robert Stupperich (Gütersloh, 1960), I, 161 23-24. Whatever his later evaluation was to be, according to his report of 30 April 1518, Bucer had bought the *Scripta Thomae* with an advance from the Prior in 1516. Cf. "Bucers Bücherverzeichnis", *ibid.*, I, 281-82.

[3] Cf. François Wendel, *Calvin : Sources et évolution de sa pensée religieuse* (Paris, 1950), pp. 99 ff.

[4] Since the discovery of Hans Volz that the marginals of Luther to the 1514 Lyon edition of Biel's *Collectorium* and *Canonis misse expositio* were written partly by the young Luther - shortly before 4 September 1517 - but partly also many years later, we know that Luther continued to consult this copy. Hence we are well advised not to restrict our investigation of the influences of the *via moderna* to the years of dissociation around the "Disputatio contra Scholasticam theologiam". See Volz, "Luthers Randbemerkungen zu zwei Schriften Gabriel Biels : Kritische Anmerkungen zu Hermann Degerings Publikation", *ZKG*, LXXXI (1970), 207-19; 217. The often quoted *WA Tr*, III, 564 5-7, no. 3722 can best be understood by relating the first ("meo iudicio") and the second evaluation in the one sentence as applying to two periods in Luther's life : "Gabriel scribens librum super canonem missae, qui liber meo iudicio tum optimus fuerat; wenn ich darinnen las, da blutte dein hertz. Bibliae autoritas nulla fuit erga Gabrielem."

Luther's theology as articulated in the tradition from Denifle to Lortz [1] is gradually disappearing. Residues of this view, however, are still operative within the concomitant Protestant apologetics. Generally it may be said that Protestant scholarship tends to reject a real connection between Luther and Ockham or nominalism. Leif Grane for example finds no "decisive influence of Occamism" in the years around the disputation against scholastic theology (1517).[2] Reinhard Schwarz argues concerning the preceding stage of the *Dictata* that "the Occamistic school indeed sharpened Luther's mind," but holds that it was as an interpreter of the Scriptures and not as an Occamist that Luther came to be "the Reformer." [3]

In recent Roman Catholic Luther studies, on the other hand, we find a greater openness to the opposite thesis.[4] Among the more recent

---

For a critical discussion of efforts to relate Luther to representatives of late medieval nominalism from Grisar to Weijenborg, see Gordon Rupp, *The Righteousness of God : Luther Studies. A reconsideration of the character and work of Martin Luther* (London, 1953), pp. 96 ff., 175 ff.

[1] Cf. Heinrich Denifle, *Luther und Luthertum in der ersten Entwickelung* (Mainz, 1909), II, 297 ff.; Joseph Lortz, *Die Reformation in Deutschland* (4th ed.; Freiburg, 1962), II, 172 ff.

[2] "Aber soweit es in dieser Arbeit möglich war, den vorhandenen Stoff zu beleuchten, gibt es nichts, was dafür spricht, dass der Ockhamismus auf die Ausformung von Luthers Theologie dieser Jahre entscheidenden Einfluß gehabt hat. Kein zentraler Gedanke hat seinen Ursprung in der Ockhamistischen Theologie, weder positiv noch negativ. Dahingegen besteht Grund zu glauben, dass der Ockhamismus auf Luthers Formulierung der Rechtfertigungslehre befördernd und klärend gewirkt hat. Aber, wie gesagt, es handelt sich kaum um mehr als eine Folgeerscheinung." Leif Grane, *Contra Gabrielem : Luthers Auseinandersetzung mit Gabriel Biel in der Disputatio Contra Scholasticam Theologiam 1517* (Gyldendal, 1962), pp. 380-81. Cf. the clear article by Bengt Hägglund, "Voraussetzungen der Rechtfertigungslehre Luthers in der spätmittelalterlichen Theologie", *Lutherische Rundschau*, XI (1961), 28-55, in English, "The Background of Luther's Doctrine of Justification in Late Medieval Theology", *Lutheran World*, VIII (1961), 24-46.

[3] "Luther manipulierte nicht die Traditionen, wie es im Grunde genommen die Autoren der Devotio moderna machten. Gewiss trat Luther, der seinen Verstand in der ockhamistischen Schule geschärft hatte, in die Bahnen der Devotio moderna, er griff die monastische Theologie auf, er liess sich von Bernhard anregen, vor allem suchte er die Person und Theologie Augustins zu erfassen. Dennoch wurde Luther weder als Ockhamist, noch als Anhänger der Devotio moderna, noch als monastischer Theologe, auch nicht als Vertreter einer bernhardinischen Frömmigkeit oder augustinischen Theologie zum Reformator. Zum Reformator wurde er als der Lehrer einer neuen Theologie, die in der inneren Auseinandersetzung mit den Traditionen beim Schriftstudium herangereift war. Dieser Reifeprozeß war während der 1. Psalmenvorlesung in vollem Gange." Reinhard Schwarz, *Vorgeschichte der reformatorischen Busstheologie* (Berlin, 1968), p. 297.

[4] Cf. however Jared Wicks : "His later assertions that he was of Ockham's school

authors, Francis Clark points to Luther's use of d'Ailly in his attack on transubstantiation in *De captivitate Babylonica* and to the doctrine of the ubiquity of the Body of Christ.[1] Erwin Iserloh finds proof of the radicalization of the nominalistic separation of human and divine action in the Ninety-five Theses when Luther denies that the Church can provide forgiveness through indulgences.[2] It is again Iserloh who discerns Luther the nominalist in the theses that images and ceremonies are neutral entities, *adiaphora*, in contrast to such realists as Karlstadt and Müntzer, who find the images so important that they call for their immediate removal.[3]

When it is said that Luther's *sola scriptura* is part of the Occamistic heritage,[4] the basis for such an assumption can be found only in a letter Luther wrote his teacher Jodocus Trutvetter on 9 May 1518. In answer

---

must refer to his philosophical training in Erfurt from 1502 to 1505 ... Luther had no interest in the dominant themes of the *via moderna* ..." *Man Yearning for Grace : Luther's Early Spiritual Teaching* (Wiesbaden, 1969), p. 267.

[1] *The Eucharistic Sacrifice and the Reformation* (London, 1960), p. 320. Cf. *WA*, VI, 508 7-26. See here Leif Grane, "Luthers Kritik an Thomas von Aquin in 'De captivitate Babylonica'", *ZKG*, LXXX (1969), 1-13.

[2] "Schon in der nominalistischen Theologie war göttliches und menschliches Handeln weitgehend getrennt, insofern Gott das Tun der Kirche nur zum Anlass nimmt für sein Heilshandeln, ohne darin wirklich einzugehen. Luther führt diese Trennung des Menschlich-Kirchlichen vom Göttlichen so weit, dass er der kirchlichen Strafe bzw. ihrem Erlass nicht einmal mehr interpretative Bedeutung hinsichtlich der von Gott auferlegten Sündenstrafen zumass. Hier scheint mir eine Wurzel der baldigen Leugnung des hierarchischen Priestertums als göttlicher Stiftung bei Luther zu liegen." Erwin Iserloh, *Luthers Thesenanschlag. Tatsache oder Legende?* (Wiesbaden, 1962), p. 38; repeated verbatim in *Luther zwischen Reform und Reformation: Der Thesenanschlag fand nicht statt* (Münster i.W., 1966), p. 87.

[3] "Luther nimmt als Nominalist die Frage der Bilder, Zeremonien und der äusseren Gestalt nicht wichtig. Es sind für ihn Adiaphora; sie dürfen bleiben und können wegfallen, weder dem einen noch dem anderen darf man Heilsbedeutung zumessen. Für ihn ist deshalb auch nicht die Bilderverehrung, ihre vermeintliche Anbetung, der Anstoss, sondern der falsche Heilsglaube, zu meinen, durch Stiften von Bildern, Kirchen und Altären Verdienste sammeln zu können... Die Bilderstürmer Thomas Müntzer und Andreas Karlstadt nahmen die Sprache und die Bilder ernster. Es ist sicher nicht zufällig, dass sie ihrer theologischen Schule nach Realisten waren. Sie wollten und konnten sich nicht damit begnügen, daß die Texte der Messe erklärt wurden, sondern drängten um der 'Errettung der armen elenden, blinden Gewissen' willen zur Verdeutschung der Liturgie. Weil sie die äußere Gestalt ernst nahmen, ..." Erwin Iserloh, "Bildfeindlichkeit des Nominalismus und Bildersturm in 16. Jahrhundert", *Bild-Wort-Symbol in der Theologie*, ed. W. Heinen (Würzburg, 1969), pp. 119-38; 134-35.

[4] Cf. Friedrich Kropatschek, *Das Schriftprinzip der lutherischen Kirche. Die Vorgeschichte. Das Erbe des Mittelalters* (Leipzig, 1904), I, 309, 312.

to Trutvetter's obviously severe criticisms of the Ninety-five Theses,
Luther says that Trutvetter was indeed the very first to teach him that
"one owes faith only to the canonical books, and a serious hearing to
all other (authorities)." [1] Now apart from the fact that it is a common
medieval *dictum* that only the literal sense of Holy Scripture can provide for a theological *assertio*, it is precisely Ockham and the Occamists,
in contradistinction to the nominalist Gregory of Rimini, who uphold
Scripture *and* tradition as the basis of theology.[2] Hence Trutvetter's
teaching on this point is by no means an "extra-occamisticum." Rather
to the contrary! Luther reminds his teacher of a basic principle which,
when carried through, means the reform—or the end—of all scholastic
theology.

A few weeks earlier, Luther had already indicated what he thought
about the scholastic and particularly Trutvetter's use of dialectics:
"Instead of being useful to theology, (dialectic) is rather an obstacle to
theological studies, because theology uses the same vocabulary in a
manner quite different from that of dialectics. In what way therefore,
I asked, can dialectics be of use, since once I begin to study theology I am
forced to reject the dialectic meaning of a word and have to accept its
(theological) meaning." [3] Hence we may conclude that the word of explicit praise, "Occam solus intellexit dialecticam..." [4] refers to the application of logic in its own domain, not to its use as a tool for theology
proper. Particularly in the field of eucharistic theology Luther employs

---

[1] "... sed si pateris discipuli tui et obsequentissimi famuli tui, id est meam confidenti-
am, ex te primo omnium didici, solis canonicis libris deberi fidem, caeteris omnibus
iudicium, ut B. Augustinus, imo Paulus et Iohannes praecipiunt. Sine ergo mihi licere
id idem in Scholasticos, quod tibi et omnibus licitum fuit hucusque : volo sequi, si per
Scripturas aut ecclesiasticos Patres meliora fuero doctus, sine quibus volo Scholasticos
audire, quoad sua firmaverint ecclesiasticis dictis, et ab hac sententia nec tua autoritate
(quae apud me certe gravissima est), multo minus ullorum aliorum deterreri propositum
est." *WA Br,* I, 171 71-80. Luther to Trutfetter, 9 May 1518.

[2] Cf. my *The Harvest of Medieval Theology. Gabriel Biel and Late Medieval Nominalism*
(Cambridge, Mass., 1963), pp. 375 ff.

[3] "Scripsi denique ad d. Isennacensem, nostra aetate (ut videtur) principem dialecti-
corum, in eandem rem, potissimum allegans id, quod negari non potest, videlicet ideo
non posse Dialecticen prodesse Theologiae, sed magis obesse, Quod eisdem vocabulis
grammaticis longe aliter utatur Theologia quam Dialectica. Quomodo ergo, inquam,
prodest Dialectica, cum, postquam accessero ad Theologiam, id vocabuli, quod in Dialectica sic significabat, cogar reiicere & aliam eius significationem accipere ?" *WA Br,* I,
150 21-28; Luther to Spalatin, 22 February 1518. I use the translation *LW,* XLVIII, 57.

[4] *WA Tr,* I, 85 27-28 (a. 1532), no. 193.

nominalistic arguments and some of its terminology, such as d'Ailly's *transaccidentatio*, to show the arbitrariness of the Fourth Lateran (1215) in opting for the *opinio Thomae* without warrant of Scripture or reason. To this extent we can therefore agree with Leif Grane's conclusion in contrast to Clark's understanding of the *De captivitate* : Luther shows his indebtedness to Occamism in his attack against Thomism and indeed, as far as Luther's view of the *ratio*-speculation is concerned, the *via moderna* is "dem Thomismus überlegen". Grane goes on to argue that this merely applies to superiority in an area which, from the perspective of the *vere theologia*, is taboo and to which entrance is to be regarded as "impious human curiosity." [1]

This last conclusion seems to me to call for correction in one respect. Aristotle is indeed seen as the perverter of the theology of all schools, including the Occamists,[2] in paving the way to curiosity by disregarding the borderline between reason and revelation. And admittedly there is for Luther a knowledge of God which to attempt to penetrate with human reason is mere curiosity or worse. [3] Yet the triad reason-Aristotle-dangerous curiosity is only one side of the coin. On the other side Luther's attack is expressly addressed to Aristotle as authority in the

---

[1] "[Luther] ist ... in seiner Polemik gegen Thomas abhängig von dem Verständnis des Aristoteles, das er durch den Ockhamismus gelernt hatte. Mehrere Dinge in dieser Polemik deuten auf eine direkte Benutzung des Sentenzenkommentars von Pierre d'Ailly hin. ... Aber indem Luther sich in diese Diskussion hineinwirft, d.h. sich auf Gebieten bewegt, die seines Erachtens prinzipiell jenseits der Grenzen der christlichen Theologie und weit innerhalb der Grenzen der ungebührlichen und frechen menschlichen Neugierigkeit liegen, dann muss er sich der hier sich befindenden Waffen bedienen. Das heisst für ihn, von der ockhamistischen Aristotelesdeutung Gebrauch zu machen. Dass er also im Verhältnis zum Thomismus als Ockhamist auftritt, darf aber die Anhänger der Theorie von der Bedeutung der 'verdorbenen' Scholastik für die Reformation nicht allzu sehr freuen. Das bedeutet nämlich nur, dass er an der Überzeugung festhielt, dass die *via moderna* auf dem Gebiet der 'Vernunft' dem Thomismus überlegen war, d.h. auf dem Gebiet, wo sich seines Erachtens die *ganze* Scholastik befand. Selbst wünschte er, sich an einer ganz anderen Stelle zu befinden, und da fand er weder Thomismus noch Ockhamismus." Grane, *Luthers Kritik*, pp. 12-13.

[2] See here G. Ebeling, *Luther : Einführung in sein Denken* (Tübingen, 1964), pp. 90-91.

[3] "Legi mille et omnes doctores, nullus melius solvet hanc quaestionem. Scotus distinguit ea formaliter, moderni ratione, antiqui realiter. Ex quibus omnibus colligitur omnes eos nescire quid loquantur. Cum enim ista nemo viderit, quicquid supra fidem additur, certissimum est figmentum esse humanum. Similiter de anima." *WA*, IX, 62 19-24; quoted by Karl-Heinz zur Mühlen, "Ratio", *Archiv für Begriffsgeschichte*, XIV (1970), 192-256; 252, no. 375.

field of theology and as interpreted *apud latinos*.[1] This does not imply that reason has no valid function of its own or that the *ratio naturalis*, when based on experience, is not a source of truth. Luther at Worms publicly acknowledges Scripture *and* reason as the two ways to convince him of his errors.[2] In *De captivitate* he rejects transubstantiation as *figmentum humanae opinionis*, because neither Scripture nor reason supports it.[3] A year earlier Luther appeals to St. Augustine for the thesis that nothing is to be believed "nisi divinis literis *aut* ratione probabili persuadeat."[4] To grasp the Gospel is beyond the reach of reason ("extra rationem")[5] and to think properly about God "non ratio, sed sola fides potest."[6] Yet it is not improper *per se* to reach beyond the domain of Scripture; to the contrary, when Scripture is silent, as in the case of purgatory, what is improper is to reach beyond the domain of reason (experience) : it is *temeritas* to hold a certain opinion "in iis quae nos ratio naturalis non docet."[7] Again, it is granted that in Luther's view to argue with probable arguments is not to do theology but dialectics, "id est probabilia tantummodo tradere, non credibilia";[8] yet it cannot be minimized that Luther proclaims Ockham as the *facile princeps* in this field. It is not by chance that Luther in *De captivitate* calls upon an argument of d'Ailly; and finally it is not mere cynicism when Luther writes in the fall of 1516 to his friend Johannes Lang, who is just about to lecture in Erfurt on the second book of the

---

[1] *WA*, I, 226 28.

[2] *WA*, VII, 838 4. Cf. Bernhard Lohse, "Luthers Antwort in Worms", *Luther*, XXIX (1958), 124-34; Kurt-Victor Selge, "Capta conscientia in verbis Dei : Luthers Widerrufungsweigerung in Worms", *Der Reichstag zu Worms von 1521 : Reichspolitik und Luthersache*, ed. Fritz Reuter (Worms, 1971), pp. 180-207; 200-1.

[3] *WA*, VI, 509, 20-21; see further zur Mühlen, pp. 214-17.

[4] *WA*, II, 447, 16-17.

[5] *WA*, XL 1, 371 5.

[6] *WA*, XL 1, 376 25. I regard it as an explicit rejection of — i.a. — the program of nominalistic theology when Luther in 1520 formulates the thesis : "8. Si quis terminos logice et philosophie in theologiam ducat, necesse est, ut horrendum cahos errorum condat." Conclusiones quindecim, *WA*, VI, 29 19-20. See further Bernard Lohse, *Ratio und Fides : Eine Untersuchung über die ratio in der Theologie Luthers* (Göttingen, 1958), pp. 95 ff.; Brian A. Gerrish, *Grace and Reason : A Study in the Theology of Luther* (Oxford, 1962), pp. 69 ff., 137.

[7] *WA*, I, 663 15-16.; cf. 664 25.

[8] *WA*, I, 665 2; cf. 664 36.

Sentences : [1] "Scio quid Gabriel dicat, scilicet omni bene, praeterquam ubi de gratia, charitate, spe, fide, virtutibus dicit." [2]

The *initia Lutheri* as Luther's quest for the Gospel was a path which implied a hard-fought, conscious break with theological nominalism, with the theological alliance and compound of Occam and Scotus, with the whole realm of issues where Biel "cum suo Scoto... pelagizet." [3] Instead of the nominalistic duality of God and Church *de potentia absoluta*, we find in Luther that grace and justification as well as the word of absolution and forgiveness are glued together on the basis of God's promises.

Against Iserloh's thesis of Luther's nominalistic dissociation of God and Church it is to be pointed out that Luther called for faith in the preached and sacramental word as the word of God Himself and the *opus Dei*. Luther's insistence on the word "est" in "Hoc est corpus meum" stands contrary to the quest of late medieval mysticism and the *devotio moderna* for reform through inwardness, as is reflected in the pneumatology of the left wing of the Reformation. After his early discovery of the antitheses between faith and speculative reason (1509), the process of dissociation had reached the breaking point by 1516. After a last effort in 1515 to harmonize the *meritum de congruo* of the *doctores moderni* with the unmerited mercy of God in the *pactum misericordiae*, an imprint of nominalism can no longer be found in the content of the new theology.[4] Yet in discussing "how a nominalist

---

[1] Cf. *WA Br*, I, 73 27.

[2] *WA Br*, I, 66 32-34. Cf. Melanchthon's comment on Luther's continuing work with Biel and d'Ailly : "Nec tamen prorsus relinquit Sententiarios. Gabrielem et Cameracensem pene ad verbum memoriter recitare poterat." *CR*, VI, 159 (1 June 1546).

[3] *WA Br*, I, 66 34.

[4] "Hinc recte dicunt Doctores, quod homini facienti quod in se est, deus infallibiliter dat gratiam, et licet non de condigno sese possit ad gratiam preparare, quia est incomparabilis, tamen bene de congruo propter promissionem istam dei et pactum misericordie. Sic pro adventu futuro promisit, 'ut iuste et sobrie et pie vivamus in hoc seculo, expectantes beatam spem'. Quia quantumvis sancte hic vixerimus, vix est dispositio et preparatio ad futuram gloriam, que revelabitur in nobis, adeo ut Apostolus dicat : 'Non sunt condigne passiones huius temporis &c.' Sed bene congrue. Ideo omnia tribuit gratis et ex promissione tantum misericordie sue, licet ad hoc nos velit esse paratos quantum in nobis est." *WA*, IV, 262 4-13. The twice repeated "*bene de congruo*" is too explicit for me to agree with our *doctores moderni* who interpret this phrase as merely terminology without content, "Das 'facere quod in se est' der Scholastik ist zwar ... terminologisch noch zu finden, aber sachlich ist es schon jetzt überwunden." So Erich Vogelsang, *Die Anfänge von Luthers Christologie nach der ersten Psalmenvorlesung* (Leipzig, 1929), p. 70. Cf. Grane : "Hiermit ist das Bielsche Dispositionsschema trotz der Beibehaltung der Terminologie

doctrine came to be pressed into the service of Augustinianism,"
Brian Gerrish puts it very well : "Luther finds himself attacking reason
in characteristic Nominalist style precisely in order to destroy the
other characteristic of Nominalist thought, its optimism concerning
the powers of the human will."[1]

Luther's interpretation of the saints' images as *adiaphora* in *De libertate christiana* is clearly based on the freedom of Christian service as
the realization of the bondage of the Christian man. If the irrelevance
of the images *coram Deo* as belonging to the external man is proof of
nominalism, Paul could be called a nominalist when he said, "The true
Jew is not one who is such in externals..." (Rom. 2 : 18). Karlstadt for
his part insists on the removal of the images not because he is a realist
but because of his understanding of the Gospel as the New Law. St.

---

in Wirklichkeit durchbrochen worden." *Contra Gabrielem*, p. 299. A survey of the earlier
literature was made by James S. Preus, *From Shadow to Promise* : *Old Testament Interpretation from Augustine to the Young Luther* (Cambridge, Mass., 1969). Preus does not
regard this text as the rest of an old, but as the beginning of a new theology : "Like
the Nominalist ideas it finds helpful, it is indeed subversive of the medieval doctrine of
grace — but that is exactly what makes it new." *Ibid.*, p. 265 n. 79; cf. p. 271. New
elements are here also found by Steven E. Ozment, *Homo spiritualis* (Leiden, 1969),
p. 166, who points to the fact that the called for *expectio* stands "in uncompromising
opposition to *meritum*". Schwarz interprets the passage à la Vogelsang, *Vorgeschichte
der reformatorischen Busstheologie*, pp. 255 ff. Cf. Jared Wicks, p. 304, n. 31. An important
advance is made by Oswald Bayer who after a comparison of the nominalistic (Biel) and
Luther's *meritum de congruo* concludes : "Aber trotz dieser Unterschiede gehört unser
Leittext auf die Seite Biels, wenn wir ihn von *De captivitate* aus betrachten." *Promissio* :
Geschichte der reformatorischen Wende in Luthers Theologie (Göttingen, 1971), p. 135. Two
elements expressed here are of lasting significance for Luther. First is the *semper incipiens*
motif, according to which there is no categorical or "vertical" progress on the *via salutis*
from the preparation for grace to the preparation for glory. This theological horizon instead of being an unverifiable psychological "komplex-artige Hemmung" of Luther
indicates rather the limits of the *fides incarnata*. Cf. Peter Manns, "Fides absoluta - Fides incarnata. Zur Rechtfertigungslehre Luthers im Großen Galater-Kommentar",
Reformata Reformanda : *Festgabe Hubert Jedin*, ed. E. Iserloh - K. Repgen (Münster
i.W., 1965), I, 265-312; 276. Secondly the "prius" category of the *iudicium Dei* before justification is to be preserved later in the relation of *persona* and *opera* (*arbor-fructus*)
and of *lex* and *evangelium*, since "das Gesetz am Anfang und das Evangelium am Ziele der
Bewegung steht". Wilfried Joest, *Gesetz und Freiheit* : *Das Problem des tertius usus legis
bei Luther und die neutestamentliche Parainese* (Göttingen, 1956), p. 43. The first element
which I relate to monastic passion-piety, as documented by Jordan of Sachsen, and not
to Aristotle, as O. Bayer has suggested, *Promissio*, p. 139, eliminates increasingly the
temporal dimension of the "prius". Cf. *Dictata*, *WA*, III, 292 2; *WA*, IV, 278 28.

[1] Gerrish, p. 56.

Paul is for him "ein reicher prediger... des Evangelien und newen ge-
setzs, der die tiffe Moysi erreicht und tzu lichte gebracht hat." [1]

In retrospect it can be said that when applying Luther's own distinction between *credibilia* and *probabilia*, the nominalistic tradition
has been consciously stamped out as far the *credibilia* are concerned.
In the realm of the *probabilia*, i.e., in that of applied *logica*, Luther can
respect Occam and use nominalistic tools and achievements in his own
revolt against the *meta*-categories in so far as it concerns the liberation
of the realm of secular experience from heteronomous authorities and
the distorting *vis traditionis*.

III. VIA GREGORII

In his investigation of the relation of German humanism to the beginnings of the Reformation Bernd Moeller comes to the well-argued conclusion : "Ohne Humanismus, keine Reformation." [2] At the same
time the inner distance between Luther and the humanistic "Anliegen"
is not be overlooked. Though Luther owes his victory to the support of
humanists, especially the younger ones, he himself remains the "grosse
Aussenseiter und Unzeitgemässe." [3]

When we understand humanism in terms of the attraction it exerted
on German court circles and city sodalities, this movement stands for
the rediscovery of poetry, rhetoric, and epistolography as marks of the
man of learning. Where philosophy is concerned, it included as well a
clear emphasis on ethics. Thus an educational ideal is furthered which
tends to transform the school-system, also including the university
curriculum. This pedagogical concern is so much one of the characteristics of what we are calling the *initia reformationis*, that humanism
is not only the context in which this Reformation could flower, but, at
least for a time, it was also to be its inseparable partner through the
inner association of the *studia humanitatis* with the concern for religious
sanctification.

Though Luther joined in the humanistic campaign against obscurantism, as may be seen in his engagement in university reform, there is a

---

[1] Andreas Karlstadt, *Von Abtuhung der Bilder und das keyn Bedtler unther den Christen
seyn sollen*, ed. H. Lietzmann (Bonn, 1911), p. 22 11-12.

[2] "Die Deutschen Humanisten und die Anfänge der Reformation", *ZKG*, LXX
(1959), 46-61; 59.

[3] Moeller, p. 61.

sense in which one can put into Luther's mouth the words of Giles of
Viterbo, the General of Luther's Order, expressed at the opening cere-
mony of the Fifth Lateran Council : "...homines per sacra immutari fas
est, non sacra per homines." [1] Early in 1517 Luther can praise Erasmus
for his attack upon the "inveterata inscitia," but adds the observation :
"humana praevalent in eo plus quam divina."[2]

Over against a humanism based on the optimistic anthropology implied in the *mutatio sacrorum per homines*, Luther must be regarded as
an outsider. Another tradition feeding into humanism, however, apparently did reach Luther, namely the humanism developed and nurtured in his own Order. In the first half of the *Quattrocento* we find a
group of influential Augustinians in close contact with Petrarch. They
had strong classical interests and were concerned with literary research
and hunting for old manuscripts. Dionigi da Borgo S. Sepolcro (d. 1342),
Bartolomeo da Urbino (d. 1350), and Jean Coci (d. 1364) are three names
among the first to participate in the new movement which soon would
give itself the proud name "Renaissance." Their involvement can be
traced back to such early times that the Order can be said to have provided if not the cradle of Italian humanism then certainly the first allies,
eagerly exploiting the new scholarly vistas for the study of St. Augustine. The work of Bartolomeo da Urbino's *Milleloquium S. Augustini*
must have supported Petrarch in his intense Augustine studies, as is
suggested by Petrarch's dedicatory letter : "Hinc sibi posteritas stillas
studiosa salubres hauriat, hinc lectos componat in ordine flores." [3]

---

[1] J.D. Mansi, ed., *Sacrorum conciliorum nova et amplissima collectio* (Florence-Venice,
1757-1798), XXXII, 669. Cf. John W. O'Malley, *Giles of Viterbo on Church and Reform :
A Study in Renaissance Thought* (Leiden, 1968), pp. 139, n. 1 ; 161-2.

[2] *WA Br*, I, 90 19-20.

[3] Rudolph Arbesmann, *Der Augustiner-Eremitenorden und der Beginn der humanistischen Bewegung* (Würzburg, 1965), p. 54. Petrarch does not express his respect for
Augustine to the exclusion of others (as for instance Jerome) ; but in view of the debate on
the relative antiquity of the several rules it is significant that in *De otio religioso*, while
discussing the great examples and representatives of the monastic tradition, he does not
include "the well-known medieval founders of monastic orders and the medieval saints".
Charles Trinkaus, "Humanist Treatises on the status of the Religious : Petrarch, Salutati,
Valla", *Studies in the Renaissance*, XI (1965), 7-45 ; 17. Terrence Heath in dealing with
the changing text books for *grammatica* as part of the late medieval reform of the *trivium*
refers to a request of the Augustinian house in Tübingen which takes on special meaning
in the context of our discussion. In 1496 the university is asked to permit the use of
Perotti's *Grammatica nova* instead of the usual but clearly "meta-grammatical" *Doctrinale*
of Alexander de Villa Dei. See Universitätsarchiv Tübingen XV, 17 ; fol. 35ʳ ; quoted by
J. Haller, *Die Anfänge der Universität Tübingen 1477-1537* (Stuttgart, 1929), II, 82, and

The increasingly employed new style of quoting within the *schola Augustiniana* is an external index to the quest for authenticity and historical concern for the sources. The anonymity of the *quidam* gives way to an exact quotation with name, title, and chapter. [1] It is in this scholarly climate, which gives birth to the *Milleloquium* and source-oriented precision quoting, that a new theology is emerging, personified by Gregory of Rimini (d. 1358), the most significant General of the Augustinian Order after Giles of Rome. Damasus Trapp has indicated the basis of this development : "What is so new in Gregory is the fact that he is the best Augustine scholar of the Middle Ages..." [2] What before Gregory had been the *schola Aegidiana* can henceforth best be called the *schola moderna Augustiniana*,[3] since in Gregory we reach a turning point away from Giles. Instead of the *cognitio universalis*, now the *cognitio particularis rei* is emphasized as the epistemological point of departure; Scripture has become the programmatic source of theology; theology is not a *scientia*, because it stands for the ability to grasp the *sensus sacrae scripturae*; [4] a much more extensive knowledge of a

---

interpreted by Heath as "concession to the Augustinians." Cf. T. Heath, "Logical grammar, grammatical logic, and humanism in the three German universities", *Studies in the Renaissance*, XVIII (1971), 9-64; 29. While Niccolò Perotti wrote his grammar in 1468 under the title *Rudimenta Grammatica*, it was adapted by Bernard Pirger and repeatedly published during the eighties in South-Germany as *Grammatica nova*. See Heath, pp. 16-17. The *Grammatica nova* of Jacob Locher is held to be spurious. Heath, p. 24, n. 64. Whereas the influential reform activity of the Brethren of the Common Life intended the critical pruning of the *Doctrinale* and its commentaries, Perotti's *Grammatica nova* provides an alternative textbook. In either case the chief aim is to liberate grammar from its logical and metaphysical encasement. The request of the Augustinians is granted, until in 1505 Donatus and Alexander are again required under oath and reign for another quarter of a century.

[1] Damasus Trapp, "Augustinian Theology of the 14th Century", *Augustiniana*, VI (1956), 146-274, 152 ff.

[2] Trapp, p. 181.

[3] "Influxus nominalismi potius est externus ac formalisticus quam intrinsecus et doctrinalis, cum magis in nimia subtilitate argumentationum atque in quadam tortuositate et obscuritate sermonis quam in novitate opinionum appareat : primum est signum temporis ac defectus communis prolapsus theologiae scholasticae, a quo rarissimi scriptores illius aetatis immunes permanserunt; perseverantia in doctrina recepta, est bonum peculiare doctorum huius scholae, ut periti fatentur, quod proculdubio connexioni cum primis magistris eiusdem tribuenda est." D. Gutiérrez, "Notitia historica antiquae scholae aegidianae", *Analecta Augustiniana*, XVIII (1941/42), 39-67, 44.

[4] Gregorii Ariminensis, O.E.S.A., *Super Primum Et Secundum Sententiarum* (Venice, 1522; Repr. Louvain-Paderborn, 1955), Prol. q. 2, art. 2, fol. 8 M.

larger number of works of Augustine's than were used either by Thomas or Giles leads to a more intensive and exclusive reliance on the *Doctor gratiae*; [1] Gregory highlights justification *sola gratia* with Augustine rather than Giles' hierocratic-curialist interpretation of *De civitate Dei*. [2]

Gregory does not remain isolated; his authority is amazingly soon established and the high honor of the title *Doctor authenticus* assigned to him. Among his disciples we find Dionysius of Montina (*magister artium* 1374) and Hugolin of Orvieto (*sententiarius* in Paris 1348/49, d. 1374), whose Sentences commentary was available in Wittenberg. [3] All three combine nominalistic elements with a clear emphasis on the insufficiency of human works and the necessity of grace. [4] A most intriguing figure is Augustinus Favaroni (d. 1443), general of the Order, who almost a century later than Gregory [5] expresses sentiments which must have been and *de facto* were offensive to all those *Doctores*, whether curialists or conciliarists, [6] who were one with Giles of Rome in thinking of the Church as a *corpus politicum*. Alphons Victor Müller repeatedly has called attention to Favaroni as an unknown source of Luther's

---

[1] John O'Malley has pointed to the fact that notwithstanding Gregory's programmatic insistence on the "ipsae sacri canonis veritatis", in practice "he seems to forget all about them and, with gay abandon, throw Paul, Augustine and Euclid together ..." "A note on Gregory of Rimini. Church, Scripture, Tradition", *Augustinianum*, V (1965), 365-78, 372. This "gay abandon" is explainable in terms of the arguments with which Gregory is confronted : when derived from (meta-)physics he will answer in kind "removendo dubia" : Prol. q. 1, art. 2, fol. 3 K. Though Gregory's emphasis on Scripture as the sole source for theology is explicit, O'Malley can rightly point to the fact that the Church universal is for him *validissima auctoritas*. In all cases where he contrasts Augustine with the *communis opinio* Gregory does so with explicit but traditional *reverentia*.

[2] See Wilhelm Kölmel, *Regimen Christianum : Weg und Ergebnisse des Gewaltenverhältnisses und des Gewaltenverständnisses, 8. bis 14. Jahrhundert* (Berlin, 1970), pp. 304 ff.

[3] Cf. Adolar Zumkeller, "Die Augustinertheologen Simon Fidati von Cascia und Hugolin von Orvieto und Martin Luthers Kritik an Aristoteles", *ARG*, LIV (1963), 15-37.

[4] Adolar Zumkeller finds with all three in combination "mit einer nominalistischen Akzeptationstheorie ... die typische Haltung des spätmittelalterlichen Augustinismus in der Beurteilung der Werke der Heiden und in der Forderung eines auxilium speciale." *Dionysius de Montina : Ein neuentdeckter Augustinertheologe des Spätmittelalters* (Würzburg, 1948), p. 82.

[5] Cf. G. Ciolini, *Agostino da Roma (Favaroni d. 1443) e la sua Cristologia* (Florence, 1944), pp. 13-26; Salesius Friemel, *Die theologische Prinzipienlehre des Augustinus Favaroni von Rom O.E.S.A. (d. 1443)* (Würzburg, 1950), pp. 19-26. N. Toner, "The Doctrine of original sin according to Augustine of Rome", *Augustiniana*, VII (1957), 100-17, 349-66, 515-30.

[6] At the Council of Basel an investigation is carried through, resulting in the condemnation of seven articles during the 22nd session on 15 July 1435. Cf. *Mansi*, XXIX, 109 B f.

theology; yet Müller's biting, ironic criticism, directed especially a-
gainst Denifle, Scheel, and Grisar, and his single-minded, undifferen-
tiated identification of trends in late medieval Augustinianism and
the *initia Lutheri*, provoked so much reaction that this line of research
has not been pursued with sufficient energy. The scholarly form of Müller's argumentation also raised more questions than it claimed to answer.
Yet notwithstanding the generally sharp and largely appropriate
criticism, the existence as such of a late medieval Augustinian school
cannot be contested.[1]

In Favaroni's recently discovered *Defensio contra quosdam errores
hereticorum*, soon to be published,[2] this Augustinian theologian indicates that though he does not deny that the Church in one sense of the
word means the *corpus mixtum*, in which the evil ones have their place
ratione sacramentorum, the *ecclesia* as article of faith *sine macula et ruga*
is the church of the elect. Of this church only Christ is the head; when
the pope is *prescitus*, he is not a member of this Church, or even—as the
accusation reads—of the Church militant.[3]

When we investigate the writings which led to the accusation against
Favaroni, it becomes clear that his particular ecclesiology is the alle-
gorical counterpart to the tropological *commercium admirabile* between
Christ and the believer, as we find it with Johann von Staupitz and
Martin Luther. On the basis of the union of Christ and his Body, "totus
et solus Christus est ecclesia," Favaroni comes to the challenging thesis :
"Christus quotidie peccat."[4]

---

[1] Cf. the reception of Müller's interpretation with Eduard Stakemeier, *Der Kampf um
Augustin auf dem Tridentinum* (Paderborn, 1937), pp. 22-60. Sharply criticized by
Hubert Jedin, *Theologische Revue*, XXXVII (1938), 425-30. Cf. Steinmetz, *Misericordia
Dei*, pp. 31-34.

[2] To be edited by W. Lewis from Basel Ms. A IV, 17, fol. 320^r - 328^v; discovered by
W. Pfeuffer. Cf. Adolar Zumkeller, *Manuskripte von Werken der Autoren des Augustiner-
Eremitenordens in mitteleuropäischen Bibliotheken* (Würzburg, 1966), p. 83, no. 159.

[3] Art. VI : "Petrus non est nec fuit caput ecclesie sancte catholice." *Defensio*, fol.
324^v. Art. VII : "... si papa est talis, si papa est malus et presertim si est prescitus, tunc
ut Judas Apostolus est dyabolus, fur et filius perdicionis et non est caput sancte mili-
tantis [!] ecclesie, tamen nec sit membrum eius." *Defensio*, fol. 325^v.

[4] "... Ista conclusio non ponitur ut aperiatur via sophistis, sed ut sacramentum unitatis, quod magnum est in Christo et in ecclesia, cum magna attentione notetur." *Tractatus
de sacramento unitatis Christi et Ecclesiae sive de Christo integro*. Ms. Bibl. Vat. cod. B VII.,
118, fol. 122ra - 130va; 125ra. Dr. W. Eckermann, O.S.A. kindly provided me with his
transcript. In the *Defensio* Favaroni claims a thoroughgoing basis in Augustine for the

Whereas Müller argues that Favaroni anticipated Luther by some seventy years,[1] Favaroni's doctrine is clearly justification *sola caritate* [2] rather than *sola fide*. Hence a continuing line should be drawn from him to Staupitz rather than to Luther, who in his *De libertate christiana* significantly describes first a union with the word in faith [3] before he speaks about the *fröhliche Wechsel*. Furthermore, there exists no evidence pointing to a broad distribution of Favoaroni's writings. Nevertheless much is gained, also for Luther research, as we reach a point where Staupitz no longer seems to arise *ex nihilo*.

It is important for us to keep in mind the words of Gordon Rupp in his splendid opening address to the Third International Congress for Luther Research : "If we are far from the end of the discussion of 'Luther and... Augustine,' it is because we await the elucidation of Augustine's theology in the later Middle Ages." [4] This elucidation is particularly to be expected from further work on Luther's immediate life-context after 1505, i.e., the Augustinian Order.

The aspect most difficult to establish is of course the sphere of the daily spiritual life in an Augustinian convent such as the one at Erfurt. An important beginning has been made by Martin Elze in pointing to the *De passione Domini* of the Augustinian Jordanus of Sachsen, whose *Vitas fratrum* is intensively used and quoted within the Order and taken over almost *in toto* in the *Vita Christi* of Ludolf of Sachsen, which found a wide readership.[5]

contested theses in this treatise : "... illa dicta mea in tractatu prefato omnia fundata sunt in doctrina et dictis beati Augustini ... nec aliquid dixi novum et inconsuetum cui non apposuerim testimonia et motiva beati Augustini." *Defensio*, fol. 320ʳ.

[1] Alphons Victor Müller, "Agostino Favaroni e la Teologia di Lutero", *Bilychnis*, III (1914), 1-17.

[2] "Sola caritas in homine est per essentiam suam vera iustitia per quam homo iustificatur et iuste vivit coram Deo." *Tractatus de merito Christi et condigna satisfactione pro electis*. Ms. Bibl. Vat. cod. B VII, 118, fol. 224ʳᵃ - 241ᵛᵇ; 225ᵛᵃ.

[3] *WA*, VII, 53 15-23. For the ecclesiological theme of union between Bride and Bridegroom in Luther's *Dictata* see Joseph Vercruysse, *Fidelis Populus* (Wiesbaden, 1968), pp. 28-32. For its relation to the medieval tradition, particularly Augustine, see Scott H. Hendrix, *Ecclesia in via : Ecclesiological Developments in the Medieval Psalm Exegesis and the Dictata super Psalterium (1513-1515) of Martin Luther* (Tübingen, 1970), ch. I, p. 4.

[4] *Kirche, Mystik, Heiligung und das Natürliche bei Luther* : Vorträge des dritten internationalen Kongresses für Lutherforschung, Järvenpää, Finnland, 11.-16. August 1966, ed. Ivar Asheim (Göttingen, 1967), p. 14.

[5] Martin Elze, "Züge spätmittelalterlicher Frömmigkeit in Luthers Theologie", *ZThK*, LXII (1965), 381-402; *idem*, "Das Verständnis der Passion Jesu im ausgehenden Mittelalter und bei Luther", *Geist und Geschichte der Reformation : Festgabe H. Rückert* (Berlin, 1966), pp. 127-51.

A closer textual analysis of the *Rosetum*, explicitly quoted by Luther,[1] and of the *Himmlische Fundgrube* and the *Coelifodina* of Johannes von Paltz shows the continuation of this tradition of affective meditation as it reaches Luther's immediate environment. Apart from Luther's fundamentally new theological hermeneutic and hence apart from the new connection between *affectus* and *effectus*, we find here the same warnings against speculative "high mysticism" [2] as well as the emphasis on

---

[1] Elze, "Züge spätmittelalterlicher Frömmigkeit", pp. 390-9. As one example of a possible relationship between Paltz and Luther, Robert H. Fischer refers to a common quotation assigned to Albertus Magnus. "Paltz und Luther", *Luther-Jahrbuch*, XXXVII (1970), 9-36, 16. Though no dependence can be established, the juxtaposition of the two texts documents the extent of continuity in this tradition of meditation piety. "Der heilige susse lerer sant Bernhart uber das buch der lobeseng spricht, dass kein nutzer oder krefftiger ding sey tzu heylen die wunden der sunde, dan die betrachtunge der wunden Christi. Dar tzu spricht Albertus Magnus : 'Welcher mensch alle tag oben hin, als man erbes oder bonen erliseth, uberlaufft oder bedenckt das leyden Christi, der erlangeth da mit mer nutz dan das er alle freitag das gantz iar fastet. Czu dem andern ist es im nutzer, dan das er ym selber geb alle wochen ein disciplin, das das blut ernach ging durch das gantz iar. Czu dem dritten male ist es ym nutzer, dan das er alle wochen das gantze iar eynen psalter beteth.' Dartzu als man auß vil leren mag vorsteen, so ist kein nutzer ding gotes huld tzu erwerben tzu gunst der muter gotes und aller heyligen und aller engel, dan die betrachtunge des heiligen leydens Christi. Auch ist keyn nutzer ding..." Johann von Paltz, *Das bucheleyn wirt genannt die hymmelische funt grube* (Leipzig, 1497), sig. A II^v-A III^r (London, British Museum, Bench mark, I.A. 1203). - Cf. Johann von Paltz, *Coelifodina* (Leipzig, 1504), sig. G II^r-G II^v (Munich, Bayr. Staatsbibliothek, call no. : P. lat. 947a [1]. 4°). - Cf. Bernhard, *Sermones in Cant. 62,7* : "Quid enim tam efficax ad curanda conscientiae vulnera, nec non ad purgandam mentis aciem, quam vulnerum sedula meditatio ?" Migne, *PL*, 183, 1079 B. See Luther, "Ein Sermon von der Betrachtung des heiligen Leidens Christi" (1519) : "Zcum andernn haben ettlich angezeygte mancherley nutz und frucht, ßo auß Christus leyden betrachtung kummen. Darzu geht yrre eyn spruch, S. Albert zu geschrieben, das es besser sey, Christus leyden eyn mal oben hyn uber dacht, dan ob man eyn gantz jar festet, alle tag eyn Psalter bettet etc. Dem folgen sie blind da hyn und geratten eben widder die rechte frucht des leydens Christi, dan sie das yhre darynnen suchen. Darumb tragen sie sich mit bildelein und buechlein, brieffen und creutzen, auch ettlich ßo ferne faren, das sie sich vor wasser, eyßen, fewr und allerley ferlickeyt zu sicheren vormeynen, und alßo Christus leyden eyn unleyden yn yhn wircken sol widder seyn art und natur." *WA*, II, 136 11-20. - "Zcum zehenden. Wer alßo gottis leyden eyn tag, eyn stund, ja eyn viertel stund bedecht, von dem selben wollen wyr frey sagen, das es beßer sey, dan ob er eyn gantz jar fastet, alle tag eynn psalter bettet, ja das er hundert messen horet, dann dißes bedencken wandelt den menschen weßenlich und gar nah wie die tauffe widderumb new gepiret. Hie wircket das leyden Christi seyn rechtes naturlich edels werck, erwurget den alten Adam, vortreybt alle lust, freud und zuvorsicht, die man haben mag von creaturen, gleych wie Christus von allen, auch von got vorlaßen war." *WA*, II, 139 11-15.

[2] In this sense one can agree with Elze's conclusion, "dass alle diese Gedanken Luthers

the specific application of the Passion of Christ to the individual, which
suggests the context of Luther's insistence on the *pro me*.[1] The final
sentence of Jordan's *Prologus* documents not only this tendency but
also provides a key to Staupitz's seemingly unprecedented campaign
against the scholastic *gratia gratum faciens*. Whereas Staupitz wants to
reinterpret *gratia gratum faciens* not as the grace which makes us acceptable to God but vice versa as the grace which makes God acceptable to
us,[2] we read with Jordan : "Omnia quae Christus passus est, ita debent
homini esse accepta et grata, ac si pro ipsius solummodo salute ea sit
passus."[3] Out of this tradition emerges, finally, that aspect of the first
of Luther's Ninety-five Theses according to which penance is a lasting
mark of the Christian life.

We encounter here the paradox that an intense preoccupation with
Augustine does not always guarantee that Augustine himself comes to
his own. Rather, it is the heritage of the mature Augustine marked by
and protected against a long history of attack or of benign condescen-
sion to the "excessive" Augustine. Quite appropriately Eck confronts
Luther right at the outset in his first proposition for the Leipzig Debate [4]
with the argument that Luther cannot appeal to Augustine for his thesis of life-long penance. Since this idea is an organic development of
Augustine's heritage (*humilitas*) within the order, Eck's attack came as a
surprise to Luther. With some of the opponents and most of the other
reformers, particularly Melanchthon and Zwingli,[5] we find an equally
intensive but generally more precise use of St. Augustine. With Melanchthon, for instance, we encounter the precision of a centuries-skirting
Augustine scholarship, not marked by the Augustinian's pious commitment to and reverential meditation on the works of the Founding

---

aus der Tradition jener unmystischen Frömmigkeit gespeist sind." Elze, "Züge spätmittelalterlicher Frömmigkeit", p. 399.

[1] Elze, "Das Verständnis der Passion Jesu", p. 134.

[2] Cf. David C. Steinmetz, *Misericordia Dei : The Theology of Johannes von Staupitz
in Its Late Medieval Setting* (Leiden, 1968), pp. 84-85.

[3] Elze, "Das Verständnis der Passion Jesu", p. 134.

[4] *WA*, IX, 208 32-33. While not answering this challenge directly Luther points, not
too convincingly, to a text in the *Enchiridion* on a related issue at the very end of the
Disputation. *WA*, II, 377 13-17. Cf. *WA*, II, 374 4-9 (Quotation from Augustine's *Enchiridion*, Migne, *PL*, 40, 265; CChr, 46. 88, 12-13). Yet at Eck's "tangit Augustinus ut
refert Gratianus", Luther cannot forego the chance to characterize this as "auctoritates
consarcinare". See *WA*, II, 376 37.

[5] Cf. Arthur Rich, *Die Anfänge der Theologie Huldrych Zwinglis* (Zürich, 1949), pp.
127-30.

Father. Modern scholarship cannot but agree with Melanchthon against Luther when he argues that *sola fide* does not characterize Augustine's doctrine of justification.[1] Indeed, to be immersed in and to emerge from late medieval Augustinianism does not *ipso facto* mean a better grasp of the historical Augustine.

The indicated thrust *ad fontes Augustini* by no means establishes an unbroken tradition in the Order. Curialistic ecclesiology like that of Giles of Rome continues at least till the times of the Council of Basel.[2] Similarly the prior of Luther's Erfurt monastery, Johann von Paltz, can by no stretch of the imagination be regarded as a partisan of either the *solus Christus* ecclesiology of Favaroni or the *sola gratia* soteriology of Gregory of Rimini. Yet the one who integrated these elements and sharpened the impact of this tradition seems to have been Staupitz, whose impact on Luther should not be underestimated. Furthermore, after Luther's Ockham-oriented *artes* training and lectorate in Erfurt,[3] he finds the nominalistic *via moderna*, referred to as the *via Gregorii*,[4] next to the *via antiqua* in Wittenberg.

When we take stock of the present state of scholarship, there are at least four potential agents of transmission of the indicated Augustinian tradition.

---

[1] *WA Br*, XII, 193 88-94. Luther invokes the *vox Augustini*, but quotes Bernard of Clairvaux ! In the contrast between Luther and Augustine, the role of the Augustinian's tradition should be given more weight. Cf. the observation of T. van Bavel in his review of R. Schwarz, *Vorgeschichte der reformatorischen Busstheologie* : "The most striking aspect of this book, in my opinion, is the rather slight influence of Augustine on Luther." *Augustiniana*, XXI (1971), 353.

[2] See Adolar Zumkeller, "Die Augustinereremiten in der Auseinandersetzung mit Wyclif und Hus, ihre Beteiligung an den Konzilien von Konstanz und Basel", *Analecta Augustiniana*, XXVIII (1965), 5-56. Cf. the contemporary of Gregory, Hermann von Schildesche, (d. 1357) by whom the political predominance of the Church is argued with a "sola Ecclesia": "... dependet rectus usus temporalium principaliter ab Ecclesia, in quantum a gratia dependet, quae in sola Ecclesia datur." *Hermanni de Schildis OSA, Tractatus contra haereticos negantes immunitatem et iurisdictionem Sanctae Ecclesiae...*, ed. A. Zumkeller (Würzburg, 1970), I, cap. 13; 35, 67-68.

[3] Cf. the document dated 18 April 1508, published by Reinould Weijenborg, "Luther et les cinquante-et-un Augustins d'Erfurt d'après une lettre d'indulgences inédite du 18. avril 1508", *RHE*, LV (1960), 819-75.

[4] The new Wittenberg University statutes of 1508 establish for the arts faculty all three 'ways' : the *via Thomae, via Scoti* and the *via Gregorii*. Karl Bauer draws the conclusion : "Als Vertreter der *via moderna* übernahm er in Wittenberg den auf das Augustinerkloster gestifteten Lehrstuhl für Ethik..." *Die Wittenberger Universitätstheologie und die Anfänge der Deutschen Reformation* (Tübingen, 1928), p. 10.

1. In the library of the Augustinians in Wittenberg, Luther had at his disposal both *De gestis Salvatoris* of Simone Fidati and the only manuscript known to us of the Sentences Commentary of Hugolin of Orvieto.[1] Either writing brings a sharper critique of Aristotle than we find with the Erfurt teachers Trutvetter and Usingen; either one carries in its own way the marks of the *via Gregorii*.

2. As is generally acknowledged, during the years of his first lectures on the Psalms, 1513-1515, Luther may well have used the main work of the Augustinian James Pérez of Valencia (d. 1490). In his doctrine of sin and grace Pérez proves his proximity to Gregory of Rimini and his school.[2]

3. The relation between Johann von Staupitz [3] (d. 1524) and Luther is intimate and hence complex, posing intricate problems, particularly during the period 1515-1518, when the roles of teacher and disciple may have been reversed. Yet it cannot be contested that in 1518 Luther assigns the role of *originator* and *movens* to Staupitz in his (Luther's) own discovery of *vera poenitentia*.[4] This ascription finds its partly verbatim, striking parallel in Luther's 1545 recollection of having grasped the Pauline sense of the *iustitia Dei*.[5] As with Gregory, we find with the later Staupitz after the period of the Tübingen Sermons, the *acceptatio* doctrine as interpretation of the *sola gratia*, which he has combined with the tropological application of 'Favaroni's' theme of the exchange of *iustitia* and *peccata* between Christ and the believer.[6]

---

[1] Zumkeller, "Die Augustinertheologen Simon Fidati von Cascia und Hugolin von Orvieto", pp. 22-23, 26 ff.

[2] Wilfried Werbeck, *Jacobus Pérez von Valencia: Untersuchungen zu seinem Psalmenkommentar* (Tübingen, 1959); Adolar Zumkeller, "Die Augustinerschule des Mittelalters : Vertreter und philosophisch-theologische Lehre", *Analecta Augustiniana*, XXVII (1964), 167-262, 250.

[3] See Steinmetz, *Misericordia Dei*; *idem, Reformers in the Wings* (Philadelphia, 1971), pp. 18-29 (Lit.).

[4] *WA*, I, 525 4-14.

[5] Cf. Ernst Wolf, *Staupitz und Luther : Ein Beitrag zur Theologie des Johannes von Staupitz und deren Bedeutung für Luthers theologischen Werdegang* (Leipzig, 1927), pp. 223 ff., 253 ff. Wolf argues for formal rather than material parallels : "Gerade in ihnen ist ein wesentlicher Teil der Einwirkung Staupitzens zu suchen..." *Ibid.*, p. 248.

[6] "Nondum misericordiae domini satisfactum putes, quod nos sua iustitia iustos fecit, quod coniugium cum peccatrice non horruit. Accedit aliud, quod nostra peccata sua facit, quatinus, sicut christianus Christi iustitia iustus, Christus christiani culpa iniustus sit et peccator." *Libellus de executione aeternae praedestinationis* (Nürnberg, 1517), cap. XI, 71. Cf. the almost three weeks earlier German translation by Scheurl.

4. Indebtedness to Staupitz is acknowledged by a second member of the Wittenberg coalition which was formed on the platform of the theology of Paul and Augustine in late 1516-early 1517. About this same time Andreas Bodenstein von Karlstadt dedicates his commentary on Augustine's *De spiritu et litera* to Staupitz and describes how, after Luther's first influence, Staupitz had freed Karlstadt from scholasticism by showing the "Christi dulcedinem" in the right relation of spirit and letter.[1] Karlstadt designates the brand of scholasticism he had turned away from prior to his lectures according to Scotus as the "secta Capreolina."[2] To have taught theology according to the *Princeps Thomistarum* (d. 1444) implied an intensive preoccupation with Gregory, since Capreolus saw the reconciliation of Gregory and Thomas as an important task; he had transcribed Gregory page after page into his *Defensiones*.[3] This considerably strengthens the argument of Ernst Kähler that the Wittenberg discussion about the Augustinianism of Gregory has to be placed early in 1517 at the latest, i.e., more than two years before Luther praises Gregory as the only scholastic theologian to oppose the modern Pelagians.[4] In Gregory, Luther publicly and explicitly was to hail a tradition which was waiting to be used by him in his own assaults *contra modernos*.

Thus there is indeed reason to reopen the discussion about the *via Gregorii* in Wittenberg. When Luther was called in 1508 to teach philosophical ethics in the faculty of arts and later, in 1512, succeeded Staupitz in the theological faculty as Doctor of Scripture, he was supposed to represent the *via moderna*, instituted at Wittenberg by his

---

Exact description by Maria Grossmann, "Bibliographie der Werke Christoph Scheurls", *Archiv für Geschichte des Buchwesens*, X (1970), 371-96, 385, no. 41 and 42. Cf. H.A. Oberman, *Forerunners of the Reformation : The Shape of Late Medieval Thought* (New York, 1966), pp. 175-203, 189-90.

[1] Kähler, *Karlstadt und Augustin*, p. 5 17-19.

[2] Cf. Kähler, p. 3 20. Already in his very first work Karlstadt employs Capreolus : "... hoc confirmat Sancti Thomae acerrimus tutor et defensor Capreolus." *De intentionibus. Opusculum compilatum ad S. emulorum Thomae eruditionem* (Leipzig, 1507), fol. 50r.

[3] For a detailed analysis of the relevant texts, see my forth-coming article "Gregor von Rimini und die Anfänge der Wittenberger Universitätstheologie".—In his *Distinctiones Thomistarum* (1508) Karlstadt quotes from a compendium of Capreolus' *Defensiones* by Prierias, *Opus in Ioannem Capreolum* (Cremona, 1497), in which Gregory is often mentioned and quoted. The name of Gregory is not mentioned by Karlstadt.

[4] *WA*, II, 394 29 ff.; Kähler, p. 22*, n. 5. Leif Grane argues acutely for the summer of 1519 as the time of Luther's Gregory studies : "Gregor von Rimini und Luthers Leipziger Disputation", *Studia Theologica*, XXII (1968), 29-49, 44.

predecessor and Erfurt teacher Trutvetter.[1] On the basis of the revised
University statutes of 1508, first edited by Muther,[2] and the comprehensive critical edition by Friedensburg,[3] Scheel and Bauer concluded [4]
that the *via moderna* at Wittenberg was designated in 1508 as "via
Guilelmi," the way of Ockham. Muther, however, based his work on
only one manuscript in which, as he noted, a later hand corrected "via
Gregorii" into "via Guilelmi." Friedensburg makes use of a second
manuscript which reads "Gregorii," so that in two passages in two
manuscripts the three admitted "ways" are described as "via Thomae,
via Scoti, via Gregorii." On the basis of this textual evidence we cannot
but draw the conclusion that whatever the later practice, the statutes
intended to allow for the *via Gregorii* from Luther's course unfortunately no lecture notes are preserved. In any case Bauer is to be
corrected to the extent that Luther was not obliged to lecture in
ethics as a representative of the *via moderna*.[5]

Luther's second Erfurt teacher, Bartholomäus von Usingen, had
already emphasized the significance of the great *Doctor autenticus*. Indeed, Ockham is for him the *Venerabilis inceptor viae modernae*; but in
theology he has the highest regard, after Petrus d'Ailly, for Gregory
of Rimini. Hence Luther did not come to Wittenberg unprepared.[6]
The implications of teaching according to the *via Gregorii* are by no

---

[1] Cf. *Christoph Scheurls Briefbuch*, ed. F.v. Soden - J.K.F. Knaake (Potsdam, 1867)
I, 142; quoted by Bauer, p. 9.

[2] "Indifferenter profiteatur Via Thomae, Scoti, Guilelmi (Gregorii Cod. Manus poster-
ior loco Gregorii correxit Occam)." Statuta Artistarum. Caput Decimum. *Die Wittenberger Universitaets- und Facultaetsstatuten vom Jahre MDVIII*, ed. Theodor Muther
(Halle, 1867), p. 45. Cf. Caput Tertium where Muther also replaces "Gregorio" with
"Guilelmo"; *ibid.*, p. 41.

[3] Walter Friedensburg reads "Gregorio" both times, but comments at cap. 3 : "So AB.;
ob Guilelmo [von Occam] zu lesen ?" at Cap. 10 : "So AB.; in B. Gregorii ausgestrichen,
von anderer Hand darüber : Occam." *Urkundenbuch der Universität Wittenberg* (1502-
1611) (Magdeburg, 1926), I, 53, 56, 57-58. The change in one Ms. convinced Muther and
influenced Friedensburg; even though we no longer possess the original copy, the total
evidence speaks clearly for "Gregorii".

[4] Otto Scheel, *Martin Luther : Vom Katholizismus zur Reformation* (Tübingen, 1917),
II, 395, n. 46; Bauer, p. 9, n. 4.

[5] Bauer, p. 10.

[6] Luther's critique of Aristotle with its unprecedented intensity stands at the very
beginning of his road to reformation. Later, in 1519, he can praise Gregory of Rimini for
refuting an opposing Aristotle with the sole weapons of Augustine and Scripture : " [Gre-
gorius Ariminensis] est enim totus aliud nihil quam Augustinus et divina scriptura,
resistens quidem omnibus doctoribus scholasticis, tum maxime Aristoteli, sed nondum

means clear, and neither is the reason why Gregory's name is replaced in one manuscript by Ockham's. When we look for a comparison we find that at Heidelberg the *via moderna* can be referred to as the "via Marsiliana" [1] after Marsilius of Inghen (d. 1396). Here again the distinction between nominalism and Occamism applies. Whereas Marsilius calls Gregory "magister noster,"[2] there is no indication in his work of exposure to Ockham's writings.[3] It is good to remind ourselves of the conclusion of Gerhard Ritter which also sets the context for understanding Gregory : the spirit of Augustine along with the philosophical elements of nominalism is the mark of a theological education which later would inform the thought of Luther as a beginning teacher.[4]

It is not difficult to be alert to the vast differences between Gregory and Marsilius on the one hand and Luther on the other, differences so obvious and far-reaching [5] that they cannot be explained merely in terms of a time interval. It is all the more important for us that beyond all reconstructions we now possess a newly discovered document from the hand of one of Luther's Augustinian brethren in the Erfurt monastery, to be dated around 1509. The text is well-known to Luther scholars since it was held until recently to be genuine Luther material.[6]

---

ab ullo confutatus est." *WA*, II, 303 12-15. But when he tries in 1517, well over a year before his last efforts during and after the Heidelberg Disputation, to win his former Erfurt teachers for the cause of the Reformation, he chides both of them for wasting their time in meaningless work ("prorsus inutiles") in commenting on the "illusor" Aristotle. (*WA Br*, I, 88 4-89 30; 8 February 1517 to Joh. Lang.) There is no indication that he does appeal to Gregory of Rimini at a time when this would have enhanced the force of his argument. This helps us to realize that we continue to be dependent on reconstruction rather than on unambiguous evidence.

[1] G. Ritter, *Studien zur Spätscholastik* : *Marsilius von Inghen und die okkamistische Schule in Deutschland* (Heidelberg, 1921), I, 46 (Sitzungsberichte 12).

[2] Ritter, p. 11, n. 4, p. 38, n. 3.

[3] "Nicht genannt wird Egidius Romanus, der sonst so beliebte; noch auffallender ist das völlige Fehlen der Originalschriften Okkams." Ritter, p. 42.

[4] "Das sola gratia ist A und O dieser Theologie. Der Geist Augustins, der sie durchdringt, in Verbindung mit den philosophischen Elementen der nominalistischen Erkenntnislehre war auch das Kennzeichen der theologischen Bildung, die dereinst das Denken Martin Luthers in den Anfängen seiner theologischen Lehrtätigkeit beherrschen sollte." Ritter, p. 183.

[5] Cf. Gordon Rupp : "You might add a double dose of Augustine to the pre-existing mixture of Peter Lombard and Aristotle, but the result would be a Gregory of Rimini, or a Bradwardine, a recognizably mediaeval Augustinianism worlds apart from Luther's theology as it developed in these formative years." *The Righteousness of God*, p. 140.

[6] *WA*, IX, 29 4-26. In a joint effort with Hans Volz to verify Buchwald's edition of Lombard's Sentences, the Buchwald text could be confirmed on the basis of a micro-

This manifesto-like *cri de cœur* is now much more precious and crucial than before, when it was ascribed to Luther. It now serves to document the factors constitutive for the Augustinian spirituality and attitude we have been pointing to, in time and space closer to the very beginning of Luther's theology than any other text we know : first, the authority of St. Augustine *nunquam satis* praised as *apex* of the tradition; secondly, the critical stance over against scholastic philosophy with its idle questions—*nugis meris* (The philosophers can be useful for theology but they are dangerous and to be regarded as "opiniosos dubitatores"); and finally there are humanistic touches in this "Declaration of Independence" in its use of Greek mythology and its alliance with the *poetae* against the philosophers.

Taking stock of this cumulative, admittedly circumstantial evidence, we can point to the *schola Augustiniana moderna*, initiated by Gregory of Rimini, reflected by Hugolin of Orvieto, apparently spiritually alive in the Erfurt Augustinian monastery, and transformed into a pastoral reform-theology by Staupitz, as the *occasio proxima*—not *causa* !—for the inception of the *theologia vera* at Wittenberg.

As we saw in the case of the *via Gregorii* and the *via Marsiliana*, nominalism is readily incorporated into this tradition. In Luther's case we know that he continues to be proud of his Erfurt association with the *secta Occamica* as far as logic and dialectics are concerned. He uses their tools, e.g., in 1520 against a Thomistic and in 1528 against a spiritualist or "Wycliffite" doctrine of the Eucharist. Ockham, d'Ailly, and Biel could function in the field of theology for Luther in 1515-1517 in a negative sense as a magnifying glass to discover the deviation of scholastic theology *in toto* from the *vera theologia*, particularly in its transition from a philosophical to a theological anthropology. Whereas in 1515 Luther is still able to use the nominalistic terminology of the *facere quod in se est*[1] for the role of the human will before the reception of grace and glory, though now reduced to *expectatio*, *gemitus* and confession of sin as the human *conditio sine qua non* in the *pactum miseri-*

---

film of the Zwickau original except for minor corrections. The relatively long opening statement "auf der inneren Seite des vorderen Einbanddeckels", however, is undoubtedly not from Luther, but from another hand, comtemporary, probably slightly older. *WA*, IX, 29,1.

[1] *WA*, IX, 28, n. 1, is the most eloquent parallel text to the one discussed above, written about the same time and presented in the same context, Schol. to Rom. 3,21 : "Non enim dabitur gratia sine ista agricultura suiipsius." *WA*, LVI, 257 30-31.

cordiae,[1] we see that at the outset the nominalistic, experience-oriented revolt against meta-theology and the Augustinian awareness of the distance between God (*sapientia*) and man (*scientia*)[2] combine to move Luther to a decisive break with the nominalistic confidence in the *facere quod in se est* of human reason.

In the relation of Luther to humanism, I discern the peak of affinity during the period around the Leipzig Debate, when Luther in Pico-like words exclaims against Eck's claims for papal prerogatives : "Omnes homines aequales sunt in humanitate, quae est omnium summa et admiranda aequalitas, ex qua omnis dignitas hominibus..." [3] A *sic et non* relation seems to apply in the same real sense in which it characterizes the Reformer's relation to mysticism.[4] As a recent overall assessment of the theme "Luther and humanism" shows, an even more striking parallel with Luther's respect for nominalism "in its own domain" emerges : "... Luther gave enthusiastic support to humanist culture in its sphere, but sharply rebuffed its encroachments in the domain of theology where God's Word and not human letters reigns supreme." [5]

Weighing the evidence now available, it can be said that humanism, nominalism, and Augustinianism do not reach Luther as three separate

---

[1] See *WA*, IX, 28, n. 1. In addition to the texts indicated in my article "Wir sein pettler. Hoc est verum. Bund und Gnade in der Theologie des Mittelalters und der Reformation", *ZKG*, LXXVIII (1967), 232-52, see Luther's marginal to Augustine's *De Trinitate*, I, 3 (Migne, *PL*, 42. 822; CChr, 50. 32, 5-6). "Et hoc placitum : i.e. pactum", *WA*, IX, 16 4; and "pepigit nobiscum fedus, ut daret nobis petentibus gratis ac mendicantibus", *WA*, IV, 350 13-14.

[2] "Sicut rancidae logicorum regulae somniant et puncto nulleitatis suae : infinitam deitatis latitudinem metiuntur." *WA*, IX, 47 6-7; cf. *WA*, IX, 29 20-26; 31 31-34; 65 10-22. As early as 1510 Luther argues *contra omnes*, against all schools : "Legi mille et omnes doctores, nullus melius solvet hanc questionem. Scotus distinguit ea formaliter, moderni ratione, antiqui realiter. Ex quibus omnibus colligitur omnes eos nescire quid loquantur." *WA*, IX, 62 19-22; quoted by zur Mühlen, p. 252, n. 375. In the years to come Luther frequently uses the argument that an opponent 'does not understand himself what he is saying', whenever an argument is not based on Scripture or experience : "Cum enim ista nemo viderit, quicquid supra fidem additur, certissimum est figmentum esse humanum. Similiter de anima." Continuation of above quotation, *WA*, IX, 62 22-24.

[3] *WA*, II, 631 1-2.

[4] See my "Simul gemitus et raptus : Luther und die Mystik", *Kirche, Mystik, Heiligung und das Natürliche bei Luther*. Vorträge des dritten internationalen Kongresses für Lutherforschung, Järvenpää, Finnland, 11.-16. August 1966, ed. Ivar Asheim (Göttingen, 1967), pp. 20-59, 24 ff.

[5] Lewis W. Spitz, *The Religious Renaissance of the German Humanists* (Cambridge, Mass., 1963), p. 238.

and unrelated forces. Both nominalism and humanism are domesticated and put into the service of a new Augustinian theology. With their aid the authentic Augustinian emphasis on the distinction between *sapientia* and *scientia* can be preserved without being doomed to slide back into a pious conservatism, as had been the case whenever no compromise was made with the Aristotelian academic centers of learning. Yet the two movements are domesticated in different ways and put to different uses. Whereas nominalism tends to shape the prolegomena of the *schola moderna Augustiniana* [1] and thus to secure a bridge to the world of the senses, of science and of experienced reality, humanism as the quest for the *mens Augustini* by returning to the *fontes Augustini* relates to the inner core of its program. It is Luther's liaison to this "school" which suffices to explain his initial readiness to exchange Lyra for Faber and the Vulgate for Erasmus' edition of the New Testament; but it also explains his critical appraisal of the high anthropology of Erasmus from the very beginning,[2] long before German Erasmians started to discover that the Wittenberger did not represent their ideals. Luther never shared the heroic vision of man, or as Charles Trinkaus has put it, the "new religious vision of *homo triumphans*," even if at times this heroicism is argued on the basis of a theology of grace.[3] Rather than Luther's contacts with individual humanists or humanistic sodalities, it is his life in the Order itself that provides us with the key to this curious mixture of respect for the historical perspective on sources and authorities, with the early preference for Augustine over Jerome,[4] and the pastoral option

---

[1] This aspect is to be taken into consideration when Otto H. Pesch observes in his impressive study of the relation Thomas-Luther : "Eher als mit dem Ockhamismus scheinen die Anfänge der Theologie Luthers mit einer augustinischen Reaktion gegen die *via moderna* verwoben zu sein." *Theologie der Rechtfertigung bei Martin Luther und Thomas von Aquin: Versuch eines systematisch-theologischen Dialogs* (Mainz, 1967), p. 4, n. 4.

[2] "Tempora enim sunt periculosa hodie, et video, quod non ideo quispiam sit christianus vere sapiens, quia Graecus sit et Hebraeus, quando et Beatus Hieronymus quinque linguis monoglosson Augustinum non adaequarit, licet Erasmo aliter sit longe visum. Sed aliud est iudicium eius, qui arbitrio hominis nonnihil tribuit, aliud eius, qui praeter gratiam nihil novit." *WA Br*, I, 90 21-26; letter to Joh. Lang, Wittenberg, 1 March 1517.

[3] "*In Our Image and Likeness*" : *Humanity and Divinity in Italian Humanist Thought* (Chicago, 1970), I, xxi, 447, n. 39. The different anthropology of Luther can be shown with respect to all major humanists discussed, whether Petrarch (p. 12), Salutati (pp. 51, 76) or—especially—Valla (p. 168).

[4] The difficulty in placing the preference for Augustine over Jerome within a definite theological tradition becomes clear, however, when one observes that the young Eck takes the same position as Luther in criticizing the opposite view of Erasmus. See Eck's letter to Erasmus, 2 February 1518; *Opus Epistolarum Des. Erasmi Roterodami*, ed.

for the "verbositas" of the German language instead of the subtlety of refined latinity.[1] The significance of the *schola Augustiniana* for Luther's development just as much as that of nominalism and humanism cannot be restricted to the *initia Lutheri*. Our understandable preoccupation with the "reformatorische Durchbruch" should not prevent us from giving more thought to another period in Luther's life, the late twenties and thirties, when the forces of the past by no means have run their full course. In his Table Talks of the early thirties, perhaps sobered by the revolutionary effect of his proclamation of Christian liberty, Luther mentions again the name of Staupitz, frequently and with great warmth, after a long period of silence.[2] In the revealing dispute with Melanchthon in 1536, Luther, unlike the *Praeceptor*, was still unwilling to admit that Augustine had at times spoken "excessively." He insists that "eum (Augustine) nobiscum sentire" as regards justification by faith alone.[3] These two examples suffice to point out that much work still is to be done on the *initia Lutheri senioris*. As far as the *initia* of the young Luther are concerned, however, the role of the *schola Augustiniana moderna* cannot be easily overestimated in our effort to assess the forces that shaped him in the years of decision. It is most certainly over-estimated, however, when a causal connection is constructed which does not take into account the contribution this same *schola* was to make to Catholic reform theology as represented by Contarini and Seripando and, at least partly, as reflected in the dogmatic decisions of the Council of Trent.

P.S. Allen (Oxford, 1913), III, no. 769, 80-99. Cf. Theodor Wiedemann, *Dr. Johann Eck* (Regensburg, 1865), pp. 326-28.

[1] "Sed nec, si quam maxime vellem, aliquid possem efficere, quod Latinis auribus tolerabile fieret, quanto minus nunc, cum dedita opera vulgi tarditati servire statuissem. Igitur te obsecro, ut e virorum eruditorum conspectu eas submoveas, quantum potes." *WA Br*, I, 93 8-94 12; Luther to Scheurl, 6 May 1517.

[2] E.g. *WA Tr*, I, 512 18-20; II 121 9-11; 227 21-25; 582 16-27.

[3] "Phil. : Augustinus, vt apparet, extra disputationes commodius sensit quam loquitur in disputationibus. Sic enim loquitur, quasi iudicare debeamus nos iustos esse fide, hoc est nouitate nostra. Quod si est verum, iusti sumus non sola fide, sed omnibus donis ac virtutibus. Idque sane vult Augustinus. Et hinc orta est scholasticorum Gratia gratum faciens. ... Augustinus non hoc sentit Gratis saluari hominem, sed saluari propter donatas virtutes. Quid vobis de hac Augustini sententia videtur ?... Phil. : Apud Augustinum Sola fide tantum excludit opera praecedentia. Luth. : Sit hoc vel non, tamen ista vox Augustini satis ostendit eum nobiscum sentire, vbi dicit : 'Turbabor, sed non perturbabor, quia vulnerum Domini recordabor'. Hoc enim clare sentit fidem valere principio, medio, fine et perpetuo, sicut et Dauid : 'Apud te propitiatio est'. 'Non intres in iudicium cum seruo'." *WA Br*, XII, 191 1-5; 23-24; 193 88-94.

IV. Epilogue

The distinction between the *initia Lutheri* and the *initia reformationis* has its limitations and accordingly its considerable dangers. It may isolate the Reformer in exactly the way in which Luther scholarship has isolated the "great and therefore lonely" man too long. It is good to remind ourselves that Luther could state in May 1518, that the part of his Ninety-five Theses which dealt with works and grace did not originate with him alone or with him first. He points for example to Karlstadt and to Amsdorf [1] as other members of the Wittenberg schoolteam. Yet in the very passages where he indicates that others have preceded him in the resistance against "modern Pelagianism" and in discovering God's initiative in the *vera poenitentia*, Luther shows his awareness that he has gone beyond this program based on an Augustinian interpretation of St. Paul. The view of the insufficiency of human works nurtured in the Order,[2] and perhaps most radically formulated by Staupitz as *opera finita* on which no hope can be built,[3] was to lead in another direction, namely to the doctrine of the *duplex iustitia* so eloquently defended at the Council of Trent by the Augustinian General Jerome Seripando.[4] Whereas the inherent "insufficient" righteousness of the *duplex iustitia* still allows for a search for the signs of election in us, a *parallelismus practicus* as described by Staupitz, this position is inverted and abandoned by Luther in his scholion on Rom. 8 : 28 [5]. Here

---

[1] "Deinde Positiones meae displicent, atque ita futurum suspicabar. Verum de iis, quae gratiam et opera tangunt, scias, optime vir, me neque solum neque primum esse earum assertorem. Scis ingenia eorum, qui apud nos sunt, puta Carlstadii, Amsdorfii, D. Hieronymi, D. Wolfgangi, utriusque Feldkirchen, denique D. Petri Lupini. At ii omnes constanter mecum sentiunt, imo tota Universitas, excepto uno ferme Licentiato Sebastiano, sed et Princeps et Episcopus ordinarius noster; deinde multi alii Praelati, et quotquot sunt ingeniosi cives, iam uno ore dicunt, sese prius non novisse nec audivisse Christum et Euangelium." *WA Br*, I, 170 20-29.

[2] Cf. Adolar Zumkeller, "Das Ungenügen der menschlichen Werke bei den Deutschen Predigern des Spätmittelalters", *ZKTh*, LXXXI (1959), 265-305.

[3] "... in homine formaliter sunt et non nisi extrinseca denominatione dei sunt et finita sunt"; "... opera personae finitae natura finita sunt. Ergo infinitum praemium..." *Libellus de executione*, cap. VII, 40, 43.

[4] Seripando once appeals to Jacobus Pérez, *Concilium Tridentinum* XII, 664-65; see Zumkeller, "Augustinerschule," p. 251, n. 298 (quoted p. 78, n. 2).

[5] Compared with the three kinds of love as signs of election in Staupitz's *Libellus de executione*, cap. XV, 117-120 Luther describes the third "gradus signorum electionis" as 'amara in subiectum' : "Sed Amor desiderii Ille, inquam, est sicut infernus, durus et robustus, et in hoc exercet suos electos Deus in hac vita miris modis. Sic sponsa in Can-

he says that the move from the requirement of self-analysis (*contritio*) to trust (*fiducia*) in the *iustitia Christi extra nos* [1] marks the end of medieval religious introspection and sets the Christian free for service, no longer in terms of his own salvation but in terms of the needs of his fellow-man : "Eyn Christen mensch ist eyn dienstbar knecht aller ding und yderman unterthan."

Our distinction between the *initia Lutheri* and the *initia reformationis* has allowed for the enlargement of part of the picture of the total Reformation movement in order to focus both on Luther's own theological voyage and on the extent to which it intersects with a number of contemporary crosscurrents. Our search for the headwaters has led us to the conclusion that the contributions of these three tributaries—nominalism, humanism and Augustinianism—are much more effective as categories in mapping the course of the *initia reformationis* than in locating the *initia Lutheri* before they surface in the flood of the early Reformation. In one perspective this conclusion would seem to put us on the side of those who venerate the mysterious Luther as a latter-day Melchizedek—"a man without beginnings." Efforts have been made in the past to find the key in Luther the nominalist, Luther the Augustinian or Luther the humanist—the first modern man assailing obscurantism. The opposite view that Luther's path to Reformation is determined by none of the these but rather by his study of the Scriptures would

---

ticis : 'Amore Langueo'. Ideo Sub nomine Amoris Vel charitatis semper Crux et passiones intelligende sunt, Vt patet in textu isto. Sine quibus anima languescit, tepefit et Dei desiderium negligit neque sitit ad Deum, fontem viuum. Est quidem res dulcis, Sed non in recipiendo seu passiue, Sed actiue et in exhibendo, hoc est, Vt vulgarius dicam, dulcis in obiectum et amara in subiectum. Quia omnia bona optat aliis et exhibet, omnium vero mala suscipit in se tanquam sua. Quia 'non querit, que sua sunt, et omnia sustinet, omnia suffert'." *WA*, LVI, 388 19-28.

[1] "Phil. :... Vos vero, vtrum sentitis hominem iustum esse illa nouitate, vt Augustinus, an vero imputatione gratuita, quae est extra nos, et fide, id est fiducia appraehenditur ex verbo ? Luth. : Sic sentio et persuasissimus sum ac certus hanc esse veram sententiam Euangelii et Apostolorum"; "Phil. : ... Vos conceditis duplicem iusticiam et quidem coram Deo necessariam esse, scilicet fidei et illius alterius, videlicet bonae conscientiae, in qua hoc, quod deest legi, supplet fides. Hoc quid aliud est quam dicere, quod homo iustificetur non sola fide. Certe enim iustificari non intelligitis Augustini more de principio regenerationis"; "Luth. : Hominem sentio fieri, esse et manere iustum seu iustam personam simpliciter sola misericordia"; "Phil. : Vtrum haec propositio sit vera : Iusticia operum est necessaria ad salutem. Luth. : Non quod operentur seu impetrent salutem, sed quod fidei impetranti praesentes seu coram sunt, sicut ego necessario adero ad salutem meam." *WA Br*, XII, 191 6-10, 18-22, 27-28; 193 95-99.

seem to find ample support in the sources, in view of his explicit rejection of theological nominalism, his early critique of religious humanism, and his awareness that he had to go beyond Augustine and Gregory, Karlstadt and Staupitz when the Wittenberger coalition disintegrated. Yet the conclusion that Luther became the Reformer as "Schrifttheologe" is a confessional rather than a historical answer to our problem since it begs the question of through what spectacles he read Scripture. On the basis of the foregoing considerations we are indeed not prepared to argue that Luther made his discovery as a nominalist, as a humanist or as an Augustinian.[1] Furthermore it is clear that the headwaters of the Reformation are much too widespread and interconnected to be reduced to the three indicated currents. We have not discussed the *devotio moderna*, late medieval mysticism, or the reemergence of apocalyptics, nor have we taken account of the numerous non-rational factors in a man's life, psyche and society which are so difficult to assess in the formal framework of stylized movements. We can say, however, that already in the earliest documents Luther thinks and writes as if Favaroni, Gregory of Rimini, and James Pérez combine in constituting his working library. Above all, this tradition is personified in Johann von Staupitz, to whose impetus Luther felt so deeply indebted. Luther for his part was willing to attest to Staupitz's role as forerunner of the *vera theologia* : "qui olim praecursor extiti sanctae euangelicae doctrinae et quemadmodum etiam hodie exosam habui captivitatem babylonicam."[2]

We have the optimal chance therefore to do justice to the *initia Lutheri* when we see his development and discoveries as those of the Augustinian monk finding and founding a new direction for the already established *via Gregorii*. That must suffice, for in seeking to understand the emergence of a man in relation to what he was before, we can never hope to lift the veil of mystery shrouding the birth of an original mind.

---

[1] We are still at the stage of *initia* in this field of research. Hence Bernhard Lohse's call for caution still fully obtains : "Es hat den Anschein, daß für den jungen Luther wichtiger als der Einfluß eines Augustinismus derjenige von Augustin selbst gewesen ist", and "der sog. Augustinismus des Spätmittelalters ist vielmehr eine höchst komplexe Größe." "Die Bedeutung Augustins für den jungen Luther", *Kerygma und Dogma*, XI (1965), 116-35; 118 with n. 6.

[2] *WA Br*, III, 264 34-36.

HEADWATERS OF THE REFORMATION

Studia Humanitatis, Luther Senior, et Initia Reformationis

LEWIS W. SPITZ

Around the year 40 B.C. Sallust said of historical writing : *In primis arduum videtur res gestas scribere*! In addition to the usual difficulties confronting the student of what Schopenhauer described as "the infinite subject matter of history," the Reformation as the first great historical movement in the post-Gutenberg era provides mountains of printed material. Luther's own works are noted not only for their vast extensiveness, but for their circumstantial nature. Robert of Melun in the twelfth century wrote of the church fathers, *Sacri patres quod non appugnabantur non defendebant*! Luther's writings, too, were frequently polemical, apologetic, or occasional. Moreover, his thought was paradoxical and he at times took a malicious joy in giving the "contradictionists" occasions for exercizing their misguided ingenuity. But the extent and difficulty of his writings, given the fact that he was a man of outsized mentality, make his work an ever fresh source of insight and inspiration.

Dr. Oberman's paper illustrates again the possibility of gaining new perspectives even on a subject so much examined as the *initia Lutheri et reformationis*. Three major intellectual currents, nominalism, humanism, and Augustinianism, can be identified and delineated quite clearly as tributaries to the Reformation movement. Their importance for Luther personally constitutes a more difficult and delicate problem. Luther's development can best be understood in terms of nominalism and humanism domesticated and put into the service of a new Augustinian theology which conditioned him. For that reason a reexamination of the *via Gregorii* as an important element in Luther's theological conditioning is called for. Our new knowledge about Pierre d'Ailly's extensive dependence upon Gregory of Rimini (d. 1358) suggests that another look at the importance of the *via Gregorii* in the 15th and 16th centuries and especially for Erfurt and Wittenberg is mandatory. Relating the intellectual forces contributing to the Reformation and those operative in Luther sheds light upon the beginnings of both. To acknowledge that Luther's *Werdegang* occurred in a specific intellectual context by no means minimizes his emergence as a creative thinker and original mind, a man who reshaped his inheritance and then reformed the church. Dr. Oberman allows for the "X" in the equation, as E. Gordon Rupp put it in his beautiful opening address to the Third International Congress for Luther Research, "the point at which great men cease to be explained by heredity and environment, and the thought world of their contemporaries."

Dr. Oberman is a man who, like Dr. Johnson, was born to grapple with libraries, and the notes reveal that he has done so. I find his methodology and conception of history most congenial to my own personal predilection. He replaces the natural science paradigm so commonly adopted by historians with homonistic conceptions with a humanistic approach. Historians sometimes substitute "factors" for "causes", thus as Professor Jack Hexter has observed, progressing sideways. The imagery of tributaries, emergence, creativity, impetus, event, movement, the provision for the paratactic element in history and the acknowledgement of the irrationality by which a *felix culpa* can move history ahead all make for a descientized and sound humanistic history. Moreover, he treats the gossamer web of intellectual history with caution and sensitivity. The intellectual history approach has its distinct limitations, of course, for it does not encompass the socio-psychological elements operative in the individual nor the social, psychological, economic, and political forces at work in the broader movement. For some historians, for example, Gabriel Biel's role as superior of the "Clerics of the Common Life" at Butzbach and the part he played in the founding of the University of Tübingen, as well as his progressive views on political economy, are as essential to understanding the man's place in history as is analyzing his exposition of the Canon of the Mass or distinguishing a Scotist from an Occamist influence in the last three books of his commentary on the Sentences. For some, an understanding of the political and legal aspect of Luther's "cause" or "case" is as essential as the theological argument itself.[1] Nevertheless, within carefully defined limits intellectual history as applied here to the problem of *initia Lutheri—initia reformationis* is perfectly legitimate.

I. COGNITIO INITIORUM DUPLEX AND THE LUTHER SEPTICEPS

The account offered of Luther's development to 1521 is authentic,

---

[1] See Wilhelm Borth, *Die Luthersache (Causa Lutheri) 1517-1524 : Die Anfänge der Reformation als Frage von Politik und Recht* (Lübeck, 1970).

letter perfect in utilizing the latest discoveries of new materials and interpretations.[1] Especially fascinating is the insight that <u>Luther was a member of a reform team including Karlstadt and Amsdorf</u> at the university, and <u>at first not even the most prominent member</u>. The importance of the year <u>1518</u> and of the <u>Heidelberg disputation</u> before the Augustinian order, "to which he owed far more than to any other single influence," so often lost in the valley between the years 1517 (95 Theses) and 1519 (Leipzig Debate), is properly assessed.[2] Moreover, the difference between Luther's teaching on justification by faith and the reception accorded his proclamation by Bucer, Karlstadt, Müntzer, or Calvin is neatly drawn. Particularly acute is his observation that after Heidelberg Bucer informed Beatus Rhenanus that for Luther man is justified through the *lex spiritus*.[3] However, a cautionary word is in order at the

---

[1] For example, Kenneth Hagen, "An Addition to the Letters of John Lang: Introduction and Translation," *Archive for Reformation History*, LX (1969), 27-32, and Oswald Bayer and Martin Brecht, "Unbekannte Texte des frühen Luther aus dem Besitz des Wittenberger Studenten Johannes Geiling," *Zeitschrift für Kirchengeschichte*, LXXXII (1971), 229-58.

[2] Oswald Bayer, *Promissio : Geschichte der reformatorischen Wende in Luthers Theologie* (Göttingen, 1971) stresses the importance of the years 1518 to 1520 from the theses *Pro Veritate* on for the development of Luther's theology, understood in the light of the *Promissio* concept. Père Daniel Olivier will soon publish a detailed study of the Heidelberg Theses of 1518.

[3] Bucer described the impression Luther made on the reform-minded humanists in April 1518, when he defended his theses before the Augustinian congregation in Heidelberg, saying that Luther agreed with Erasmus in everything except that he excelled him in one thing, namely that he taught openly and freely what Erasmus merely hinted at. See Helmar Junghans, ed., *Die Reformation in Augenzeugenberichten* (Düsseldorf, 1967), pp. 214-15; Humanismus, pp. 214-38. An excellent analysis of Bucer's interpretation of Luther's justification by grace alone in terms of the *Lex spiritus* is to be found in Karl Koch, *Studium Pietatis* (Neukirchen, 1962), pp. 10-15. W.P. Stephens, however, holds that Koch overemphasizes Bucer's humanism, *The Holy Spirit in the Theology of Martin Bucer* (Cambridge, 1970), p. 11, n. 3. On the identification of the *lex Christi* and *lex regni* in both Karlstadt and Müntzer, see E. Gordon Rupp, *Patterns of Reformation* (Philadelphia, 1969), pp. 49-353, where he perceptively tags the former as "puritan." Martin Brecht, *Die frühe Theologie des Johannes Brenz* (Tübingen, 1966), p. 31, observes that Brenz, like his friends Bucer and Oecolampadius, was under the influence of Augustinian spiritualism and that this distinguished him from Luther, who very soon founded the church exclusively on the Word. Luther was fond of referring to Zwingli and Oecolampadius as Daedalus and Icarus, perhaps with their lofty spiritualizing tendencies in mind. Joachim Rogge, "Die Initia Zwingli und Luthers': Eine Einführung in die Probleme," *Luther Jahrbuch*, XXX(1963), 107-33, contrasts Luther's broad theological base in the exegetical work of the years 1513-1519 and relative indifference to the external form of the church

point where a clear contrast is drawn between Luther's emphasis upon faith effected by the *verbum dei* and that of Zwingli, Bucer and Calvin upon faith as effected by the *operatio spiritus sancti* (pointing up the *extra-Calvinisticum*), for Luther consistently held to the catechetical truth that "the Holy Ghost calls me by the gospel, enlightens me with his gifts, sanctifies and keeps me in the one true faith." Although the Word produces faith, for Luther, too, the Holy Spirit is the operative agent in inducing faith in the Word. His statements on this point are very numerous such as those following from *The Bondage of the Will* : "Unless the Spirit revealed them [the principle articles of our faith], no man's heart would know anything about the matter"; again, "For no man on earth, unless imbued with the Holy Ghost, ever in his heart knows of, or believes in, or longs for, eternal salvation, even if he harps upon it by tongue and pen." [1] The assessment that Occamism was not important for the *initia reformationis* seems to be well-founded. The importance of humanism, on the other hand, for the beginnings and transmission of the Reformation are rightly stressed in the light of recent research. [2]

The structure of the argument is deceptively simple : *Duplex est cognitio initiorum—Lutheri et Reformationis.* The dual beginnings are related to three tributaries, nominalism, humanism, and Augustinianism, the first two domesticated in the third. The image evoked is that of a three-headed Luther rather than Cochlaeus' *Luther septiceps* in Brosamer's well-known woodcut. The seven heads might well be : 1. nominalism, 2. humanism, 3. Augustinianism, 4. mysticism, 5. apocalypticism, 6. *Historia sacra*, and 7. social conditions and actual ecclesiastical practices and teachings, all attached to the psychosomatic finitude known to us as Dr. Luther. When Luther saw the woodcut he was very

---

with Zwingli's strong humanist background, relatively narrow theological base, and immediate concern with the external form of the church and its relations to the state. The recent volume by Robert C. Walton, *Zwingli's Theocracy* (Toronto, 1967), illustrates the Swiss reformer's ethics which can be regarded as one of the hallmarks of city and social reform. His view of society and its aim, Walton concludes, represented a particular version of the theocratic ideal which dominated political thought in the 16th century.

[1] J.I. Packer and O.R. Johnston, eds., *Martin Luther on the Bondage of the Will* (London, 1957), pp. 139-40.

[2] Herbert Schöffler, *Wirkungen der Reformation* (Frankfurt a. M., 1960), pp. 126-32: Die jugendlichste Fakultät, *et passim*; Bernd Moeller, "Die deutschen Humanisten und die Anfänge der Reformation," *Zeitschrift für Kirchengeschichte*, LXX (1959), 46-61; Lewis W. Spitz, "The Third Generation of German Renaissance Humanists," *Aspects of the Renaissance*, Archibald Lewis, ed. (Austin, Texas, 1967), pp. 105-21.

amused and observed that "Kochleffel" had trouble getting all seven heads on one neck. Three is simpler, and this supplementary lecture will indulge in further reductionism by concentrating upon the importance of one of the three, humanism, for the Reformation movement. It will examine the role of the religious in Renaissance humanism, particularly the Augustinians with an eye to their importance for the *initia Lutheri et Reformationis* and the attitude of *Luther Senior* from 1530 to 1546 toward the *studia humanitatis* as it affected the course of the Reformation.

Humanism is to be defined less in the confining terms of Paul Oskar Kristeller, who relates it closely to the profession of rhetoricians and city-secretaries in the medieval *ars dictamini* tradition, than in the broader sense employed by Hanna Gray in her brilliant articles on rhetoric, Lorenzo Valla and other topics of Italian humanism, or by Paul Joachimsen, who many years ago described humanism as an intellectual movement, primarily literary and philological, which was rooted in the love of and desire for the rebirth of classical antiquity.[1] Humanism stressed the importance of classical languages, grammar and philology, cultivated epistelography, elevated rhetoric over dialectic, cherished poetry and music, emphasized moral over speculative philosophy, presented history as philosophy teaching by example, and held education at a premium. The key phrase came from Cicero's *De Oratore* : "For eloquence is nothing else than wisdom speaking copiously."

II. Renaissance Humanism and Augustinianism

The regular clergy contributed significantly to Renaissance culture and uniquely to the fusion of humanist and religious concerns. The role of the "religious," just as the revival of Christian antiquity during the Renaissance, has received far too little attention in scholarship.[2] From

---

[1] Hanna H. Gray, "Renaissance Humanism : The Pursuit of Eloquence," *Journal of the History of Ideas*, XXIV, 4 (October-December 1963), 497-514. P. 503 : True eloquence can be derived only from the "harmonious union between wisdom and style." Hanna H. Gray, "Valla's *Encomium of St. Thomas Aquinas* and the Humanist Conception of Christian Antiquity," Heinz Bluhm, ed., *Essays in History and Literature* (Chicago, 1965), pp. 37-51.

[2] Carlo Angeleri, *Il Problema Religiosa del Rinascimento : Storia della Critica e Bibliografia* (Florence, 1952) pays much attention to the historiography dealing with Franciscan naturalism and its supposed influence upon Renaissance realism in art and letters, but he offers no systematic treatment of the role of the religious or place of the orders in Renaissance culture. The concern of the humanists with the life of the religious, the *vita contemplativa* and *otium religiosum*, is examined by Charles Trinkaus, "Humanist Trea-

its very inception Renaissance humanism owed much to the regular
clergy. In Florence the Augustinian monk Luigi Marsigli (c. 1330-1394),
a friend of the cleric Petrarch, did a commentary on two Petrarchan
poems. He gathered a group of intellectuals together at the church of
Santo Spirito where they discoursed on the classics. The Camaldulensian
Ambrogio Traversari (1386-1439) contributed in an important way to
the revival of patristic studies.[1] The Carmelite prior general Baptista
Mantuanus (1448-1516) wrote Christian poems with classical accouter-
ments to counteract the pagan influence of Greek and Latin literature.
Pico called him the most learned man of the period and contemporaries
hailed him as a second Virgil. The young Luther and many other
Northerners read his poems with deep appreciation.

Of special interest for the *initia reformationis* problem is the role played by Augustinianism and by the Augustinians in the development of the
Renaissance culture. During the two centuries preceding the Reformation there was a lively resurgence of Augustinianism in European
intellectual life of which the Reformation itself was in a sense at one
point a manifestation. The influence of Augustine persisted, of course,
in those medieval disciplines which carried through to the sixteenth
century such as scholastic theology.[2] On the popular level, too, much
religious and ascetic literature revealed the influence of Augustine. The
Augustinian Canons and the Augustinian Hermits persisted in medieval
piety, debated as to whether Augustine had been a monk, revived the
cult of Monica, and copied their patron's works. But beyond the traditional concerns, Augustine had a critically important influence upon the
two most characteristic intellectual currents in Renaissance intellectual
life, humanism and Neo-Platonism. Petrarch, the father of humanism,
and Ficino, the founder of the Florentine Platonic Academy, illustrate

---

tises on the Status of the Religious : Petrarch, Salutati, Valla," *Studies in the Renaissance*,
ed. M.A. Shaaber, XI (1964), 7-45. See also the excellent comprehensive work, Charles
Trinkaus, "*In Our Image and Likeness*" : *Humanity and Divinity in Italian Humanist
Thought* (2 vols. Chicago, 1970).

[1] See Charles Stinger, "Humanism and Reform in the Early Quattrocento : The Patristic Scholarship of Ambrogio Traversari (1386-1439)," unpublished Ph. D. dissertation,
Stanford University, 1971 ; Agnes Clare Way, "The Lost Translations Made by Ambrosius
Traversarius of the Orations of Gregory Nazianzen," *Renaissance News*, XIV (1961),
91-96. Traversari's influence reached to the North where Lefèvre d'Étaples used his
translation of Dionysius in his 1499 edition, though he might have used Ficino's had he
known it.

[2] Karl Werner, *Die Scholastik des späteren Mittelalters*, III, *Der Augustinismus in der
Scholastik des späteren Mittelalters* (Vienna, 1883).

the essential place of Augustine's Platonized and somewhat mystical theology in the central literary and philosophical movements of the Renaissance. Wherever Aristotle did not reign supreme, there was room for a burgeoning of Augustinian thought.[1]

Augustine played a key role in the humanists' cultural reorientation of the West. The humanists in turning away from medieval culture and theology developed a new intellectual norm, classical letters and pre-scholastic theology, specifically the church fathers and preeminently Augustine. Petrarch, Valla, and other humanists realized that Augustine lived while the Roman empire still existed and they cited him along with classical writers on matters of literary concern. Vives, Erasmus, and other humanists translated, edited, and commented on the fathers and especially on Augustine, with the same philological care as they devoted to the classics. The Platonism derived in part from the Augustinian current of the medieval period was reinforced by the discovery by Petrarch and other humanists that Augustine and Cicero both had preferred Plato to Aristotle. Ficino derived many substantive aspects of his Neo-Platonic philosophy from Augustine rather than from the school of Plotinus, Iamblichus, or Proclus.

The important role played by the Augustinians in conjunction with the Brethren of the Common Life in the revitalized spiritual life of the *Devotio Moderna* in the Netherlands and lower Rhinelands as well as their influence supportive of education must be recognized. Not only was this spiritual and educational force crucial for the northern Renaissance, providing an early introduction to the classics for Erasmus among others, but for the Reformation as well, not least of all through Luther's brief and mysterious encounter with the *Nollbrüder* in Magdeburg.[2] Augustine and Augustinianism had a pervasive influence also

---

[1] Paul Oskar Kristeller, "Augustine and the Early Renaissance," *The Review of Religion*, VIII, 4 (May 1944), 339-58. For Augustine's influence in general Kristeller, p. 340, n. 2, refers to the dated work by J.F. Nourrisson, *La Philosophie de Saint Augustine*, (Paris, 1865), II, 147-276, and to E. Portalie, "Augustinisme," *Dictionnaire de Théologie Catholique*, I, 2501-2561.

[2] P.O. Kristeller, "Augustine and the Early Renaissance," p. 345, n. 23, draws attention to the fact that Augustine exercized a powerful influence on Gerard Groote, the founder of the Brethren of the Common Life and that the decisive chapter 31 of their statutes, *De vita communi et paupertate*, begins with a quotation from Augustine. Despite R.R. Post's strictures against the thesis of Albert Hyma, Augustin Renaudet, and other scholars that the *Devotio Moderna* contributed to the growth and development of humanism and indirectly of the Reformation in the North, the significance of both the Brethren

on French humanism, Platonism, and Stoicism, but the direct line of
impetus for the *initia Reformationis* involved rather Italy and Germany.[1]

A statistical survey of the regular clergy who contributed to humanism in Italy and Germany, most of them writing both neo-classical and
religious treatises, reveals large numbers, important figures, and a
fascinating ratio of Augustinians to other regulars. The data provided by
a compilation from four sources yields a combined total of some 184
monks and brothers from the late Trecento through the Quattrocento
to the mid-Cinquecento or approximately the time of Luther's death.[2]
Of these, 41 were Dominicans, 36 Benedictines, 35 Augustinians, 30
Franciscans, 11 Camaldulensians, 11 Carmelites, and 21 others from
other orders such as the Carthusians, Servitians, Humiliati, Vallumbrodians, or new groups like the Theatines. It is clear that the Augustinians played a larger role relative to their numbers than the other
major orders.

---

and the Augustinians was basic. See the excellent review by Helmar Junghans of R.R.
Post, *The Modern Devotion : Confrontation with Reformation and Humanism* (Leiden, 1968),
in *Luther-Jahrbuch, 1970*, pp. 120-29. A far more positive assessment of the role played by
the Brethren in education than that given by Post can be found in Julia S. Henkel, "An
Historical Study of the Educational Contributions of the Brethren of the Common Life,"
unpublished Ph. D. dissertation, University of Pittsburgh, 1962 ; William M. Landeen,
"The *Devotio Moderna* in Germany," Part III, *Research Studies of the State College of
Washington*, XXI (1953) ; Kenneth A. Strand, "Luther's Schooling in Magdeburg : A
Note on Recent Views," *Essays on Luther*, Kenneth A. Strand, ed. (Ann Arbor, Michigan,
1969), pp. 106-12. A picture of humanism in the Netherlands which is hardly complimentary is given by P.N.M. Bot, *Humanisme en Onderwijs in Nederland* (Utrecht and Antwerp, 1955), arguing that the humanists replaced complete classics with excerpts, produced
lengthy pedantic books, and preferred moralizing Euripedes to the truly dramatic Aeschylus.

[1] See N. Abercrombie, *Saint Augustine and French Classical Thought* (Oxford, 1938),
pp. 1-17, for a useful and reliable survey of Augustine's influence upon Renaissance
thought. Jean Delumeau, *Naissance et Affirmation de la Réforme* (2nd ed. Paris, 1968),
pp. 367-71, "Prédestination et Augustinisme" discusses the ongoing influence of Augustine
on Catholic and Protestant thinkers alike and sees this historical fact as an ecumenical
point of theological contact. On page 370, n. 2, he cites important articles on the Augustinianism of Luther by L. Saint-Blancat, L. Christiani, M. Bendiscioli, J. Cadier, P. Courcelle, as well as the books of A.V. Müller and P. Vignaux.

[2] Paul Oskar Kristeller, "The Contribution of Religious Orders to Renaissance
Thought and Learning," *The American Benedictine Review*, XXI, 1 (March, 1970), 1-55 ;
P.O. Kristeller, *Iter Italicum* (2 vols. ; London and Leiden, 1963-1967). Rudolph Arbesmann, *Der Augustiner-Eremitenorden und der Beginn der humanistischen Bewegung*
(Würzburg, 1965) ; L. Lauchert, *Die italienischen literarischen Gegner Luthers* (Freiburg,
1912).

A brief introduction to a few typical representatives of the *Ordo Eremeticorum Sancti Augustini* involved in the world of humanism may prove to be instructive. The three Augustinians cited in the preceding paper, Dionysius de Burgo S. Sepulchri, Bartholomaeus de Urbino, and Jean Coci did indeed contribute to the development of early Renaissance culture. One thinks immediately also of such major figures as Giles of Viterbo,[1] Girolamo Seripando,[2] Mariano da Genazzano, who was Savonarola's eloquent competitor in the Florentine duomo,[3] Paul of Venice, an Augustinian who transmitted Franciscan physics to the school of Padua,[4] and the renowned humanist Maffeo Vegio, who like Petrarch was personally involved in Augustine's thought and wrote a *Life of Saint Monica* which honored Augustine indirectly.[5] But six more average figures will better represent the group and a quick glance at their works will provide an overview of their intellectual interests and range.

Guilielmus Becchius, bishop of Fiesole (d. 1491 ?), wrote commentaries on Aristotelian *Economics, Ethics,* and *Politics,* a *Protesto,* dedicated a treatise *De Cometo* to Piero d'Medici, did a commentary on Porphyry's *Isagoge,* and wrote an apologetic *De falso dogmate Maumethi, De potestate spiritum,* and *De potestate papae et concilii.*

---

[1] John W. O'Malley, *Giles of Viterbo on Church and Reform : A Study in Renaissance Thought* (Leiden, 1968). The famous "Address to the Fifth Lateran Council" is translated in John C. Olin, ed., *The Catholic Reformation : Savonarola to Ignatius Loyola. Reform in the Church 1495-1540* (New York, 1969), pp. 44-53.

[2] Hubert Jedin, *Girolamo Seripando* (Würzburg, 1937).

[3] See Pasquale Villari, *La Storia di Girolamo Savonarola e de'suoi tempi* (Florence, 1930), I, 80 ff. on Genazzano as a popular preacher; II, 97, on Genazzano's conspiracy in Rome against Savonarola. Roberto Ridolfi, *Vita di Girolamo Savonarola*, secunda edizione, I (Rome, 1952), capitola V, "Predicatore dei disperati." La "giostra" col Genazzano, pp. 56-65. A thorough study of Italian "humanist homiletics" would be a very welcome addition to our knowledge of rhetorical culture.

[4] Bruno Nardi, *Saggi Sull'Aristolelismo Padovano da Secolo XIV al XVI* (Florence, 1958), pp. 75-93.

[5] Vittorio Rossi, *Il Quattrocento* (Milan, 1945), pp. 283-84, writes "Le Confessioni di Sant 'Agostino gli erano state alla riconquista della Verità e alla purificazione del costume e avevano acceso nel suo cuore quel fuoco d'amore e di pietà che tutto pervade il libro *De perseverantia religionis,* dedicato nel 1448 all sorella monaca." Anna Cox Brinton, *Maphaeus Vegius and his Thirteenth Book of the Aeneid* (Stanford, 1930), p. 12, discusses St. Augustine as the "unrivalled master of Vegio's heart" and lists eight of his works which bear witness to his special veneration of Monica and Augustine. Vegio's humanistic achievements were largely his Petrarchan poems and his treatise *De educatione liberorum*; Giuseppe Saitta, *Le Pensiero Italiano Nell'umanesimo e nel Rinascimento,* I (Bologna, 1949), 273-80.

Aurelius Lippus Brandolinus (1440-1497) did poems, orations, letters and sermons. He wrote *Paradoxa Christiana* (ed. 1531), *De humanae vitae conditione* (ed. 1543), *De ratione scribendi* (ed. 1549), *De comparatione rei publicae et regni* (ed. 1890 ?), *Epithoma in sacram Judeorum historiam, Rudimenta grammaticae,* in addition to commentaries on Virgil's *Georgics* and a translation of Pliny's *Panegyricus.*

Gabriel Buratellus attempted a *Praecipuarum Controversiarum Aristotelis et Platonis Conciliatio,* a harmonizing ambition shared with both Pico and Melanchthon.

Ambrosius Massarius de Cora (d. 1485) was more of an organization man or company hand. He published orations, a life of Augustine, a commentary on "his rule," a chronicle of the order, a *Defensarium ordinis Heremitorum S. Augustini* (against the Augustinian Canons), and a *Vita B. Christianae Spoletanae,* but also a commentary on Gilbertus Porretanus' *Liber sex principiorum,* and a treatise *De animae dignitatibus.*

Nicolaus Tridentinus Scutellius (d. 1542) was of a more philosophical bent of mind and could do Greek. He translated Iamblichus' *De mysteriis* and *De vita Pythagorae* (ed. 1556), a dialogue of Lucian and four hymns, Pletho's treatise on the difference between Plato and Aristotle, Orpheus' *De gemmis,* a treatise of Proclus, Porphyry, pseudo-Plato's *De iusto,* and other philosophical texts.

Sigfridus de Castello (c. 1500) corresponded with the German humanist Jacob Wimpfeling on the question of whether St. Augustine was a monk, which Wimpfeling had raised in chapter 31 of his *De Integritate.* Luther read it with approval at the time although in later life he referred to this controversy as the kind of quibble on which people under the papacy wasted their time.[1]

Humanism also penetrated the order of the Augustinian hermits in Germany. Relatively early the preacher from the Osnabrück Augustinian house, Gottschalk Hollen (d. 1481), disseminated humanist views which he had learned while studying in Italian convents. In his sermons he showed a preference for Ovid, Horace, Valerius Maximus, but also cited Petrarch and contemporary Italian humanists, as well as the Bible. Another humanist Augustinian in Germany was Casper Amman, who was provincial of the Rhenish-Swabian Province of the Order, a

---

[1] P.O. Kristeller, "The Contribution of Religious Orders," pp. 34, 36, 37, 46, 51. Paul Oskar Kristeller, *Le Thomisme et le Pensée Italienne de la Renaissance* (Montreal, 1967), pp. 51-56, discusses Dominican savants of theological and philosophical importance.

student of Hebrew. Johannes Lang of Erfurt was an excellent Graecist. Johann Altensteig was a pupil of the German humanist Heinrich Bebel. Hieronymus Streitel of Regensburg wrote history of a humanist type. The library of the Munich monastery contained works not only of antiquity but of Italian humanists as well.[1]

In the Catholic opposition to Luther during the decades prior to Trent, the Augustinians along with the friars provided leading polemicists. Ambrosius Flandinus (d. 1531), for example, a Platonist who published several volumes of humanist sermons, *Conciones quadragesimales* (Venice, 1523), *Conciones pre adventum*, and *De mundi genitura*, wrote against Pomponazzi in defense of the immortality of souls and against fatalism. Against Luther he wrote an *Examen vanitatis duodecim articulorum Martini Luther* (Parma ms.) and *Contra Lutheranos de vera et catholica fide conflictationes* (Genoa ms.). Augustina Steuco (1496-1549), celebrated for his biblical studies, coined the term *philosophia perennis* in 1540 for the combined Christian and Platonic tradition.[2]

A survey of the entire scene suggests the following conclusions and invites further study:

1. During the two centuries preceding the Reformation, there was a clear continuity of Augustine's influence in traditional theological and philosophical lines in areas less affected by Aristotelianism. There was also a general resurgence of Augustinianism which extended far beyond the new vitality within the order of hermits. This resurgence was manifested in the preoccupation with Augustine of Petrarch, Vegio, and many other Italian humanists, as well as Mutian, Pirckheimer, Erasmus, and other northern humanists, including adherents to the *Devotio Moderna* which had some impact on Luther himself.

---

[1] Helmar Junghans, "Der Einfluss des Humanismus auf Luthers Entwicklung bis 1518," *Luther-Jahrbuch*, XXXVII (1970), 54-55, cites the humanistic Augustinians in Germany named here, drawing on the older work of Hedwig Vonschott, *Geistiges Leben im Augustinerorden am Ende des Mittelalters und zu Beginn der Neuzeit* (Berlin, 1915), pp. 103-6, 134-36, 141-43, 157-59.

[2] L. Lauchert, pp. 239-40. Charles B. Schmitt, "Perennial Philosophy from Augustino Steuco to Leibniz," *Journal of the History of Ideas*, XXVII (1966), 505-32. Adolar Zumkeller, O.S.A., who has provided impressive source materials drawn from the Würzburg archives, *Urkunden und Regesten zur Geschichte der Augustinerklöster Würzburg und Münnerstadt von Anfängen bis zur Mitte des 17. Jahrhunderts* (Würzburg, 1966), p. 4, comments that a thorough history of these Augustinian monasteries satisfying all modern requirements has not as yet been written, a statement applicable to the entire history of the order in Germany.

2. The predominant thrust of Augustinian humanists South and North was naturally strongly in support of Platonism and Neo-Platonism in the later Quattrocento and early Cinquecento, a predilection which often led them to undertake an anti-Aristotelian polemic, against contemporary Aristotelians as well as against Aristotle himself. The Augustinians were therefore in phase with the most characteristic form of Renaissance philosophy of which the priest Marsiglio Ficino was the leading exponent. In April 1518, Luther expressed his strong preference for Plato and even Pythagoras over Aristotle, an order of priority that he retained in later years.

3. In view of the demonstrable steady intellectual commerce between Italy and Germany, the broader intellectual milieu within the order South and North merits further intensive study. Luther's *Romreise* is no more enlightening than the knowledge we have of his experience with the *Nollbrüder*, but it does illustrate the North-South contact. Such a study should encompass the traffic in books and manuscripts, as well as people, and the penetration of humanist ideas into septentrional Augustinianism.[1]

4. While there is a special point in beginning with Luther's immediate situation, his teachers and the Augustinian and nominalist and humanist books known to be available in the Erfurt library or prescribed for study, much can be gained by casting a wider net in the analysis of pre-Reformation Augustinianism. Such a study should be coupled with a comprehensive analysis of the conversion of regular clergy of all orders to the evangelical faith and their reeducation, in many cases for the Lutheran ministry, as well as an examination of their contribution to Protestant literature in subsequent decades. The humanist learning of the regulars, and specifically of the Augustinians, is important not only for the *initia Lutheri* but for the *initia Reformationis* as well. For it may well have been an important element favorable to the continuity of humanism in Protestant culture in the first critical decades of the Reformation, and during the centuries which followed. The resistance

---

[1] A comparison of the ideas representative of humanism and Augustinianism would be of interest, similar to Heiko Oberman's article "Some Notes on the Theology of Nominalism with Attention to its Relation to the Renaissance," *The Harvard Theological Review*, LIII, 1 (1960), 47-76, a study not entirely satisfying since it operates with only one side of the humanists' thought, stressing the *dignitas hominis* aspect without bringing out the *miseria hominis* underside of humanist anthropology. See Lewis W. Spitz, "Man on this Isthmus", *Luther for an Ecumenical Age*, Carl S. Meyer, ed. (St. Louis, 1967), pp. 43-49, 63-65, notes 50-64.

of highly spiritual and somewhat humanistic Augustinians to evangelical theology on the other hand reveals how wide the moat was over which Luther leaped in his own appropriation of the Biblical message.

III. LUTHER SENIOR AND THE STUDIA HUMANITATIS

One noted Augustinian reared in a nominalistic climate of thought bitterly resented his scholastic upbringing and monastic entrapment. In his *Address to the Municipalities* Luther exclaimed :

> How much I regret that we did not read more of the poets and the historians, and that nobody thought of teaching us these. Instead of such study I was compelled to read the devil's rubbish—the scholastic philosophers and sophists with such cost, labor and detriment, from which I have had trouble enough to rid myself.

Luther's own relation to humanists and humanism, his personal interest in the *studia humanitatis*, his contribution to curricular reform at Wittenberg, and yet that theological gulf that separated him from the optimistic anthropology of humanism and from the synergistic moralism of Christian humanism have been examined closely by a number of scholars.[1] On the other hand, much work does indeed remain to be done on the *initia et exitus Lutheri senioris* with regard to humanism, a qualified and relative good which remained even after the young Luther had consciously turned against monasticism and scholasticism. One may well find in the voluminous writings of Luther's last three lustra clues to his earlier thought or how he came to understand himself. If in the early tension years he felt cultural deprivation, did he in later years compensate for the deficiency by study ? Can one make a choice between the passages in the *Explanation of the 95 Theses* in which he came close to the religious expressions of a Pico or Reuchlin, and his assertion against Eck at the time of the Leipzig debate that *"Omnes homines aequales sunt in humanitate, quae est omnium summa et admiranda aequalitas, ex qua omnis dignitas hominibus"* as the peak of Luther's affinity with humanism, when in the *Disputatio de homine* of 1536 he can speak of divine reason as a god and in his last great *Commentary on Genesis* can grow ecstatic over the qualities of man and the glories of nature ? The attitude of the mature Luther toward the *studia humanitatis*, moreover, was of critical

---

[1] The most recent examination of the problem is Helmar Junghans, "Der Einfluss des Humanismus auf Luthers Entwicklung bis 1518," pp. 37-101. See also Peter Meinhold, "Die Auseinandersetzung Luthers mit dem Humanismus und dem Spiritualismus," *Luther Heute* (Berlin und Hamburg, 1967), pp. 100-8.

importance for the beginnings and the development of the Reformation movement which accepted and transmitted the educational and cultural values of Christian humanism.

A reading of Luther's treatises from 1530 to 1546, of the *Tischreden* which begin in the summer of 1531, and of his voluminous correspondence may embolden one to venture a few judgments. There is little help to be found in secondary works, for Oswald G. Schmidt's old monograph *Luthers Bekanntschaft mit den alten Klassikern* (Leipzig, 1883) has not as yet been replaced by a more complete modern study. There are grave difficulties to be overcome in a reading of the sources as well. Not only is the authenticity of the *Table Talks* open to question, but, as Peter Meinhold has demonstrated in his impressive study of classical references in the Genesis commentary, it often remains difficult or impossible to establish whether a citation was Luther's or the transcriber's and editor's.[1] Despite these difficulties, at least a preliminary assessment may be made of the three most relevant points : 1. The older Luther's knowledge and utilization of the classics; 2. Luther's cultivation of the humanist discipline; and 3. Luther's relation to Italian and northern humanists from 1530 to his death.

1. Four months after Luther's demise Melanchthon wrote of him in the *Vita* :

> ... legit ipse pleraque veterum Latinorum scriptorum monumenta, Ciceronis, Virgilii, Livii et aliorum. Haec legebat non ut pueri verba tantum excerpentes, sed ut humanae vitae doctrinam, aut imagines, Quare et consilia horum scriptorum et sententias proprius aspiciebat, et ut erat memoria fideli et firma, pleraque ei lecta et audita in conspectu et ob oculos erant.[2]

Melanchthon seems to imply that Luther did his heavy reading in the Latin classics during his school days and as a student in the arts and with his marvellous memory retained and used what he had learned for life.

In 1531 Luther reminisced very touchingly about a certain young man who sold his *corpus iuris* and other books to a dealer but took his

---

[1] Peter Meinhold, *Die Genesisvorlesung Luthers und ihre Herausgeber* (Stuttgart, 1936), pp. 332-41 : "Luther war ein gründlicher Kenner der griechischen und römischen klassischen Literatur. Für seine genuinen Werke beweist das die Fühle der von ihm beigebrachten Zitate aus den alten Klassikern. Die Frage für die Genesisvorlesung ist, ob die sich hier findenden klassischen Zitate auf Luther oder auf die Bearbeiter zurückgehen." See also *LW*, I, x-xi.

[2] *CR*, VI, 157, no. 3478.

Virgil and Plautus along into the monastery.[1] With respect to Luther's frequency of citation, Melanchthon was quite right in pointing to Virgil and Cicero as Luther's favorite classics, for in the *Tischreden* alone there are 59 references to and from Cicero and about 50 from Virgil, although Livy fell aside, and there are 61 references to Aristotle. In his writings and correspondence (although his letters contain very few classical references), Aristotle, Cicero, and Virgil are most frequently cited and far more so than any other classical authors. The next in order of frequency of reference to and quotation from their works are Terence, Horace, Plato, Quintilian, Homer, and Ovid roughly in that order. Individual scattered references are to be found to Aesop, Plautus, Suetonius, Herodotus, Xenophon, Ammianus Marcellinus, Juvenal, Caesar, Aeschylus, Minucius Felix, Pliny, Tacitus, Demosthenes, Apuleius, Polycrates, Plutarch, Sulpetius, Severnus, Parmenides, Zeno, and a few others.[2]

Frequency of citation does not, of course, tell the whole story. Aristotle figures very prominently because of Luther's polemic against his intrusion into scholastic philosophy. Luther praised Aristotle's physics, metaphysics, and the *De anima* as his best books, but he regrets that Aristotle denies God tacitly.[3] Although he preferred Plato to Aristotle, he reproaches him for saying in the *De Ente* that "God is nothing and God is everything."[4] Philosophers in this tradition describe God as a circle in which He as midpoint is coterminous with the circumference, a kind of speculation which leads to pantheism. In Luther's clearly discernible hierarchy of classical authors Cicero is firmly established at the top. In his repeated comparisons of Cicero and Aristotle he pronounces Cicero more learned by far, a clear teacher, and, in books such as *De Officiis*, very wise. "If I were a youth," Luther exclaims, "I would devote myself to Cicero, but with my judgment nevertheless confirmed in the Sacred Scriptures." [5] Aristotle knows nothing about God and the immortality of the soul, but *Cicero longe superat Aristo-*

---

[1] *WA Tr*, I, 44, no. 116.

[2] For a list of the classical authors and Italian humanists whose works were published in Germany between 1465 and 1500 and the classical and humanist authors printed in German translations up to the year 1520, see Rudolph Hirsch, "Printing and the Spread of Humanism in Germany : The Example of Albrecht von Eyb," *Renaissance Men and Ideas*, Robert Schwoebel, ed. (New York, 1971), pp. 28, 31. Most of the classical and humanist authors whom Luther cited frequently had been published in Germany by 1520.

[3] *WA Tr*, I, 57, no. 135.

[4] *WA Tr*, I, 108, no. 257.

[5] *WA Tr*, III, 612, no. 5012.

telem, for in his *Tusculan Disputations* and *On the Nature of the Gods* he writes about the immortality of the soul, and his *De Officiis* is superior to the ethics of Aristotle.[1] He hopes that God will be merciful to Cicero and men like him, for he was the best, wisest and most diligent man.[2]

2. *Luther senior* retained a positive interest in the characteristic humanist disciplines. He had been the prime mover in the curricular reform at Wittenberg which introduced the humanist subjects at the expense of Aristotle and dialectic. In subsequent years he took an active interest in professional appointments to the chair of Greek, rhetoric, or similar subjects in the arts faculty.[3]

In the choice between rhetoric and dialectic Luther consistently held the former to be superior. Dialectic teaches and rhetoric moves the audience; dialectic belongs to reason, rhetoric to the will. He refers to Moses and St. Paul as great rhetoricians. St. Paul in Romans 12 distinguished between teaching and exhorting and except for one passage, all of Romans 4 is rhetorical.[4] On 22 February 1518, Luther wrote to Spalatin :

> I absolutely do not see how dialectic can be other than a poison to a true theologian. Grant that it may be useful as a game or an exercise for youthful minds, still in sacred letters, where pure faith and divine illumination are expected, the whole matter of the syllogism must be left without, just as

---

[1] *WA Tr*, III, 451, no. 3608d. Again in *WA Tr*, IV, 16, no. 3928, Luther relates that Cicero could comfort himself very nicely against death in the *Tusculan Disputations* so that Christians who have Christ as the conqueror of death should be able to do so much more. *WA Tr*, III, 4, no. 2808a, Luther observes that Cicero was the wisest and most prolific of all the philosophers and had read thoroughly the books of all the Greeks, but he could not rise above human wisdom.

[2] *WA Tr*, IV, 14, no. 3925.

[3] Thus he favored Veit Örtel in August 1541 for the Greek professorship since he had been taught in Deventer by Bartholomäus of Cologne, *WA Br*, IX, 482-84, no. 3649. Elector John Frederick wrote to Luther about appointing Mag. Holstein to teach rhetoric, *WA Br*, IX, 487-89, no. 3651.

[4] *WA Tr*, II, 360, no. 2199b. *WA Tr*, I, 120, no. 287 : Philippus Melanchthon : Duplex est orationis genus, dialecticum, id pertinet ad scholam, rhetoricum pertinet ad contiones publicas, ibi enim sunt tractandi loci pathetici in scholis tractandae disputationes, etc. *WA Tr*, I, 127, no. 309 : In omni oratione aut est exhortatio aut doctrina: doctrina dialectica, exhortatio rhetorica. *WA Tr*, II, 555-56, no. 2629a : "Dialectica ist, wen man ein ding unterschidlich und deutlich sagt mit kurtzen worten, rhetorica autem versatur in suadendo et dissuadendo; quae habet suos locos, bonum, honestum, utile, facile. Quae Paulus brevissime complexus est dicens : Qui docet in doctrina, qui exhortatur in exhortando...".

Abraham, when about to sacrifice, left the boys with the asses. This, Johannes Reuchlin in the second book of his *Cabala* affirms sufficiently. For if any dialectic is necessary, that natural inborn dialectic is sufficient, by which a man is led to compare beliefs with other beliefs and so conclude the truth. I have often discussed with friends what utility seemed to us to be gained from this so sedulous study of philosophy and dialectic, and truly with one consent, having marveled at, or rather bewailed, the calamity of our minds, we found no utility, but rather a whole sea of hindrance.[1]

Luther held this position also in later years. Even when he allowed the disputations to be reintroduced at Wittenberg, he did so only because they provided a useful exercise for youthful minds who would soon be obliged to engage in apologetics, much as he himself made use of syllogisms in controversy with scholastics to "beat them at their own game". In his treatise *On Christian Doctrine* St. Augustine had written that "the science of disputation is of great value for solving all sorts of questions that appear in sacred literature." Luther was less impressed with this thought than were Abelard and the dialecticians. When in later years Luther praised Ockham, his "dear master", as a great dialectician, he had in mind the utility of dialectic as a mental tool but not as an aid in theology.

Ockham alone understood dialectic [said Luther] that it has to do with defining and distinguishing words, but he was not able to speak out [eloquently]. But now, O God, I have truly lived to see such a noble time, so many revelations, and truly as Christ says about the time of the last day : There will be a flowering and then judgment day will come. All the arts flourish and when that happens, as Christ says, summer is not far off.[2]

Luther repeats elsewhere the criticism that while Ockham was very wise and learned he was deficient in rhetoric.[3] Cicero's rhetorical power and Quintilian's instruction in rhetoric strongly attracted Luther to them. Reading Quintilian is such a pleasure, he observed, and he draws the reader along so that he is continuously impelled to proceed with

---

[1] *WA Br*, I, 149-50, no. 61. In the same letter Luther continues by saying that he had written to Trutvetter, the prince of the dialecticians in our age (so it seems), that dialectic "instead of being useful to theology is rather an obstacle to theological studies, because theology uses the same vocabulary in a manner quite different from that of dialectic. In what way therefore, I asked, can dialectic be of use, since once I begin to study theology I am forced to reject the dialectic meaning of a word and have to accept its [theological] meaning." This footnote translation is from *LW*, XLVIII, 57, no. 19.

[2] *WA Tr*, I, 85-86, no. 193.

[3] *WA Tr*, 137, no. 338.

reading, for he presses into one's heart.[1] Quintilian is opposed to ambiguity and offers other sound rhetorical advice.[2]

Luther's knowledge of classical poetry was limited in scope but he very much cherished what he knew, and cited certain lines quite freely and repeatedly. "Baptista Mantuanus was the first poet whom I read," he reminisced, "then the Heroiads of Ovid, and then Virgil, and afterwards I read nothing in the poets, for scholastic theology said it was an impediment." [3] Poets and playwrights portray the real world. Terence, Homer, and other poets were no lazy-dog monks but saw how things are with real people.[4] Terence is good for boys and girls, he thought, though Virgil is superior for adults. "I love Terence," he said, "for I see that it is good rhetoric to make a comedy out of a man sleeping with a maid; then he imagines what the father, what the servant, what the circle of friends say to that. *Sic ex qualibet causa potest fieri comoedia.*" [5] He advised a schoolmaster in Silesia who had been criticized for having his boys play a comedy of Terence to continue as he had done. For the boys should be encouraged to put on the plays, practice Latin, develop good artistry, see people well portrayed and all reminded of their duties. There is no reason because of obscenities not to do the comedies.[6] Luther was not about to see his Terence bowdlerized.

Luther's native genius for language carried over to a keen curiosity about philology, and an interest in historical and place names and etymologies reminiscent of Celtis, Aventine, and other German humanists. There is some doubt as to whether he himself was the author of a piece attributed to him, *Aliquot nomina propria Germanorum ad priscam etymologiam restituta*, 1544. However, he enjoyed playing with words, comparing Graecisms with Germanisms and toying with etymologies from Tacitus.[7]

---

[1] *WA Tr*, II, 411, no. 2299. *WA*, III, 73 fn., Quintilian's *Institutio oratoria* cited.

[2] *WA Tr*, I, 195, no. 446.

[3] *WA Tr*, I, 107, no. 256. A typical classical allusion is his *WA Br*, XI, 6-7, no. 4062, 4 January 1545, in counseling patience against one's enemies he cites Virgil's *Aeneid*: "Dabit Deus his quoque finem." *WA Tr*, III, 459, no. 3616a : Ovid excells all poets, even Virgil, in expressing feelings.

[4] *WA Tr*, I, 119, no. 285.

[5] *WA Tr*, 203-4, no. 467.

[6] *WA Tr*, I, 430-32, no. 867.

[7] *WA Tr*, III, p. 588, no. 3748; *WA Tr*, I, 110, no. 262; *WA Tr*, I, p. 123, no. 297. An excellent study of Luther's language skill in his Bible translation is that of the noted Germanist Heinz Bluhm, *Martin Luther Creative Translator* (St. Louis, 1965).

As a young *dozent* Luther had lectured on the ethics of Aristotle and he continued throughout his life to refer especially to the *Nichomachian Ethics*.[1] But, of course, he waged his theological battle against the Aristotelian premise that good works make a man good rather than that a good man does good works. And on a deeper level he fought the intrusion of Aristotelian anthropology and dialectic into scholastic theology. The fundamental difference between Aristotle and *Ecclesiastes*, he noted, is that Aristotle measures honesty by the best reason of life, but *Ecclesiastes* by the observance of the precepts of God.[2]

Luther's own very personal contribution to the cultivation of moral philosophy and prudential wisdom in the young was his edition of Aesop's *Fables, Etliche Fabeln aus Äsop 1530* done at the Coburg after meals, "to rest his weary head as great men need to do," said Mathesius in *Sermon VII* on Luther's life. The German humanist Heinrich Steinhöwel had published an edition with Johannes Zainer in Ulm between 1476 and 1480 based on the Phädrus-Romulus collection of the 4th and 5th centuries. In the front of that edition is a life of Aesop and in the appendix the fables of Avian and the facetiae of Petrus Alfonsus and Poggio with translations by Steinhöwel. Luther prepared his edition in 1530, although it was not printed until 1557, after his death. In a letter to Wenceslas Link in Nuremberg, 8 May 1530, he wrote, "I have also proposed to prepare the fables of Aesop for the youth and the common crowd so that they may be of some use to the Germans." [3] The fables which he chose taught moral lessons about folly, hatred, disloyalty, envy, greed, frivolousness, force. In the preface Luther quotes Quintilian's *Institutio oratoria* (V,11, 19) as saying the fables came from a wise Greek like Hesiod. Some of them, however, he believed to have been composed by two Christian bishops to teach schoolboys in a cryptic way at the time of the suppression of Christians by Julian the apostate.[4]

From the Aesop edition it is obvious that Luther's early emphatic advocacy of education for the youth continues throughout his life. His *Predigt, dasz man Kinder zur Schule halten solle* (1541) glows with the same fervor as his earlier sermon on keeping children in school and his *Address to the Councilmen of All Cities in Germany that They Establish*

---

[1] For example, *WA Br*, X, 575-76, no. 3992 (15 May 1544).

[2] *WA Tr*, I, 79, no. 168.

[3] *WA Br*, V, 309, no. 1563.

[4] *WA Tr*, VI, 16, no. 6523.

and Maintain Christian Schools (1524). The *Fakultäts-Zeugnissen* given
to the university graduates and signed by Luther emphasized the young
men's achievements in arts and letters, religion and piety, as well as
their mastery of Latin, Greek, and Hebrew.

Similarly in his old age music provided Luther comfort as it had provided solace in his stormy youth. He wrote prefaces for musical works,
περὶ τῆς Μουσικῆς, a *Vorrede auf alle guten Gesangbücher, Frau
Musica, 1543*, and a *Praefatio zu Symphonicae iucundae*. He asked Elector John Frederick to appoint a musician to the university.[1] He sent his
son John to study music with Marcus Crodel in Torgau.[2]

Luther's preoccupation with history actually increased during the
last decade and a half of his life, as though his own advancing years developed in him a deeper interest in past ages. He wrote prefaces to a
variety of "historical" works : *Vorrede zu Spalatin, magnifice con-
solatoria exempla et sententiae ex vitis et passionibus sanctorum... collectae;
Vorrede zu Robert Barnes, Vitae Romanorum Pontificum; Vorrede zu
Johannes Kymäus, Ein alt christlich Konzilium...zu Gangro; Vorrede zu
Historia Galeatii Capellae, 1539; Vorrede zu Epistola S. Hieronymi ad
Evagrium de potestate, 1538; Praefatio zu Georg Major Vitae patrum,
1544; Vorrede zu Papstreue Hadrian IV. und Alexandrus III. gegen
Kaiser Friedrich Barbarossa, 1545*. From these various prefaces it is
clear that Luther viewed history as a weapon in controversy. Twenty
years after the Leipzig Debate of 1519 Luther reflected that at that time
he had not been well versed in history and had attacked the Papacy *a
priori* on the basis of Scriptures, but that now he appreciated the correspondence of the histories and Scripture and could attack the Papacy
a posteriori from the histories.[3] The polemical and apologetic uses of
history, whether the history of the patristic period, of the medieval
papal period, or of lives of the saints are stressed most vigorously in the
prefaces which Luther wrote. Moreover, in 1537 he wrote a blast of his
own at the monstrous papal fraud of the Donation of Constantine,
Einer aus den hohen Artikeln des päpstlichen Glaubens, genannt Donatio

---

[1] *WA Br*, IX, 340, no. 3583.

[2] *WA Br*, X, 132-35, no. 3783.

[3] *WA*, L, 5. John M. Headley, *Luther's View of Church History* (New Haven, 1963),
p. 51. On the importance of history for Wittenberg theology in the first years of the
Reformation, see D. Karl Bauer, *Die Wittenberger Universitätstheologie und die Anfänge
der Deutschen Reformation* (Tübingen, 1928), pp. 80-98 : "Die Bereicherung der Wittenberger Theologie durch die Geschichte."

Constantini. He knew Hutten's edition done by Schöffer in 1520 of Valla's 1448 treatise. As a younger man Luther had been led by it to the conviction that the pope must be the anti-Christ.

Certain features of his view of history remain consistent with his more youthful period such as his idea that God calls out certain "wonder men" or "sound heroes" gifted with superior endowments to perform certain epochal deeds,[1] his conviction that the *verae historiae* show that the will of God is done also among the heathen nations,[2] and that history is philosophy teaching by example.[3] He still refers to the "histories" which provide an example of faith, but the "exemplarism" is considerably attenuated after the sobering experience of Müntzer and of the Münster radicals. He cautioned against mimesis or literally imitating in detail the lives of saints, heroes, or of Christ himself. Undoubtedly the discourse on history which most nearly approaches the humanist "pragmatic view" of history is his *Preface to Galeatius Capella's History* (1538) in which Luther tells us that historians are useful people and that rulers should support them, that the Germans should learn and write about their own early history, that God is everywhere at work in history so that at every point in time there are noteworthy deeds, that heroes are important in the scheme of things, and that historians are obligated to describe things as they actually happened without prejudice or flattery to men of power.[4]

---

[1] In his commentary on Psalm 101 of 1534-1535, for example, he adduces his theory of the role of the miracle men of history. *WA*, LI, 214-15 : "The healthy heroes are rare, and God provides them at a high price... In addition, we also follow the advice of the best people who live in our midst, until the time comes in which God again provides a healthy hero or a wondrous man in whose hand all things improve or at least fare better than is written in any book."

[2] *WA Tr*, I, 192, no. 441 : "Verae historiae apud gentes ostendunt voluntatem Dei tanquam mutae literae." *WA Tr*, I, 75, no. 158, one of the repeated references to the incident related in Theodoret's *Historia Ecclesiastica* which tells of the Persian king killed by flies in the siege of Nisibis by Sapor II.

[3] *WA Tr*, I, p. 374, no. 389 : Historiae sunt exemplar fidei.

[4] *WA*, L, 383-85; *LW*, XXXIV, 271-82. Perhaps Luther's focussing on the need for more knowledge of early German history was a reflection of Melanchthon's publication in 1538 of *Arminius dialogus Huttenicus, continens res Arminij in Germania gestas. P. Cornelii Taciti, de moribus et populis Germaniae libellus. Adiecta est breuis interpretatio appellationum partium Germaniae* (Wittenberg, 1538), *CR*, XVII, 611. A comparison of Luther's ideas of history with those of Melanchthon in his *Introduction to the Chronicon*, his preface to Hedio's *Chronicle* of 1539, or his slightly altered *Preface to Cuspinian's Caesares* of 1541, reveals many identical or similar views. On the Renaissance humanist attitude

As Luther's interest in history grew he appreciated the value of chronology as an aid to exegesis and for the light it shed on the history of the church. He prepared for his own use a *Reckoning of the Years of the World*, which was a chronological table so that he

> could always have before his eyes and see the time and years of historical events which are described in Holy Scriptures and remind himself how many years the patriarchs, judges, kings and princes lived and ruled or over how long a period of time one succeeded the other.

Inspired perhaps by Eusebius, whose chronicle he intensely admired, he worked out parallel traditions of Biblical history and secular events, with three columns, for the East, West, and German history. He projected the dates from creation forward to the year 1540, dividing the table up by millenia. He drew on contemporary histories to fix dates, but where there was a conflict between the Scriptural data and that of some other source, such as a chronology ascribed to Megasthenes he opted for the reliability of Scriptures.[1] He held that all the humanist disciplines together do not compare in value with the gospel and its promise for eternity.[2]

3. *Luther senior* distinguished among the humanists according to one basic criterion, whether or not they were favorably disposed toward the evangelical movement. As one might well expect, the older humanists, Italian and Northern, were on his blacklist and the younger who had turned evangelical for the most part received his commendation. Luther retained in later years his high regard for Lorenzo Valla. He praised him as the best Italian who disputed well in his *De libero arbitrio*, seeking simplicity both in piety and letters, while Erasmus seeks it only in letters and laughs at piety.[3] Sabellicus, the historian who had been so un-

---

toward history see Myron P. Gilmore, "The Renaissance Conception of the Lessons of History," *Humanists and Jurists* (Cambridge, Mass., 1963), pp. 1-37; Herbert Weisinger, "Ideas of History During the Renaissance," *Journal of the History of Ideas*, VI (1945), 415-35; Felix Gilbert, "The Renaissance Interest in History," *Art, Science, and History in the Renaissance*, Charles Singleton, ed. (Baltimore, 1967), pp. 373-87; and Nancy Struever, *The Language of History in the Renaissance; Rhetoric and Historical Consciousness in Florentine Humanism* (Princeton, 1970).

[1] "Supputatio annorum mundi", 1541, 1545, *WA*, LIII, 1-184. On chronology as the light of history, *WA*, XLIII, 138; on Scriptures and Megasthenes, *WA*, LIII, 24 and 27. J. Headley, pp. 51-52. Peter Meinhold, *Die Genesisvorlesung Luthers und ihre Herausgeber*, pp. 306-32, collates the *Supputatio* with the Genesis Commentary Chronology.

[2] *WA Tr*, I, 191, no. 439.

[3] *WA Tr*, I, 109, no. 259; *WA Tr*, II, 107, no. 1470. For the most part Luther considered Italians to be very superstitious and blind in their saint cults, *WA Tr*, III, 560, no. 3718.

complimentary to the Germans, wished to imitate Livy but nothing came of it.[1] With regard to Cardinal Bembo on Lutheranism, Luther merely commented that it is not fitting for a serious man to read such trifles.[2] The Erasmian Sadoleto he considered ingenious and learned, although "he wrote against us," but he showed in his commentary on the psalm *Misereri mei, Deus* that he does not understand the theological meaning of the *Deus absconditus*.[3]

Nor did Luther's opinion of the Northern humanists mellow with the years. Mutian remained for him an epicurean from whom Albert of Mainz learned the blasphemous joke that *Soli deo gloria* meant "Glory to God the Sun." [4] Crotus Rubeanus corrupted Justus Menius with his impious conversations. [5] Luther was saddened, on the other hand, by the death of Eobanus Hessus, the evangelical poet. He thought the Frenchman William Postel's effort in the *De orbis terrarum concordia libri IV* (1544) to convert the Turks, Jews, and other peoples by proving the articles of faith by nature and reason too ambitious, too much for one volume, and too "enthusiastic." [6] Luther was angered by the bawdy poems of a certain talented young poet named Simon Lemnius, who sold fifty copies of his poetry book before the church door at Pentecost in 1538. Luther thought the poems mocked university people and this suspicion was deepened by Lemnius' escape through the city gate when the town shepherd took his flock out in the morning.[7]

Erasmus remained for him a nutcracker, or mockingbird, who did not take Christ seriously. Luther considered Erasmus' *Copia* and *Adages* to be of value but thought all else would perish. Luther was ready to re-

---

[1] *WA Tr*, III, 459, no. 3616b.

[2] *WA Tr*, IV, 667, no. 5109.

[3] *WA Tr*, II, 8, no. 1248. Richard M. Douglas, *Jacopo Sadoleto, 1477-1547 Humanist and Reformer* (Cambridge, Mass., 1959), p. 47. The Commentary on Psalm 50 was Sadoleto's first exegetical work. Erasmus praised it but Luther found it to be untheological throughout, insensitive to the motive of grace, and neglectful of the role of Christ in the redemption of man. P. 118 : Commenting on Sadoleto's letter to Melanchthon Luther described the author as one "who was a papal secretary for fifteen years, certainly an able and cultivated man... but cunning and artful withal, in the Italian manner." See also Douglas, pp. 25, 27, 253 n. 64, 114, 116-17, 134, 149.

[4] *WA Br*, 11, pp. 168-69, no. 4146, Luther on Nikolaus von Amsdorf in Zeitz. Wittenberg, 19 August 1545. *WA Tr*, I, 186-87, no. 432.

[5] *WA Tr*, II, 627-28, no. 2741a.

[6] *WA Tr*, V, 472, no. 6070.

[7] *WA*, L, 348-55 : *Erklärung gegen Simon Lemnius*, 16 June 1538.

lieve Erasmus of all embarrassment at being considered a Lutheran, for it is clear that "Erasmus believes implicitly whatever Pope Clement VII believes." Erasmus remained for him the great Epicurean.[1] With the single exception of Erasmus, however, one finds many more references in Luther's later writings to John Hus, Karlstadt, Müntzer, and comets than to all the Renaissance humanists together.

IV. CONCLUSIONS

Approaching the headwaters of the Reformation from the angles both of the *initia Lutheri* and the *initia Reformationis* puts into clearer focus the point of confluence of the intra-personal and the broader societal intellectual forces at work. Following their combined course downstream deepens our understanding as to what that juncture meant to history.

1. Emphasis upon the Augustinian intellectual nexus within which Luther developed as a reformer, a nexus which combined and "domesticated" nominalist and humanist components, does make an understanding of Luther's development more intelligible. It seemed crystal clear to Luther that he owed nothing at all to humanism as such for the substance of his theology. "From Erasmus I have nothing," he asserted,

---

[1] *WA Tr*, III, 30, no. 2859a. The references to Erasmus are highly repetitive and too numerous to cite. Typical expressions are *WA Tr*, II, 346, no. 2170; *WA Tr*, IV, 574, no. 4902; *WA Tr*, III, 214, no. 3186a; *WA Tr*, III, 216, no. 3194; *WA Tr*, III, 107, no. 2939a; *WA Tr*, II, 363, no. 2205a; *WA Tr*, IV, 87, no. 4028 : Erasmi Roterodami epicurismi. One of his strongest blasts against Erasmus was *WA Tr*, IV, 37, no. 3963 : "Erasmi propositio et status fuit serviendum esse tempori. Tantum in se respexit. Vixit et mortuus est ut Epicurus, sine ministro et consolatione. Ist gefahren in bus correptam." Erasmus appears 182 times in the index to the *Tischreden*. In connection with a letter to Amsdorf Luther relieved himself of a vicious blast at Erasmus which was published separately in Antwerp, Basle, Cologne, Paris, Augsburg and elsewhere, *WA Br*, VII, 27-39, no. 2093, Luther to Nikolaus von Amsdorf, Wittenberg, c. 11 March 1534, in which he concludes, p. 38 : "Ego sane optarim totum Erasmum esse e nostris scholis explosum ; nam si etiam non esset periciosus, tamen nihil est utilis, nullas res docet aut tractat." He expressed an opinion about Erasmus not a bit more flattering probably in 1543 in a letter to his son John, who had inquired of him what he thought of Erasmus, *WA Br*, VI, 565-66, no. 2076. The *Glossen zu Erasmus, Apophthegmatum opus*, 1543, a copy of Erasmus' work with Luther's marginal comments found in the Prince Stolberg Library shows that Luther consistently saw the shadowside of Erasmus' personality, *WA*, LIV, 101-6, 497-501 (Nachtrag), for Erasmus is an epicurean, a wordling, a mocker like Lucian, a man who despises God and religion without strong religious conviction, a despicable personality, one who has more words than content.

Spitz : Luther's development :
    nominalism + humanism
Jamestocated 89

on divine be. Metaphore + dialectic
    L held former superior 104-105

Authority of Bible nothing
    to Gabriel 113 h

"for I have received everything from Dr. Staupitz, who gave me the favorable opportunity."[1] In his formal theology he was dependent upon the works of Augustinus Favorini, Jacobus Perez, Gregory of Rimini, and upon conversations with Staupitz. Erasmus provided philological instruments and a Greek text, Lefèvre contributed a highly spiritualized approach to exegesis, Reuchlin supplied a Hebrew grammar and vocabulary, but Luther's theology proper developed within the context of Augustinian thought as conditioned by nominalism and "in-house" humanism.

2. In later years Luther was consistent in relating his evangelical breakthrough to a new understanding of the Word and a categorical rejection of his scholastic background. Consider this account of his conversation with Amsdorf on 2 February 1538 :

> That evening Luther in a happy mood conversed with Amsdorf discussing many things concerning the studies of the previous age when very ingenious men were occupied with vain readings, which sophisticated words are plainly unknown and barbarous to men of our century. For Scotus, Bonaventura, Gabriel, Thomas were men of great leisure when the papacy flourished and had to phantasize something. Gabriel writing a book on the Canon of the Mass, which book was in my judgment then the best; when I read it my heart bled. The authority of the Bible was nothing to Gabriel. I still have the books which martyred me so. Scotus wrote very well on the third book of the Sentences. The very ingenious Ockham was zealous in method; his desire was to expand and to amplify things to infinity. Thomas was most loquacious because he was seduced by metaphysics. Now God has wonderfully led us out and has led me unknowing through the affair for over twenty years.[2]

In view of Luther's explicit rejection of scholasticism and specifically of theological nominalism it would indeed be a mistaken notion to find the key to his reformatory development and evangelical solution in the theology he was reacting against. Similarly it is quite clear that Renaissance humanism even in the religious expression given it by the Erasmian *philosophia Christi* was only of marginal importance. Luther credited the power of the Word for his change, exercized upon him during the course of his intense Biblical studies and quite evident already in his first commentary on the Psalms. To be sure it would be a case of *petitio principii* to argue that Luther became a reformer as a *Schrifttheologe* without considering through what medium

---

[1] *WA Tr*, I, 80, no. 173 (*anno* 1532).
[2] *WA Tr*, III, 563-66, no. 3722. For an attack on the three sects of Thomists, Scotists, and Moderns see *WA Tr*, IV, 145, no. 4148.

8

and focus he read the Scriptures. Much insight is gained by paying close attention to the Augustinian mental setting from which he emerged. However, theological terms in the Scriptures, God, sin, righteousness, law, gospel, do not occur in a hygenically sealed package or as neutral objects whose interpretation is predominantly dependent upon the subjective outlook of the observer. Rather they appear in context and not infrequently, as Luther observed, are employed by master rhetoricians such as Moses and Paul. The Biblical passages are set in a Biblical world and have an impetus of their own which, when studied intensely, may well induce a changed or reformatory perception of theology. The fact that Luther's theological change was related so intimately to his personal religious seeking (he was a stormy petrel compared with serene Thomas) made his problem-solution more than an intellectual game.

Much can be gained by comparing the evangelical discovery of other reformers who attributed their conversion to the impact of the gospel, such as Vadian, who moved from a role as a humanist to reformer. On the other hand, a number of Luther's Augustinian opponents had backgrounds analogous to his own, but lacking his encounter with the Biblical world, they remained what he might have been without his long and arduous preoccupation with the Scriptures. To see his exegetical studies as the critical determinant in his evangelical theology is more than a mere begging of the question.

3. The examination of the *initia et exitus Lutheri senioris* reveals some interesting insights into his overall relation to humanism. Despite his avowed wish that he could earlier have devoted himself more fully to the liberal arts, there was no noticeable increase in his reading or mastery of the *studia humanitatis* in his later years. That Luther possessed a very considerable store of classical learning was evident even at the time of the controversy over the will with Erasmus. There are many more classical references in Luther's treatise *De servo arbitrio* (1525), though admittedly the longer one, than in that of Erasmus.[1] Luther continued in later years to call himself a *rusticus* as he did on that occasion!

4. With respect to the classics as a norm or form for theology and anthropology Luther remained the great *Aussenseiter*. One fact which marks the transition from Renaissance to Reformation is that now there

---

[1] E. Gordon Rupp, "Luther : Contemporary Image," *Kirche, Mystik, Heiligung und das Natürliche bei Luther*, Ivar Asheim, ed. (Göttingen, 1967), p. 13. Luther's allusions, Rupp observes, were frequent and often very subtle, so that it was not a case of Luther airing his classical knowledge, as Zwingli was wont to do.

were more leading intellectuals on the "outside" with him. This included not a few prominent Italians, who turned Protestant and came to the North, although most of them veered toward Geneva.

A subtle test case for Luther's reaction to Renaissance humanism is the question of the relationship of the power of the Word to induce faith and the power of rhetoric to persuade. The temptation is always present to see Luther's formula *verbum facit fidem* as an affective rhetorical religious manifestation of the power of the written and especially of the spoken word. None of the scholastics brought *fides* and *verbum* into direct correlation in the way that Luther did.[1] Luther encountered a life-bringing Word (*vox divina*) in St. Bernard and other monastic prophetic types, and the power of words was explicitly and almost tediously emphasized by the humanists. But it would be a fundamental error to equate the *fidem facere* with the humanist *persuadere*. Faith is not for him being persuaded and agreeing with human assertions. Faith is unconditioned trust in the *promissa dei et beneficia Christi*.[2] Similar clear distinctions and sharp contrasts between Luther's conception of God and evaluation of man and those predominant in Renaissance humanism and Platonism could easily be drawn.

5. The reasons for Luther's failure to follow through on his impulse and desire to study the classics more thoroughly were largely practical ones. Juvenal declared that men narrowly constrained by heavy duties do not easily emerge from the shadows. Luther seemed to have no more leisure in his later years than in his earlier period. From 1535 to 1545 he served as dean. He wrote countless letters, many in behalf of students. Some eighteen letters for students from the fourteen years between 1517 and 1531 are still extant; from the fourteen years between 1532 and 1546, some 57 letters are still extant. He was busy with the organization of the evangelical churches. Moreover, he was intensely preoccupied

---

[1] Reinhard Schwarz, *Fides, Spes und Caritas beim jungen Luther* (Berlin, 1962), p. 422 : "Bei keinem der Scholastiker ist also von der fides in der Korrelation zum verbum und ohne ihre Unterordnung unter die formierende caritas die Rede. Anders verhält es sich bei Bernard." Schwarz stresses the critical importance of Scriptural studies in Luther's ripening into a reformer, explicitly denying that his new theology was derived from an Ockhamist, humanist, monastic (Bernard) or Augustinian theology or way of thinking, *Vorgeschichte der reformatorischen Busstheologie* (Berlin, 1968), p. 297.

[2] Heinz Otto Burger, *Renaissance Humanismus Reformation. Deutsche Literatur im Europäischen Kontext* (Berlin, 1969), pp. 418-24, especially p. 423, offers comments of special value since Burger approaches Luther from a thorough study of the German humanist background.

with teaching, preaching and defending the gospel, which had for him
a higher priority than reading *belles lettres*.

6. However, his attitude toward the humanist disciplines remained
positive, a fact of fundamental importance for the beginnings and the
development of the magisterial Reformation and the form which the
relation of evangelical religion to the learned tradition took. His
attitude toward the young pro-evangelical humanists remained most
cordial, toward Eobanus Hessus, the memory of Mosellanus, and
Joachim Camerarius. "There are many living today," he said, "who
are more erudite than Erasmus, such as our Philipp (Melanchthon),
Joachim (Camerarius) and others." [1] Thus Luther's inner relation with
Melanchthon remained harmonious despite their differences, such as
in the interpretation of Augustine.

Finally, for the *exitus Reformationis* this positive stance of Dr. Luther
toward the humanist disciplines helps to explain how many Renaissance cultural values were absorbed and transmitted by Protestantism
to the modern world. [2]

On concluding these few remarks upon the subject of such magnitude
with its vast implications, I feel very much as Luther did, not in his
heroic moments making a great stand, but when he had come down
from the pulpit feeling that he had not done so very well. "Ich habe
mich offte angespeiet," he confessed, "wan ich vom predigstuel komen
bin : Pfeu dich an, wie hastu gepredigt ? Du hast warlich wol ausge-
richtet, nullum servasti conceptum." [3]

---

[1] *WA Tr*, IV, 567, no. 4908 (*anno* 1540).

[2] See the learned article of Professor Heinz Liebing, "Die Ausgänge des Europäischen
Humanismus," *Geist und Geschichte der Reformation* (Berlin, 1966), pp. 357-76, and Lewis
W. Spitz, "Humanism in the Reformation," *Renaissance Studies in Honor of Hans Baron*,
Anthony Molho and John A. Tedeschi, eds., (Florence, Italy, 1971), pp. 643-62.

[3] *WA Tr*, IV, 446-47, no. 4719.

REPORT ABOUT THE NEWLY DISCOVERED
LUTHER MANUSCRIPTS

OSWALD BAYER and MARTIN BRECHT

The two authors presented an investigation about "Unknown Manuscripts of the Young Luther" to the Fourth International Congress for Luther Research for discussion. Shortly before that it was published.[1] We herewith present the comments made there.

I

Because of the impetus in Luther research in our century the publication of Luther's early writings was furthered. With the edition of Luther's Lectures on the Epistle to the Hebrews, 1929,[2] it seemed that the extant sources had been submitted rather completely. Since that time, apart from the fragment of the second lectures on the Psalms, published by Vogelsang,[3] scarcely any other manuscripts of the young Luther have appeared.

To be sure, the tradition about Luther's early literary activities pointed to remaining gaps, for instance, in regard to the sermons or the Lectures on the Epistle to the Galatians. The latter we know as before only in a very poor textual form, although Hans Volz could point to another copy.[4] In the future, it is possible, more sources can be found, if the books in the possession of the then Wittenberg students, now in German libraries, are investigated systematically. That could be a task for a future generation. For the present, the prerequisites, for example, card indexes of previous owners, are generally lacking.

Efforts in this direction in the relatively small library of the Evangel-

---

[1] Oswald Bayer and Martin Brecht, "Unbekannte Texte des frühen Luther aus dem Besitz des Wittenberger Studenten Iohannes Geiling", *Zeitschrift für Kirchengeschichte*, LXXXII, 2 (1971), 229-59. The complete argumentation and the exact evidences will be found there.

[2] Now WA, LVII.

[3] Erich Vogelsang, *Unbekannte Fragmente aus Luthers zweiter Psalmenvorlesung, 1518* (Berlin : W. de Gruyter, 1940).

[4] Hans Volz, "Eine neue studentische Nachschrift von Luthers erster Galaterbriefvorlesung von 1516/17," *Zeitschrift für Kirchengeschichte*, LXVI (1954/55), 72-96.

118   OSWALD BAYER AND MARTIN BRECHT

ical Stipendium in Tübingen recently led to a happy outcome. The
volume, with which we are dealing,[1] carries the ownership entry of
Johannes Geiling from Ilsfeld near Heilbronn (Württemberg). Geiling
first studied in Heidelberg and there belonged to the group of students
around Johannes Oecolampadius and Johannes Brenz. Between 1515
and 1520 he studied in Wittenberg. Later he was a follower of Luther in
southwestern Germany. As such he also subscribed to the *Syngramma
Suevicum* of 1525.[2]

In this volume three Venetian imprints from 1500-1510 are bound
together :

1. A compilation, especially of patristic authors such as Lactantius,
Chrysostom, and Tertullian ; [3]

2. Eusebius, *Praeparatio Evangelica* ; [4]

3. Cicero, *Tuscullanae Questiones cum commento Philippi Beroaldi* .[5]
Besides other texts which need not concern us here, the volume contains identifiable texts of the young Luther in marginal comments and
notes written on the blank sheets bound between the individual imprints.

We are dealing here with two excerpts from the Lectures on the Epistle
to the Romans, one each from the Lectures on the Epistle to the Galatians and on the Epistle to the Hebrews, and an older version of an
exhortation to Communion which was printed with the *Instructio pro
confessione peccatorum*, 1518.[6] The excerpt from the Lectures on the
Epistle to the Galatians has interesting variations.

Immediately in connection with the passages from the Lectures on
the Epistle to the Romans and on the Epistle to the Galatians there are

---

[1] Library of the Evangelische Stift Tübingen. Call no. : F 55.

[2] Johannes Brenz, *Werke: Frühschriften*, (Tübingen 1970), I, 222-78. The *Syngramma
Suevicum* by Johannes Brenz was one of the first and most important polemical pamph-
lets of the Upper German Lutherans in the beginning controversy about the Lord's
Supper.

[3] Habes in hoc volumine, lector optime, divina Lactantii Firmiani opera nuper per
Janum Parrhasium accuratissime castigata, graeco intergro adiuncto, quod in aliis cum
mancum tum corruptum invenitur. Eiusdem Epitome. Carmen de Phoenice. Carmen de
resurrectione Domini. Habes et Ioannis Chrysostomi de eucharistia quandam expositio-
nem et in eandem materiam Laurentii Vallae sermonem. Habes Philippi adhortationem
ad Theodosium. Et Adversus gentes Tertulliani Apologeticon : habesque tabulam noviter
impressam. (Venice : Iohannes Tacuinus, 1509).

[4] Eusebius de Evangelica praeparatione a Georgio Trapezuntio e graeco in latinum
traductus... (Venice, 1500).

[5] M.T. Cicero, Tusculane questiones cum commento Philippi Beroaldi (Venice :
Philippus Pincius Mantuanus, 1510) 113 pp.

[6] *WA*, I, 257-65.

two other documents : a Latin Lenten meditation on Luke 23:28, "Filiae Jerusalem, nolite flere super me, super filios vestros"; a more voluminous and in many respects a more significant piece, a German sermon on Ps. 113:9 (resp. 115:1), "Non nobis Domine, sed nomini tuo da gloriam." We have come to the conclusion that here, too, we are dealing with Luther documents.

Unfortunately very little is known about the story of how these documents were transmitted. The library of the Tübingen Stipendium has several other books that were in the possession of other Württemberg reformers. There are no others that belonged to Geiling. It cannot be determined when and from whom the volume under consideration came to the library of the Stipendium.

This much is known about the individual excerpts. The admonition to Communion is written as marginalia and refers to I Corinthians 11 :16-27, which is printed before a homily by Chrysostom on this pericope.

The excerpt from the Lectures on the Epistle to the Hebrews is a marginal note to that passage in Eusebius' *Praeparatio Evangelica* to which Luther alludes. Why Geiling chose not to enter especially striking passages from the scholia on Romans and Galatians on the blank pages of his valuable book, we cannot rightly perceive.

The Lenten sermon and the German sermon, as also the admonition to Communion, are certainly not mere transcripts, but are based on written copies, which are dependent directly or indirectly on a Luther autograph. In both instances the arrangement of the copy points to this. The German sermon, it is true, is colored by dialectical Upper German. It must remain open how relatively early the appearance of a German sermon manuscript by Luther came about. One must almost believe that Luther himself regarded this sermon as so important, that he already thought about the publication of a German version. That manuscript must then have come into Geiling's possession.

In the instance of the German sermon there are several points that are dependent on the question of its transmission. We present our opinion for discussion, namely, that we are dealing here not with a sermon that has been revised, but with a well transmitted, very early German sermon by Luther, until now the earliest of which we know.

Brief reference may be made yet to the fact that the volume contains numerous remarks by Geiling himself. In them both early Reformation theology and Geiling's humanism are interestingly reflected.

II

In the second part of our report we want to talk about the *references and importance* of the discovered texts. We cannot tell about everything here, only about what is most important and most interesting. The most important texts are :

1. The *varia lectio* of exhortation to Communion of 1518;
2. The Lenten meditation on Luke 23:28;
3. The German sermon on Ps. 113:9.

1. The text in the *Weimar Ausgabe* is the appendix to the *Instructio pro confessione peccatorum*, which was printed in 1518, most likely during Lent. The excerpts designated "A" and "B" [1] were originally independent exhortations to Communion. We cannot enter here into the very rich instructional history of the origin of "A". It refers to Matt. 11:28.[2] "B" expounds I Cor. 11:28.[3] Aside from the fact that both are exhortations to Communion, they are only outwardly related. This is evident in the loose connection between them.[4]

That "B" was an independent text is proved by the form which Geiling offers. For textual-critical reasons this form cannot be understood as having been taken from the printed text. For the printed text is linguistically more polished and shows in its only significant variation that it is dependent on the text which Geiling offers. (The opposite is much less likely.) This variation reads : "sitire gratiam ac credere illam consequi ibi posse."[5] Instead of that, according to Geiling, it simply reads : "sitire iusticiam, humilitatem, charitatem."

Geiling's text was corrected and now reads in "B" : "sitire gratiam ac creder illam consequi ibi posse." This correction is the only point where the two, originally independent sections, converge and are essentially connected : namely in the motif of *confident* faith that not only *thirsts* for grace, but *attains* it. Compare the two : "credant et confidant sese gratiam ibi consequuturos"[6] and "sitire gratiam ac credere illam consequi ibi posse."[7]

---

[1] *WA*, I, 264. 65.
[2] *WA*, I, 264/9-18.
[3] *WA*, I, 264/18-265/11.
[4] *WA*, I, 264/18 : "*Unde* ait Apostolus I Cor. 11 :..."
[5] *WA*, I, 264/30.
[6] *WA*, I, 264/13-14 ("A").
[7] *WA*, I, 264/30 ("B").

IX. et X.

Purissima castitas et paupertas spiritus, radicitus evulsa libidine et cupiditate, Quod in hac vita incipit quidem et proficit, sed in futura perficietur.

Spiritus vivificans.

Charitas Dei et proximi usque ad contemptum sui.
Abstinentia a rebus et nominibus Dei et oblatio sui nihili.
Abstinentia a rebus proximi et exhibitio suarum.

Adverte, quod magnus est error eorum, qui ad Sacramentum Eucharistiae accedunt, arundini illi innixi, quod confessi sint, quod non sibi conscii sint peccati mortalis vel praemiserint orationes suas et praeparatoria. Omnes illi sibi iudicium manducant et bibunt, Quia his omnibus non fiunt digni et puri, Imo per eam fiduciam puritatis peius polluuntur. Sed si credant et confidant sese gratiam ibi consequuturos, haec sola fides eos facit puros et dignos, quae non nititur operibus illis, sed purissimo, piissimo firmissimoque verbo Christi dicentis: Venite ad me omnes, qui laboratis &c. In praesumptione, inquam, istorum verborum accedendum est, et sic accedentes non confundentur. Unde ait Apostolus 1. Corin. 11: Probet autem seipsum homo, et sic de pane illo edat.

Ista probatio ab iliis refertur ad discussionem peccatorum praeteritorum, ut studio possibili peccata sua recordetur atque poeniteat. Sed haec est inicialis et adhuc rudis probatio, quae non nisi timorem et angustiam conscientiae facit, plusque retrahit a Sacramento quam attrahat. Ideo in ipsa nullo modo standum est, sed procedendum ad probationem, quae ad praesentis status conditionem refertur, ut homo probet et examinet quo affectu sit formatus, An cupiat gratiam, iusticiam, salutem, An adhuc potius sitiat vel lucrum vel honorem vel voluptatem. Hoc est quod alii dicunt satis obscure, An adhuc sit in proposito peccandi actuali. Nam summa et optima dispositio ad Sacramentum est illa: Si homo sese probans invenit se sitire gratiam ac credere illam consequi ibi posse, displiceatque sibi ac miserum se et egenum in spiritu cognoscit, plenum multis atque perversis cupiditatibus, Talis est recte dispositus, quia, secundum B. Augustinum, Iste cibus Sacramenti nihil ita odit, sicut fastidientem et saturum, Nihil ita requirit, sicut esurientem et sitientem. Qui ita facit, recte se probat. Talis etiam Apostolo satisfacit, qui ista scribit contra saturos et superbos, qui invicem alter alterum despicientes mutuo dissentiebant, qualium morbus est...

Matth. 11, 28.

1. Cor. 11, 28.

6—8 Diese drei Zeilen sind in A an der Seite des vorstehenden Abschnitts entlang geführt; in B sind sie anders untergebracht, aber die Sache verwirrend.   Zwischen Z. 5 und 9 bringt B was unter dem ersten Abschnitt als Compendium decem Praeceptorum steht und das Ende des zweiten Abschnitts, das beginnt Facile itaque bis contra charitatem Dei et proximi 20 discutionem B   33 itaque requirit A

Geiling's text therefore reveals a correction by Luther, which is especially noteworthy because it is the only substantive correction in the otherwise only stylistically polished text. It points up sharply what was important for Luther when he joined the two originally independent sections. He intends in March 1518 not to let any doubt remain about the certainty of faith.

Thus the difference between Geiling's text and the printed text, therefore Luther's correction, points emphatically to the turn which the history of his theology takes in the spring of 1518 and represents it at a decisive point. (Nothing, of course, is decided by this about the importance of this turn.)

In view of the transmission of Geiling's rendition of the text we here present the proposition for discussion, that this text is a completely separate elaboration by Luther, which Geiling had the opportunity to copy. How far this text reaches back behind the printed text of March 1518 is difficult to determine. Considering the theme and in view of Luther's habit of using casual sermons in the following years, one could accept Lent 1517.

2. We will call attention to the Lenten meditation on Luke 23:28 only very briefly. The text is not very extensive; however, it is not a fragment, but a rounded out exposition. Its basic motif is the analogy between Jesus suffering because of his oppressors and the soul suffering because of sin. The soul's state we recognize by meditating on the passion of Jesus. By a knowledge of His history we come to a knowledge of ourselves.

This motif shapes decisively the already known early Lenten sermons by Luther and in general his early Lenten meditations. By a comparison between Luther's already known Lenten sermons (between 1515 and 1518) [1] and the text transmitted by Geiling, it is evident that it indeed must be referred to them, but it cannot be identified with either one of them (also not with portions of these sermons).

Rather, here we are dealing with an independent Lenten sermon, one that may be close even in point of time to the two other Lenten sermons of 1515 and 1518. The external circumstantial evidences of the place where it was found speaks for a dating in Lent 1516.

Its significance is found in the fact that it is a link, previously unknown, in the sequence of Luther's early Lenten sermons. It enriches

---

[1] *WA*, I, 340-345 (for the dating see p. 119, n. 1, *art. cit.*, p. 238, n. 12); *WA*, I, 336-39; 339f.

and confirms our knowledge of Luther's early "sacramental text meditation"[1] by giving us an especially clear example of this meditation.

3. Without doubt the most important of the discovered manuscripts is the German sermon on Ps. 113:9.[2] We would call your special attention to it.

a) It strikes one that this sermon was delivered in German. In noteworthy contrast to that fact we see that it pertains especially to priests, who therefore must be regarded as those to whom it was primarily addressed. We can understand the combination of both characteristics, if this sermon was held on the occasion of a first mass, which had to be understood also by the laity present. By comparison we can point to a sermon by Luther held on the occasion of a first mass in the summer of 1518, which evidently was in part, at the very least, preached in German.

The sermon before us is characteristically different from the latter. It is shaped by numerous motifs which belong per se and in their configuration unexchangeably to the Luther of the years from 1515 to 1517. The closest reference is found to the sequence of scholia on Rom. 4:7, since this can be shown in exact detail.[3] The date of its composition fixes the *terminus a quo* for the dating of the sermon. On the other hand, to be noted is the extensive congruence (including the single citations from the Scriptures and the Church Fathers !) with Luther's letter to Spalatin on 15 February 1518.[4] This letter can mark the *terminus ad quem* in view of the theological turn in spring/summer 1518 (in connection with the sermons to the priests; concretely in view of the mentioned sermon for a first mass in the summer of 1518).

b) Four characteristic motifs because of their specific connection definitely argue that we are dealing with a text by Luther :

1. Confession of sin and supplication;
2. God's saints according to Ps. 31:6;
3. *semper in motu*;
4. Christ's cloak of grace.

---

[1] For this term and the phenomenon see O. Bayer, *PROMISSIO. Geschichte der reformatorischen Wende in Luthers Theologie* (Göttingen, 1971), pp. 78-100.

[2] *WA*, IV, 655-59.

[3] See above footnote 1.

[4] *WA Br*, I, 144-47, especially lines 28-38, 45, 46-49.

(In the presentation under these headings the sermon was compared especially with texts from the Lectures on the Epistle to the Romans.[1] The presentation continued as follows).

With this we discontinue the comparison of single points. If it were complete, it would have to deal exactly with the meaning of the Law together with its stricter interpretation by Christ, the meaning of good works, righteousness and sin (together with the concept of *fomes* and *concupiscentia*), as found in the German sermon. Such an investigation could, however, merely show how closely the sermon touches the questioning of the Lectures on the Epistle to the Romans and of contemporary sermons and that the specific interests of the years from 1515 to 1517 are demonstrated in it.

Within the limits chosen here, that is, in view of the purpose to locate the time and subject matter of the sermon in respect to known texts, the specific references may nevertheless suffice to ascribe the sermon to Luther. The time of its composition cannot have been very long after the composition of the scholia on Romans 4:7, with which it is most closely connected; hence in the years 1515/16, most certainly in 1516.

The significance of this sermon by Luther, previously unknown, is evident from a thorough comparison especially with the Lectures on the Epistle to the Romans. We are dealing here with a text that summarizes Luther's then willing and thinking as no other and that documents precisely the peculiarity of his theology before the turn in spring 1518. We would not be overestimating its importance, if we regard it as the most revealing sermon and one of the most important lesser documents of that time.

Non nobis domine, sed nomini tuo da gloriam (Ps 113, 9).

In den vorten des heiligen propheten David, dy er im psalter scribet, sollen mir lernen, das mir in allen dingen suchen sollen dy er gottis. Und in sunderheit dy prister dy sollen sich hutten in allen iren verken, das sy nith ir er, sunder gottis er suchen, es sy in predigen, beten, fasten und andern gutten verken. O vy ein schvere arbeith
5 ist das denen, dy sich lassen duncken, sy leben in der heilickeit, das sy goth loben und allein sein er suchen.

Dan gottis er suchen allein, ist nichtes anderß, den sich selber schenden und gantz vorachten und nicht uff sich selber halten. Das kunnen aber dy nith thun, dy sich und ire gutte verck fur guth halten, dan sy vollen alle tzeit venen, sy sindt gerecht, und
10 so mer sy sich guth und frum lassen duncken etc, so vill dester mener sindt sy ungerecht vor goth.

---

[1] See above p. 117, footnote 1.

Das man aber mog versten, vy man goth in allen vercken dy er geben soll, vill das
selbig ein venig ercleren, und von aller erst von den pristern. Dy prister sollen mercken,
ßo man in er entpitten ist, das sy dy selbig er nith auß veniger und in unitziger gestalt
15 goth zuschriben und alle zeith alßo sprechen : O eviger goth, ich bin nith virdigk, das
ich dein heyliges vorth under dein heyliges cristglaubiges volck seyen sol. Dan ein
prister sol alle zeith auß grun(d) seines hertzen erschrecken, van er sein heiliges vort
außsprechen sol, dan es ist ein unaussprechlich gros heiliges ding, gottis vort außzu-
sprechen.
20 Man findet itzund aber vill prister, dy allein predigen, das sy vollen gesehen, hoch-
geacht und gelopt darvon verden. Darauß volget auch, das sy kein gnad herlangen
by got dem heiligen geist und das volck auch kein lusth hat, in zuhoren. Das mach,
das sy nichts dan belvern kunnen, gleich vy ein boßer bauer tudt, und bredigen nichtes,
dan allein, vy man durch guth thun in himel muß kumen, und vissen nith, vas guth
25 thun ist, und geschveigen gantzs gottis marter und seines bittern sterbens, velches
doch der recht veg zum der selikeit ist. Van im also vere, das mir durch gutte verck in
himel mochten kummen, so ver es eviglich zu erbarmen, das cristus so groß marter
glitten het. Van sy aber von gotis (sohn) sagenten und von seinen heiligen exempeln,
dy er uns geben hat in allen seinem leben, vy man seinem himlischen vatter und nith
30 uns dy er zuschriben solten, so vurd goth dy gnad geben, das das volck in der lib ent-
zundeth vurdt, und vurdt in gern zuhorn und vurd das volck und dy prister gar ein
grossen nutzs darvon nemen.
Man sol kurtzlich mercken, das ein itzlicher mensch goth dy er gipdt und nith im,
ßo er sich und alle seine verck herkeneth. Dan mir seidt nichtes anders dan sunder
35 ßo lang, bis uns dy sell zum hals auß geeth und ist gantzs nichtes guttis in uns. Ja, das
nach vill mener ist, ist kein mensch under dem dach des himels, der one sunde sey;
mir seind allesampt gantz boß und schlamig und unßer natur ist gantz vergifft bis
uff das aller ergest und ist nichtes gutz in uns und kunnen und mogen nichtes guttis
thun.
40 So nun das var ist, das mir sunder sindt und aller boßheith voll, ßo muß das herauß
ervolgen, das goth gerech(t) ist, dan mussen mir im aller unßere verck heimsetzen,
leib und sel, und mussen sprechen : Allmechtiger eviger goth, dir sy lob, er und briß,
schaff es mith mir nach deinem gottlichen villen. Und mussen uns und unsere gutte
verck vornichten und nith gedencken, das uns goth durch dy selbigen in himell nem,
45 sunder mir mussen uns in allen unßern vercken gering achten, gleich vy der Evangelist
spricht : So ir alles hapt gethan, das euch muglich ist zu thun, ßo must ir sprechen,
das ir unutze diner seith (Lk 17, 10), und nith mit einem hoffertigen hertzen, sunder
mith der demuth gen himel faren, uff das euch nith geschech vy lucipern, do er volt
venen, er seß am allerhochsten, do vill er. So vurt uns auch geschehen, ßo mir uff unßere
50 gutte verck verden bauen, ßo mir vollen verden venen, mir ffaren in himel dardurch,
ßo verden sy uns in dy helle leitten. Dan van mir uff sy hoffen, ßo machen sy ein geist-
liche hoffart und hoffen, got verd uns dem himel dadurch geben. Und dyselbig hoffart
mißfelt got ßo serr, das er uns dem deuffel gibet mit lib und sel, und spricht : Ich volt,
ven ich het dich herloßt am creutz, und solltest allein mich hoffen etc. Dicunt autem
55 multi : Faciamus igitur mala, ut inde veniant bona. Absit, dicit Paulus (Röm 3, 8.6).
Vy mir aber uns halten mussen, das unsere gutten verck bei goth angenem sindt, vil
ich kutzlich sagen.
Ich hab gesaget, sol got gelobet verden und im dy er allain geben verden, so mussen

mir uns gantz vornichten und vorachten, auch nichtes uff unß und unsere gutte verck
60 bauen, allein sy got heimsetzen, das er mith mach, vas er vol.

Und so mir dan also thuen, ßo demutigen mir uns und geben goth er unßer verck
und sprechen : Got, thu hast mir leib und seel geben, und ich red nichtes und thu nichtes,
es get allain auß deiner gottlichen gnad. Darum glaub ich, das thu alle gutte verck mir
durch dein gnad gebest. Darum, almechtiger eviger goth, nim dy verck vider zu dir
65 und mach darauß, vas du vilt, dan es sindt deine gab und komen von deiner allmech-
tigen gnaden.

Das aber mir sunder sindt und gottis gebot nicht halden, das zeigen uns an dy heiligen gottis, dan si haben alle tag uber ire gutte verck geclaget und alle zeit in ubel
darbey geforcht und sich als sunder herkenneth. Das varn sy auch.
70 Zum ersten spricht S. Paulus : Infelix o ego homo, quis liberabit me de morte cor-
poris huius (Röm 7, 25) um des villen, das er alle zeit im fult dy boße volust und zun-
tiglichkeit zu der sundt.

Item spricht zu dem deuffel cristus : Ich hab ein gerechten man, ein frumen, ein
gedultigen (Hiob 1, 8). Item Job spricht och von im selber, ich meine am 13. c. : Ich
75 habe nimantz betrogen, ich hab mein handt dem armen gereicht, noch focht er im.

Item S. Augustinus schribet von seiner mutter; vy sy gantz ein frum veib sy gevest.
Gleichvol spricht er in dem selbigen buch und bith alle, dy das buch lessen, das sy seiner
Mutter och gedencken vollen, ob sy noch in gener velt etwas vider goth het. Und
knupffet der heiligk doctor den spruch hinden dran und spricht : O ve, ve, umer ve
80 allen denen, dy mith iren vercken blos fur das gericht komen, van sy verden nach inen
geurteilet werden.

Hort mein liben frundt cristi, wy gantz ein herbermkglicher spruch ist das von einem
heiligen docter. Meint ir och, vy ir besten vellent, ßo ir alßo uff euer gutte verck hin
sterbent und sprechent : Got vert mir den himel dardurch geben. Ja, liber gesell, er
85 wil dir dy hell darfur geben, darum das du nith allein dein hoffnung in in setzezesch
und sprichst : Eviger got, ich bin follen sunden, in mir ist gantz nichtes guttes, ich
stee hy vor deinen gottlichen augen gantz blos, ich hab dir mein dag ny kein er, trew,
lib bewissen.

So spricht aber cristus : Du hast var, fol sund bist du und allen deine geverck in
90 sunden folpracht und hast dy hell wol vordineth. Aber darum, das du dich herkennest
alßo ein ubelteter und richtest dich selber und herkennest, das ich allein frum bin,
ßo solt du evigk von mir nicht gericht werden, sunder bey mir in meynes vatter vonungk
bleyben.

Es muß sich der mensch alle zeit dannoch forchten, das er dy vort, ßo er sich alßo
95 demutigtet, nith auß einem gantzen hertzen reden sey. Dan es spricht der prophet :
O ver kan dy falscheit des hertzens imer erkennen ? (Ps 19, 13).

Das ich aber sprich : Mir kundt dy zehen gbot nit erfullen; und kein mensch hat
sy oder kein heylig noch ny erfullet.

Das man spricht, dy horffertigen heiligen erfullen dy gbot cristi nith, das kunnen sy
100 gantz nith leiden.

Cristus kam vom himel und must dy gebot seines vatters herfullen, darum das mir
so gantz boßhaftig varen und kunten sy nith erfullen. Szo kumen sy und sprechen :
Mir herfullen sy, mir stellen nith, ehebrechen nith, morden nith, und meinen alßo,
ßo sy dy außwenigen verck erfullen, es sey genug. O liber got, sy fellen veit !
105 Merck, vas spricht Christus Mathei 5 (28) : Si videris mulierem et concupiveris eam,
iam mechatus est in corde. Mein liben freundt cristi, hy zeiget got an, das von notten

ist, vill man dy zehen gbot halten, das nith genug ist, ßo mit außventzigen vercken, sunder och man muß kein bos gedancken nith haben.

Szo sprechen sy : Hor ich vol, das ich dy gbot nit halten kan und verd vordammeth ?
110 So spricht cristus : Ja, es ist var, O Margen, gottis mutter, das sindt herschreckeliche vort und trostliche vort. Herschreckelich vort, das uns das gebot zu schver ist und mir mogen es nith halten und fordammeth uns. Dy vorth verden viderum frolich, ßo mir dy blinden phariseyeraugen uffthun und fragen cristum : Eviger goth, ist das var, das du dy boßen gedancken ßo hart anzeuchest und vilt mich dardurch verdammen
115 und sprichest, van ich gedencke zu stelen

morden im hertzen und thu es gleich nith ehebrechen

mith den vercken, ßo sey ich ein ehebrecher ? Spricht cristus : Ja, liber mensch, du bist so hart vorgift durch den fal, den Adam und Eva haben gethon, das du an sunden und boß gedancken nith kanst sein. Die selbige gedancken machen dich gleich vol zu
120 eim glid des deuffels, als ob du sy mith den vercken tetest. Darum, liber mensch, mein himelischer vatter kunth keinen frummen menschen uff erden finden, der dy bossen gedancken nith het ghapdt. Darum musth ich mensch verden und im underdenigk hy uff erden und im dy er gottis geben und bin geborn nith noch der fleischlichen vollust vy du und bin on sundt.
125   Darum liber mensch, ven du kumest zu mir und herkennest dich als ein brichlichen menschen, so vil ich dir von meiner gnad ein teil geben, und vo du vol sundt bist, vill ich mein volkummenheit und gerechtikeith vor dein sund setzen und vil alßo gern ungerecht verden deinethhalben.

Van dy heiligen im himel nit herkennet hetten ir gebrechlichkeit, sy vern numer
130 seligk vorden. Do sis aber erkenten, do schrien sy dag und nacht zu goth, er solt sy auß dem suntlichen leben nemen. Do nam got den mantell seiner gnaden und dagkt ir unvolkumenheit mith zu und macht sy seligk.

Es ist uns gut ding um das gesetz, van es lerneth uns unßer ungluck und sundt er-kennen und lerneth uns gnad suchen bey got. Darum sindt gottis gbot gut. Darum
135 sprech S. P(aulus) : Lex dat (a) est ideo, ut abundaret delictum (Röm 5, 20).

RENAISSANCE AND REFORMATION

An Essay in Their Affinities and Connections

WILLIAM J. BOUWSMA

Since the peculiar mixture of responsibility and presumption in the title of my paper will scarcely have escaped the notice of this distinguished audience, I feel some need to explain at the outset that it represents an assignment on the part of those who planned our meeting. The significance of the problems to which it points is suggested by the great historians who have grappled with it in the past, albeit (a fact that should constitute something of a warning) with somewhat contrary results, among them Michelet, Dilthey, and Troeltsch.[1] Its practical importance lies in the need of most of us to place our more limited conclusions in some broader historical framework; we must therefore reconsider, from time to time, the relationship between Renaissance and Reformation. In spite of this, the subject has recently received little systematic attention, and many of us are still likely to rely, when we approach it, on unexamined and obsolete stereotypes. Obviously I cannot hope to remedy this state of affairs in a brief paper. Yet the progress of Renaissance studies in recent decades invites a reassessment of this classic problem, and I offer these remarks as an essay intended to stimulate further discussion.

What has chiefly inhibited larger generalization has been the extension and refinement of our knowledge, and with it a growth both in specialization and in humility. Thus we are increasingly reluctant to make broad pronouncements about either the Renaissance or the Reformation, much less about both at once. For as scholars we are divided not only between Renaissance and Reformation, or between Italy and

---

[1] The complexity of the issues involved is nicely suggested by Troeltsch's own retreat from the famous "medieval" interpretation of Reformation theology in his classic *Die Soziallehren der christlichen Kirchen und Gruppen* of 1911. Hans Baron has called my attention to Troeltsch's little known revision of his *Protestantisches Christentum und Kirche in der Neuzeit* (Leipzig and Berlin, 1922), in the second edition of part one of *Die Kultur der Gegenwart*, Abteilung IV. 1, II Hälfte, pp. 431-792.

Northern Europe; even within these categories most of us are specialists who would claim competence only in a particular aspect of Renaissance Florence or Venice, in one phase or another of Renaissance humanism, in Machiavelli or Erasmus, in later scholasticism or the history of piety, in Luther or Calvin or the sects. Under these conditions few students of the Renaissance have cared to look as far as the Reformation; and although Reformation scholars have been somewhat bolder, they have rarely pursued the question of Renaissance antecedents farther than northern humanism. Humanism is, indeed, the one subject that has recently encouraged forays into the problem of this paper; but although Breen, Dufour, Spitz, Liebing, and especially Charles Trinkaus, among others, have made valuable contributions to discussion,[1] the problem is still with us, primarily, I think, because we have not fully made up our minds about the meaning of Renaissance humanism. A result of this dificulty has been a tendency to focus special attention on Erasmus as a touchstone for the Renaissance, a role for which—for reasons that will emerge later in this paper—I think he is not altogether suited.

It is, however, one measure of the complexity of our subject that we cannot approach the question of the relationship between Renaissance and Reformation without somehow first coming to terms with the implications of humanism. I should like to do so, however, obliquely rather than directly. It seems to me that although humanism, which assumed a variety of forms as it passed through successive stages and was influenced by differing local conditions, was not identical with the more profound tendencies of Renaissance culture, it was nevertheless often likely to give them notable expression, and for reasons that were not accidental but directly related to the rhetorical tradition; whatever their differences in other respects, most recent interpretations of

---

[1] Quirinus Breen, *Christianity and Humanism : Studies in the History of Ideas* (Grand Rapids, 1968), and *John Calvin, A Study in French Humanism* (Chicago, 1931); Alain Dufour, "Humanisme et Reformation," *Histoire politique et psychologie historique* (Geneva, 1966), pp. 37-62; Lewis W. Spitz, *The Religious Renaissance of the German Humanists* (Cambridge, Mass., 1963), and, most recently, "Humanism in the Reformation," in *Renaissance Studies in Honor of Hans Baron*, Anthony Molho and John Tedeschi, eds. (Florence, 1970), pp. 643-62; Heinz Liebing, "Die Ausgänge des europäischen Humanismus," *Geist und Geschichte der Reformation* (Berlin, 1966), pp. 357-76; Charles Trinkaus, *In Our Image and Likeness : Humanity and Divinity in Italian Humanist Thought* (2 vols.; Chicago, 1970), and "Renaissance Problems in Calvin's Theology," *Studies in the Renaissance*, I, (1954) 59-80.

Renaissance humanism have at least identified it with a revival of rhetoric.[1]

What has been less generally recognized is the deeper significance of this revival. The major reason is, I think, that in our time the term *rhetoric* has become largely pejorative; we are inclined to couple it with the adjective *mere*. But for the Renaissance there was nothing shallow about rhetoric. Based on a set of profound assumptions about the nature, competence, and destiny of man, rhetoric gave expression to the deepest tendencies of Renaissance culture, tendencies by no means confined to men clearly identifiable as humanists, nor always fully expressed by men who have generally been considered humanists. I shall try in this paper to describe these tendencies, which seem to me to have exerted intolerable pressures on central elements in the medieval understanding of Christianity. And I will suggest that similar tendencies underlay the thought of the great Protestant Reformers. Thus the significance of Protestantism in the development of European culture lies in the fact that it accepted the religious consequences of these Renaissance tendencies and was prepared to apply them to the understanding of the gospel. From this standpoint the Reformation was the theological fulfillment of the Renaissance.

I

Fundamental to the cultural movements of the Renaissance was a gradual accumulation of social and political changes : an economy increasingly dependent on commerce rather than agriculture, a political structure composed of assertive particular powers, and a society dominated by educated laymen who were increasingly restive under clerical direction and increasingly aggressive in pressing their own claims to dignity and self-determination. A commercial economy and the more and more openly uncoordinated conduct of politics supplied the social base for a new vision of man's place in the world, and of the world itself. Social experience rooted in the land had perhaps encouraged a sense of

---

[1] Among more important recent works, see Paul Oskar Kristeller, *Renaissance Thought: The Classic, Scholastic, and Humanist Strains* (New York, 1961); Hans Baron, *The Crisis of the Early Italian Renaissance* (Rev. ed. ; Princeton, 1966): Eugenio Garin, *L'umanesimo italiano* (Bari, 1958) ; Jerrold E. Seigel, *Rhetoric and Philosophy in Renaissance Humanism* (Princeton, 1968) ; Hanna H. Gray, "Renaissance Humanism : The Pursuit of Eloquence," *Journal of the History of Ideas*, XXIV (1963), 497-514.

broad, natural regularities ultimately responsive to cosmic forces and inhibiting to a sense of the significance of change; but the life of a merchant community and the ambitious operations of independent rulers made all experience contingent on the interaction between unpredictable forces and the practical ingenuity and energies of men. Under these conditions the possibility of cosmic order seemed remote, but in any case of little relevance to human affairs; and the obvious rule of change in the empirical world encouraged efforts at its comprehension and eventually stimulated the awareness of history, that peculiarly Hebraic and Christian—as opposed to Hellenic or Hellenistic—contribution to the western consciousness. Meanwhile new political realities and the claims of laymen undermined the hierarchical conceptions that had defined the internal structure of the old unified order of the cosmos, within which the affairs of this world had been assigned their proper place.[1] It will also be useful to observe at this point that these developments were by no means confined to Italy; I will touch briefly at a later point on the implications of this fact for the Renaissance problem.

It is not altogether wrong to emphasize the positive consequences of these developments which, by freeing human activity from any connection with ultimate patterns of order, liberated an exuberance that found expression in the various dimensions of Renaissance creativity. Burckhardt's insight that the autonomy of politics converted the prince into an artist of sorts may require modification; yet the new situation made all human arrangements potentially creative in a sense hardly possible so long as the basic principles of every activity were deduced from universal principles. The notion of the state as a work of art points to the general process of secularization and reminds us that the culture of the Renaissance extended far beyond its brilliant art and literature, and was perhaps even more significant in its implications than in its accomplishments.

It had, however, another and darker side. It rested on the destruction of the sense of a definable relationship between man and ultimate realities. It severed his connection with absolute principles of order, not so much by denying their existence as by rejecting their accessibility to the human understanding. It deprived him of a traditional conception

---

[1] I have discussed these matters at greater length in *Venice and the Defense of Republican Liberty* : *Renaissance Values in the Age of the Counter Reformation* (Berkeley and Los Angeles, 1968), esp. chs. 1 and 8.

of himself as a being with distinct and organized faculties attuned to the similarly organized structure of an unchanging, and in this sense dependable, universe. Above all, therefore, it left him both alone in a mysterious world of unpredictable and often hostile forces, and at the same time personally responsible in the most radical sense for his own ultimate destiny. For he was now left without reliable principles and—because the directive claims of the church also depended heavily on the old conceptions—reliable agencies of guidance. These darker aspects of Renaissance culture eventually required, therefore, a reformulation of Christian belief, and we shall now examine them a bit more closely.

Renaissance thought has sometimes been represented as a reassertion of ancient rationalism against the supernaturalism of the Middle Ages. The formulation is, of course, both inaccurate and misleading. In the thirteenth century some intellectual leaders had been notably hospitable to Greek philosophy, and had tried to coordinate it with revelation. But it was precisely the possibility of such coordination that Renaissance culture—insofar as it differed from what had preceded it—characteristically denied; in this sense Renaissance thought was less rationalistic (if not necessarily less rational) than that of the Middle Ages.

In fact it was inclined to distinguish between realms, between ultimate truths altogether inaccessible to man's intellect, and the knowledge man needed to get along in this world, which turned out to be sufficient for his purposes. Thus the Renaissance attack on scholasticism had a larger implication as well as a specific target; it implied, and occasionally led to, the rejection of all systematic philosophy. From Petrarch, through Salutati and Valla, to Machiavelli, Pomponazzi, and the Venetians of the later Renaissance, the leaders of Renaissance thought rejected any effort to ground human reflection or action on metaphysics: and at the same time they insisted on the autonomy of the various dimensions of human concern and the relativity of truth to the practical requirements of the human condition. In this sense, although truth was robbed of some grandeur, it was also made more human; and if Aristotle was less and less respected as a vehicle of eternal wisdom, he could be all the more admired as a man.[1] Under such conditions philosophy could evi-

---

[1] Cf. Petrarch, *De sui ipsius et multorum ignorantia*, Hans Nachod, trans., in *The Renaissance Philosophy of Man*, Ernst Cassirer, et al., eds. (Chicago, 1948), p. 74: "I certainly believe that Aristotle was a great man who knew much, but he was human and could well be ignorant of some things, even of a great many things."

dently contribute nothing to theology; indeed, its spiritual effects were likely to be adverse since it encouraged malice and pride.

Related to the attack on metaphysical speculation was an attack on hierarchy, which rested ultimately on metaphysically-based conceptions of the internal structure of all reality. The repudiation of hierarchy was most profoundly expressed in Nicholas of Cusa's conception of the infinite, which made every entity equally distant from—and thus equally near to—God;[1] a similar impulse perhaps lurks behind Valla's rejection of Pseudo-Dionysius.[2] But partly because the formulations of Cusanus smacked too much of metaphysics, partly because the problem of hierarchy was peculiarly related to social change, the attack on hierarchy was likely to receive more overtly social expression. It took a general form in the effort to substitute a dynamic conception of nobility through virtue for the static nobility of birth,[3] a specific form in the impulse (often expressed in legislation and the practical policies of states)[4] to consider the clergy in no way superior to other men but, on the contrary, as equal in the obligations of citizenship (if generally less competent in practical affairs), at least as vulnerable to sin, and in as desperate a need for salvation as other men, whom it was their obligation to serve rather than to command. This suggested at least that social order was unrelated to cosmic order, but it also raised the possibility that order per se was of a kind quite different from what had been supposed.

For the age of the Renaissance was by no means oblivious to the need for order, which indeed historical disasters had converted into the most urgent of problems. But its very urgency intensified the necessity of regarding order as a practical rather than a metaphysical issue. Bitter

---

[1] Cf. Ernst Cassirer, *Individuum und Kosmos in der Philosophie der Renaissance* (Leipzig and Berlin, 1927), ch. 1.

[2] See Mario Fois, *Il pensiero cristiano di Lorenzo Valla nel quadro storico culturale del suo ambiente* (Rome, 1969), p. 492.

[3] For Poggio's celebrated dialogue on this subject—one of the better known pieces on the theme—see George Holmes, *The Florentine Enlightenment, 1400-1450* (London, 1969), pp. 148-50

[4] For Florence, for example, see Marvin B. Becker "Church and State in Florence on the Eve of the Renaissance (1343-1382)," *Speculum*, XXVII (1962), 509-27. More generally see Nicolai Rubinstein, "Marsilius of Padua and Italian Political Thought of His Time," *Europe in the Late Middle Ages*, J.R. Hale et al., eds. (London and Evanston, 1965), pp. 44-75; and Daniel Waley, *The Italian City-Republics* (London. 1969), pp. 87ff.

experience seemed to demonstrate that order had to be brought down to earth, where it could be defined in limited and manageable ways. And, as the occasional intrusions of the clergy into politics appeared periodically to demonstrate, the attempt to apply ultimate principles to concrete problems was likely only to interfere with their practical solution. This was a central point not only for Machiavelli and his *politique* successors; it also molded the numerous constitutional experiments of the Renaissance, with their repudiation of hierarchically-defined lines of authority in favor of order through a balance of interests and their appeal to immediate local needs and the right of local self-determination. The best arrangements, in these terms, were not those that most accurately reflected some absolute pattern but those that best served the specific and limited human purposes for which they were instituted.

But although a sense of the limitation of the human intellect was basic to the thought of the Renaissance, this negation had a positive corollary in a new conception of the human personality which also seemed to correspond better to the experience supplied by a new social environment. Men whose lives consisted in the broad range of experiences, contingencies, and human relationships that characterized existence in the bustling and complicated modern world could no longer find plausible an abstract conception of man as a hierarchy of faculties properly subject to reason; instead the personality presented itself as a complex and ambiguous unity in which the will, primarily responsive to the passions, occupied a position at the center. One result of this conception was to undermine the contemplative ideal; if man's reason was weak but his will strong, he could only realize himself in this world through action, indeed he was meant for a life of action. Another was to reduce suspicion of the body; in the absence of the old psychological hierarchy, the body could no longer be held merely base and contemptible. Action required its use, and the new integrity of the personality reduced the possibility of attributing the human propensity to evil primarily to the physical or sensual aspect of man's nature. Human passions now also acquired a positive value, as the source of action.[1] This new anthropology, articulated by Petrarch, Salutati, and Valla, required a reconsideration of the problem of immortality and led eventually to the ardent discussions of the soul in which Pomponazzi figured. It also pointed to the political and historical conceptions of Machiavelli and

---

[1] Cf. Hans Baron, "Secularization of Wisdom and Political Humanism in the Renaissance," *Journal of the History of Ideas*, XXI (1960), 140-41.

Guicciardini, who emphasized the primacy of will and passion, as well as to the psychological interests of a host of Renaissance writers.[1]

In addition man was defined as a social being; if he lost one kind of participation in a larger reality, namely his abstract position as a member of the human species in the cosmic hierarchy of being, he obtained another with, perhaps, more tangible satisfactions : his membership as a concrete individual in the particular human community in which he lived, now an essential rather than an accidental condition of his existence. Thus the values of human community now achieved full recognition. Human virtue was defined not as an abstraction but as a function of relationship with other men; man's active nature was understood to achieve full expression only in a life of social responsibility, and indeed his happiness was seen as dependent on human community. Furthermore, since effective participation in society required some wealth, the conception struck another blow at medieval asceticism.

On the other hand the demands of life in society also stimulated a vision of human existence very different from that implicit in the contemplative ideal. For life in society was patently marked by a conflict of opposing interests that could rarely (if men were honest) be identified with absolute good or evil; and to incessant struggle with other men was added, in social existence, the temptations that inevitably beset anyone who chooses to engage with rather than to withdraw from the world. The life appropriate to men in this world was thus not repose (however desperately one might long for it) [2] but a constant and morally ambiguous warfare, with the outcome ever in doubt. By the same token earthly life had also to be seen as dynamic, as subject to change in all its aspects. Human communities could be seen to rise, flourish, and decay; and the philological investigations of Renaissance humanists supplemented common experience by revealing the general outlines of ancient civilization and thus demonstrating how much had changed

---

[1] See in general Trinkaus, *In Our Image and Likeness*. On Pomponazzi see also J.H. Randall's introduction to Pomponazzi's *De immortalitate animae*, in *The Renaissance Philosophy of Man*, esp. p. 273; and on Valla, Giorgio Radetti, "La religione di Lorenzo Valla," *Medioevo e Rinascimento : studi in onore di Bruno Nardi* (Florence, 1955), II, 616-17.

[2] Cf. Petrarch, *De ignorantia*, p. 49 : "Shall we never have any respite ? Must this pen always need fight ? Shall we never have a holiday ?... Shall I never find quiet repose by fleeing almost everything for which mankind strives and fervently exerts itself ?... Most avidly craving for peace, I am thrust into war."

during the intervening centuries.[1] They also wrote histories that communicated not only this perspective on the past, with its implication that human culture is not an absolute but relative to its times, but in addition other aspects of the Renaissance vision of life : the active and social nature of man, the values of community, the inescapability of conflict and change.

This vision found its fullest expression in the rhetorical culture of the Renaissance. Humanist oratory was based on the conception of man as a social being motivated by a will whose energies stemmed from the passions. This conception led in turn to a distinctive concern with communication as the essential bond of life in society, as well as to a new human ideal of the well-rounded, eloquent, and thus socially effective man of affairs. The purpose of communication, in this view, could not be the transmission of an absolute wisdom, which the human mind was incompetent to reach, but the attainment of concrete and practical ends. Such communication had above all to be persuasive; it had to affect the will by swaying the passions, rather than merely to convince the mind ; in short it needed to penetrate to the center of the personality in order to achieve results in visible acts. And the significance of the need for persuasion should also be remarked. It implied a life in society that could not be controlled by authority and coercion through a hierarchical chain of command but depended instead on the inward assent of individuals. It was therefore no accident that the rhetorical culture of Italian humanism achieved its fullest development in republics. In addition the needs of broad communication pointed eventually to the development and use of vernacular languages, a more important concern of Renaissance humanism than has sometimes been recognized.[2]

II

It should be immediately apparent that this set of attitudes imposed great strains on traditional Catholicism.[3] It undermined the effort to

---

[1] For an introduction to this aspect of the Renaissance, see the fine piece of Theodor E. Mommsen, "Petrarch's Conception of the 'Dark Ages'," *Speculum*, XVII (1942), 226-42 and Donald R. Kelley, *Foundations of Modern Historical Scholarship* (New York, 1969), esp. ch. 2.

[2] Baron, *Crisis*, esp. pp. 332 ff., and Dufour, p. 58. Dufour emphasizes the concern for vernacular communication as a bond between humanists and Reformers.

[3] On the general point Trinkaus is particularly valuable.

base earthly existence on abstract principles identified with divine wisdom, and to relate the visible and changing world of ordinary experience to the invisible and immutable realm of the spirit. Both the comforts in this relationship and its implications for the guidance and control of lower things by higher were seriously threatened. From a Renaissance perspective the arguments by which it was supported seemed at best frivolous, at worst a specious rationalization of claims to power in this world on behalf of a group of men whose attention should be directed exclusively to the next. And behind such suspicions we may also discern the perception of man as primarily a creature of will and passion. In this light intellectual claims were likely to be construed as masks for motives that could not bear inspection; dogma itself might be no more than an instrument of tyranny. In addition, since a contemplative repose now seemed inappropriate to the actual nature of man, as well as a breach of responsibility for the welfare of others, the ideal form of the Christian life required redefinition. Finally, the problem of salvation was transformed. Alone in an ultimately unintelligible universe, and with the more fundamental conception of sin and the problems of its control opened up by the new anthropology, man could no longer count on the mediation either of reason or of other men in closer contact with the divine than himself. His salvation depended on an immediate and personal relation with God.

Here it is necessary to pause for a more searching look at one of the key terms of our title : *Renaissance*. The conceptions I have so far reviewed have been based largely on developments in Italy, and this would suggest a vision of the Renaissance, or of Renaissance culture, as initially and perhaps primarily an Italian affair. But this audience is well aware that the tendencies I have described were also present in a variety of movements outside Italy, if in somewhat different forms. It is obvious, for example, that later medieval piety exhibited similar impulses; and that, in spite of the antipathy of humanists to scholastic speculation (though here we need to be more precise about what was actually under attack), the later schoolmen played a major if largely independent part in bringing underlying assumptions to the surface and in attempting to accommodate theology to them.[1] Perhaps, therefore,

---

[1] The affinities between Italian humanism and some tendencies in later scholasticism have been recognized by Garin, *L'umanesimo italiano*, pp. 10-11, and *Medioevo e Rinascimento : studi e ricerche* (Bari, 1961).

the time has come to expand, as well as to make more specific, our conception of what was central to the age of the Renaissance, and also to abandon the traditional contrast between Italy and the North, which seems to me to have been in some measure the result of a failure to get beneath surface differences. If I have concentrated on Italian thought in this sketch, I have done so partly to bring out the fundamental unity of European spiritual development, partly because the affinities between Protestantism and later scholasticism have been more regularly a concern of Reformation scholarship than the parallels with the Renaissance in Italy. What is nevertheless increasingly clear is that the process of redefining Christianity to bring it into correspondence with the new assumptions about man and the world was gradual, and that it was taking place simultaneously throughout Europe.

Largely because of the recent profound book of Charles Trinkaus, it is unnecessary to review in detail the process by which the pressures for religious change implicit in the assumptions of Renaissance culture operated among the humanists of Italy. They are already discernible in Petrarch, and they seem to have reached a climax in Lorenzo Valla. In a general sense they may be attributed to the special loneliness and despair of men who could no longer regard religious truth as a body of knowledge of the same order as other knowledge that was communicable through similar kinds of intelligible discourse. Nor could the institutional fideism encouraged by ecclesiastical authority as an alternative to rational theology provide a satisfactory solution to the problem. Not only did the idea of implicit faith clash with the growing sense of individual spiritual dignity among pious laymen; in addition, discredited by its impotence, its worldliness, the presumed irrelevance of its abstract theology, and a sacramental and disciplinary externalism increasingly inadequate to assuage the peculiarly intense guilt of the age, the church could no longer be regarded as a dependable guarantor of truth.

Thus, driven by a profound yearning for immediate contact with the eternal,[1] the humanists of the early Italian Renaissance moved perceptibly toward a simple religion of grace based on the Scriptures and apprehended by the individual through faith. Petrarch typically began with insights into his own inner conflicts and the discovery that these could only be resolved by throwing himself on God's mercy in a faith that was at once the highest form of knowledge and at the same time

---

1 Cf. Heiko A. Oberman, "Some Notes on the Theology of Nominalism, with Attention to Its Relation to the Renaissance," *Harvard Theological Review*, LIII (1960), 47-76.

different in kind from all other knowledge; confusion on this point seemed to him the most dangerous error. Salutati, concerned as a sterner moralist to protect human freedom and responsibility within a religion of grace, wrestled with the problem of predestination. And with Valla justification by faith received an even fuller exploration, the role of priest and sacrament in the economy of salvation was correspondingly reduced, and that of Scripture, the Word whose authenticity could be established by philology and which spoke directly to the individual, was enlarged.[1]

Corresponding to the distinction between philosophy and faith was the demand for a sharper distinction between the church and the world; the separation of realms in one area seemed to lead naturally to separation in others. In its demands for a spiritual church, the new historicism of the Renaissance collaborated with the insistence of the Italian states on freedom from clerical interference and with their grievances against Rome as a political force.[2] The study of the historical church revealed the spiritual costs of the confusion of realms.[3] At the very least, as men of the Renaissance with some political experience were in a position to know, the effective use of power in the world was always morally ambiguous;[4] and meanwhile the growing participation of popes and prelates in secular politics had been accompanied by an increasing neglect of the spiritual mission of the church. Thus, if reform required a return to the past, the reason was above all that the early church had been true to its spiritual character.[5] Only a spiritual church, devoted to that which does not change, could stand above history and thus resist decay. Valla's attack on the Donation of Constantine was not an isolated document;[6] it reflects a concern with the church, its earthly role and its spiritual mission, that runs through much of

---

[1] Trinkaus, I, 40-41, 55, 76, 127, 147; II, 575. On Valla, see also Radetti, pp. 609-10.

[2] On the uses of history, see Walter Ullmann, *Principles of Government and Politics in the Middle Ages* (London, 1961), pp. 228-29.

[3] This is a central conception, for example, in the first part of Machiavelli's *Istorie fiorentine*.

[4] Cf. Guicciardini : "Political power cannot be wielded according to the dictates of a good conscience. If you consider its origin, you will always find it in violence—except in the case of republics within their territories, but not beyond. Not even the emperor is exempt from this rule; nor are the priests, whose violence is double, since they assault us with both temporal and spiritual arms." *Maxims and Reflections of a Renaissance Statesman*, Mario Domandi, trans. (New York, 1965), p. 54.

[5] Cf. Machiavelli, *Discorsi*, Bk. III, ch. 1, on the need for regular revivals in religion.

[6] See Radetti, pp. 610-12.

Rennaissance historiography, from Mussato at the beginning of the fourteenth century to Machiavelli, Guicciardini, and Fra Paolo Sarpi.[1]

The rediscovery of grace was closely related to the new vision of man; philosophy, as Petrarch recognized, was incapable of converting man at the crucial center of his being. "It is one thing to know," he declared, "another to love; one thing to understand, another to will." What was required was a transformation not merely of the intellect but of the whole personality, so that Christian conversion would find appropriate expression in a life of love and active responsibility for the welfare of others. And, as in the world, the essential means for such a transformation was not rational appeal to the intellect but rhetorical appeal to those deeper levels in man that alone could move the will. Thus Petrarch argued for the superiority over rational philosophers of moral teachers who could sow the love of virtue in the very hearts of men.[2] For Valla rhetoric was thus the only branch of secular learning (except for philology) applicable to theology.[3] The implications of this position for the importance and character of preaching seem clear.

A new conception of man was also reflected in a changed conception of God, in accordance, perhaps, not only with Renaissance emphasis on man's creation in God's likeness and image but also with Calvin's recognition of the reciprocal relationship between man's understanding of himself and his knowledge of God.[4] Like man, God could no longer be perceived as a contemplative being, as Aristotle's unmoved mover, operating in the universe not directly but through a hierarchy of intermediate powers.[5] Laymen active in the world required a God who was also active, who exercised a direct and vigilant control over all things, like that to which they aspired for themselves. God too had therefore to be perceived as primarily will, intellectually beyond man's grasp yet revealing something of himself—all, at any rate, that man needed to know—in his actions, above all as recorded in Holy Scripture. And from Petrarch's sense of the free, mysterious, and incalculable nature

---

[1] For Mussato, Manlio Dazzi, "Il Mussato storico," *Archivio Veneto*, Ser. 5, VI (1929), 361; for Machiavelli, see, for example, *Istorie fiorentine*, Bk. I, ch. 1; for Guicciardini, *Storia d'Italia*, Bk. IV, ch. 12; for Sarpi, see my *Venice*, pp. 358 ff.

[2] *De ignorantia*, pp. 103-4.

[3] Hanna H. Gray, "Valla's *Encomium of St. Thomas Aquinas* and the Humanist Conception of Christian Antiquity," *Essays in History and Literature Presented to Stanley Pargellis* (Chicago, 1965), p. 45.

[4] *Institutes*, I, i.

[5] For the point in Valla, see Radetti, p. 616.

of God,[1] Salutati went on to defend the anthropomorphic representations of God in the Bible as a form of communication appropriate to men's capacities.[2] Valla was, as one might expect, even clearer that the God of philosophy could not be the God of faith.[3]

In spite of all this, it is nevertheless undeniable that the culture of the Italian Renaissance did not culminate in Protestantism, although even on this point our old sense of the immunity of Italy to the impulses of the Reformation is no longer altogether tenable.[4] Yet it remains true that the religious thought of Renaissance Italy remained no more than an incoherent bundle of fundamental insights, and it was unable to rid itself of fundamental contradictions; again, however, the contrast with Northern Europe seems hardly absolute. Above all it failed to complete its conviction of man's intellectual limitations, which pushed him only part of the way into the realm of grace, with full conviction of his moral impotence. Even here its vision of man suggests a deepening in the understanding of sin and the human obstacles to salvation; and there is abundant evidence of a pessimistic estimate of the human condition in Petrarch, Salutati, Poggio, Valla, and later, in a different form, in Machiavelli and Guicciardini. Yet Renaissance emphasis on the central importance of the will frequently served chiefly to nourish the moralism that so deeply permeated later medieval piety,[5] contributing both to the notion of Christianity as the pursuit of moral perfection and of the church as essentially a system of government;[6] Renaissance humanism remained, in Luther's sense, Pelagian. The consequence was, however, that Renaissance culture in Italy, like scholastic theology in the north, helped to intensify, from both directions at once, the unbearable tension between the moral obligations and the moral capacities of the Christian that could at last find relief only in either a repudiation of Renaissance attitudes or the theology of the Reformation. But it could not resolve the problem itself, and we must ask why this was so.

---

[1] Trinkaus, II, 768-69.

[2] Baron, *Crisis*, pp. 295-96.

[3] Radetti, p. 616.

[4] For example, George H. Williams, *The Radical Reformation*, (Nashville, 1962) pp. 16 ff., and various works of Delio Cantimori.

[5] Cf. Heiko A. Oberman, *Forerunners of the Reformation* (New York, 1966), pp. 10-12, and Jean Delumeau, *Naissance et affirmation de la Réforme* (Paris, 1968), p. 356, quoting J. Toussaert: "... un Christianisme à 80% de morale, 15% de dogme et 5% de sacraments."

[6] Ullmann, p. 51 and *passim*. Cf. E. Delaruelle, et al., *L'Église au temps du Grand Schisme et de la crise conciliaire* (Paris, 1962), II, 899, 902.

Part of the explanation is connected with the fact that some among the figures we have cited were lacking in theological interests, while the rest were amateurs whose major activity lay elsewhere. The result was an inability to develop the full implications of their assumptions, which was supplemented by prejudice against intellectual labor too closely resembling the scholasticism they despised. In addition, closely attached to particular societies in which, traditionally, no distinction was made between Christianity and citizenship, they were unable to achieve a full sense of the radical disjunction between salvation and civilization that might have placed the Christian man fully in the sphere of grace. Thus they celebrated instead the positive implications of the spark of divinity in man.[1]

Of greater importance were the changing social and political conditions of the later fifteenth century which, at least in Italy, tended to undermine the assumptions underlying Renaissance culture, and thus to remove the sociological pressures for religious change. Foreign invasion and prolonged war produced general insecurity and a growing sense of helplessness, so that freedom presented itself rather as a threat than an opportunity; and the extension of despotism even to Florence reduced the dignity of civic life and encouraged an increasingly aristocratic and stratified social order. Meanwhile the recovery of the Papacy from the long eclipse of the conciliar period brought a vigorous reassertion of the old cosmic intellectuality, of hierarchical principles, and of claims to clerical superiority in the world.[2] The result was a movement of general, if not total, retreat from the ideals of the earlier Renaissance.

The Neoplatonism of later Quattrocento Florence may be taken as an illustration. Although this movement retained and even developed further some of the tendencies I have identified as central to Renaissance culture, what seems to me most significant in Florentine Platonism is not what it had in common with the humanism of the earlier Renaissance but the ways in which it differed.[3] Thus it was spiritually akin to the thirteenth century in its concern to reunite philosophy and

---

[1] Cf. Trinkaus, I, 74-76 (on Salutati's amalgamation of Christianity with civic life), 88-89; and Nicola Abbagnano, "Italian Renaissance Humanism," *Journal of World History*, XI (1963), 278.

[2] See L.D. Ettlinger, *The Sistine Chapel before Michelangelo: Religious Imagery and Papal Primacy* (Oxford, 1965). The development is nicely reflected also in the changing ecclesiology of Eneas Silvius Piccolomini.

[3] In this emphasis I differ somewhat from Kristeller and Trinkaus, though I am deeply indebted to both.

theology; for Ficino philosophy was not merely the handmaid of philosophy but her sister.[1] It also reasserted, if in a modified form, the conception of hierarchy; Ficino provided contemporaries with a Latin translation of Pseudo-Dionysius.[2] And with these conceptions inevitably went also a return to an understanding of man as a duality in which sovereign intellect should rule the contemptible flesh and salvation was held to consist in the separation of the spiritual man from the visible world so that he might enjoy the harmony and peace of intellectual contemplation; Ficino described the task of Christian conversion as "fishing for intellects." [3] The intellectuality here was also reflected in a spiritual elitism based on contempt for the ordinary man who lacked the capacity for such lofty detachment; it also pointed once again to the authority of a body of absolute truths guaranteed by the experts who were alone competent to grasp them.[4] With such an ideal the historical world, the changing realm of conflicting interests, of political and social responsibility, and of the intrinsic dignity of the individual layman, was unworthy of attention.[5] Rhetoric was no longer praised for its utility but denounced as an enemy of truth.[6] For truth had come to present itself in the old way again.

The problem of interpreting Erasmus, as indeed of other northern humanists of his generation, arises from the fact that he appeared on the European scene when conceptions of this kind, by no means confined to Florence, were generally attractive. They provided a resolution of a kind for the religious tensions of the age, at least for intellectuals; and the mind of Erasmus was partly formed by them.[7] The place of Erasmus in any discussion of the relationship between Renaissance and Reformation thus requires some distinctions.

---

[1] Paul Oskar Kristeller, *The Philosophy of Marsilio Ficino* (New York, 1943), p. 322. On the general point cf. Holmes, p. 243.

[2] See Josephine L. Burroughs, in *Renaissance Philosophy of Man*, p. 185. For the modification in the idea of hierarchy, P.O. Kristeller, "Ficino and Pomponazzi on the Place of Man in the Universe," in his *Studies in Renaissance Thought and Letters* (Rome, 1956), p. 286.

[3] Letter to Pico, quoted by Leland Miles, *John Colet and the Platonic Tradition* (London, 1961), p. 7. On the general point, Burroughs, p. 191.

[4] Edgar Wind, *Pagan Mysteries of the Renaissance* (New Haven, 1958), pp. 14 ff.

[5] Eugene Rice, *The Renaissance Idea of Wisdom* (Cambridge, Mass, 1958), pp. 49 ff.

[6] See the letter of Pico Della Mirandola to Ermolao Barbaro, in Breen, *Christianity and Humanism*, pp. 16 ff. On the general point, Seigel, p. 258.

[7] Roland Bainton, *Erasmus of Christendom* (New York, 1969), pp. 59-60.

This is hardly the place to attempt a general interpretation of the complex and ambiguous Erasmus, but he enters so regularly into discussions of the relations between Renaissance and Reformation that we cannot avoid him altogether. As Margolin has reminded us, one needs first of all to understand Erasmus himself; for this purpose it is inappropriate to measure his thought by standards external to it.[1] Yet this is a different problem from the problem of his historical significance; and from the standpoint of those tendencies in Renaissance culture I have been concerned to emphasize here, Erasmus seems to me at least equivocal. Sometimes he attacked the schoolmen in ways typical of the Renaissance, not only shallowly, for the barbarities of their style, but also because the kind of truth they sought to explicate was beyond the legitimate capacities of men and because of the irrelevance of their speculations to the urgent needs of spiritual life;[2] yet in the moment of personal crisis forced on him by Luther, he turned to scholastic theology and rebuked Luther for his sweeping criticism of Aristotle.[3] Nor is it altogether clear that his own *philosophia Christi* (the phrase itself suggests a concern to reunite what earlier humanists had tried to keep apart) was intended simply to reflect the practical reason of the Renaissance; at times he seems to have conceived it as an expression of ultimate wisdom, of the Logos itself.[4] Again, although he often gave eloquent articulation to the lay impulses of Renaissance piety, we must also take into account the elitist tendencies in his insistence on the allegorical meanings of Scripture and his frequent expressions of contempt for the crowd; he attacked Luther for "making public even to cobblers what is usually treated among the learned as mysterious and secret." [5] He liked to represent true Christianity as a religion of the

---

[1] J.C. Margolin, *Recherches érasmiennes* (Geneva, 1969), p. 31.

[2] See the general discussion by Eugene Rice. "Erasmus and the Religious Tradition" *Renaissance Essays*, P.O. Kristeller and P.P. Wiener, eds. (New York, 1968), pp. 175-79.

[3] See Philip S. Watson's introduction to *Luther and Erasmus : Free Will and Salvation* (London, 1969), p. 14. For Erasmus's criticism of Luther's attack on Aristotle, see his letter to Jodocus Jonas, 10 May 1521, *Opus Epistolarum Erasmi*, P.S. and H.M. Allen, eds. (Oxford, 1906-1958), IV, 488.

[4] Cf. Matthew Spinka's introduction to the *Enchiridion*, in *Advocates of Reform from Wyclif to Erasmus* (London, 1953), pp. 285-86; and Heinrich Bornkamm, "Faith and Reason in the Thought of Erasmus and Luther," *Religion and Culture : Essays in Honor of Paul Tillich*, Walter Leibrecht, ed. (New York, 1959), p. 138.

[5] Letter to Jonas, Allen, IV, 487-88.

WILLIAM J. BOUWSMA

heart [1] and defended marriage,[2] but his anthropology tended to the
familiar dualism that opposed the body to the rational soul and made
actions depend on beliefs;[3] such conceptions contributed substantially
to his belief in the value of education.[4] He described the Christian as a
soldier of Christ; but his own ideal, at both the social and personal level,
consisted in harmony and peace.[5] But if I call attention here to the
contradictions in Erasmus, my purpose is not to indict him for what
some have considered one of his more lovable traits, but only to suggest
that we should be cautious in identifying Erasmianism with the Renaissance. Thus the echoes of Erasmus in Zwingli, Bucer, Melanchthon,
and Calvin are not necessarily proof that we are in the presence of
impulses from the Renaissance; the reverse may well be true.

   Nevertheless the ambivalence of Erasmus reminds us again that the
Renaissance posed religious problems that it could not solve. It left man
alone and in desperate need, but without the means or the assurance
of salvation. It pointed to a religion of free grace, perhaps even (as in
Valla) to *sola fide*; but in the end it turned away. Indeed its refusal to
give up the dubious consolations of an intellectual definition of man,
its failure to distinguish between the temporal works of civilization
and the requirements of eternal life, and the strain which this added
to its continuing insistence on human responsibility merely left the

---

   [1] See, for one example among many, his *Paraclesis*, in *Ausgewählte Werke*, Annemarie
and Hajo Holborn, eds. (Munich, 1933), p. 144; here Erasmus expresses the hope that
there should "everywhere emerge a people who would restore the philosophy of Christ
not in ceremonies alone and in syllogistic propositions but in the heart itself and in the
whole life." John C. Olin, trans., in *Christian Humanism and the Reformation* (New York,
1965), p. 99; cf. his letter to Paul Volz, 14 Aug. 1518, Allen, III, 374.
   [2] Cf. his approval of Colet's position on this matter, letter to Jonas, 13 June 1521, in
Allen, IV, 521.
   [3] As with other aspects of Erasmus's thought, it is possible to find the most contradictory passages on this point among his various pronouncements, but it seems to me
difficult to ignore the dualism underlying his influential *Enchiridion;* and it is notable
that although he has much to say about the immortality of the soul, he says remarkably
little about the resurrection of the body. For the dependence of actions on beliefs, see
the adage *Aut fatuum aut regem*, Margaret Mann Phillips, trans., *The Adages of Erasmus*
(Cambridge, 1964), p. 217 : "The first requisite is to judge rightly about each matter,
because opinions are like sources from which all the actions of life flow, and when they
are infected everything must needs be mismanaged."
   [4] Noted by Bornkamm, pp. 135-36.
   [5] Cf. Johan Huizinga, *Erasmus and the Age of the Reformation*. F. Hopman, trans.
(New York, 1957), pp. 119-20; and Bernd Moeller, *Reichsstadt und Reformation* (Gütersloh,
1962), p. 49.

masses of men unusually vulnerable to a spiritual anxiety widely reflected in a heightened sense of sin and a fear of damnation that found no relief. Meanwhile the persistent moralism in Renaissance culture was supplemented by the demands of the church for conformity to external moral and ritual observance as the price of salvation. And as the burdens on the individual conscience grew heavier, so also did the weight of man's anxiety.[1]

Yet I would argue that among the major causes of anxiety on the eve of the Reformation was also the persistence, even in movements that in some respects disowned them, of the deep and by this time ineradicable assumptions of Renaissance culture. As long as Europeans could not come to terms in an explicit theology with the conceptions that remained implicit in their vision of man and the world, as long as the beliefs of the heart remained at war with those of the head, the Renaissance would not be complete. That it required completion was, in a sense, recognized by Erasmus himself in his conviction of the peculiar degree to which the world of his time thirsted for salvation, "by a longing ordained, as it were, by fate." [2]

III

It would be too evidently a work of supererogation to demonstrate at any length the fundamental importance for classical Protestantism of the tendencies I have identified as central to Renaissance culture. I shall therefore offer only a rapid review of the connections between them, and then attempt to deepen the argument of this paper by focusing briefly on two questions that seem to me to reveal in a special way the intimate connections between Renaissance and Reformation : the conception of God and the Protestant solution to the Renaissance problem of anxiety.

Renaissance skepticism, with its sense of the limits of the human understanding, its utilitarian conception of the knowledge appropriate to the human condition, and its clear separation between philosophy and religious belief, found expression in the Protestant insistence that the Scriptures alone communicate what is necessary for salvation. They

---

[1] Cf. Delumeau, pp. 33, 48 ff.; Trinkaus, II, 767-69; Joseph Lortz, *Die Reformation in Deutschland*, (3rd ed.; Freiburg, 1948), I, 11-12; Delaruelle, II, 872-74.

[2] *Axiomata*, in *Erasmi opuscula*, W.K. Ferguson, ed. (The Hague, 1933), p. 337, trans. Olin, p. 149.

place, therefore, a limit on speculation; they reveal God only as he chooses to reveal himself, and only insofar as such revelation is relevant to man's practical needs. Furthermore this revelation is to be grasped not after the manner of earthly wisdom, which often requires peculiar intellectual gifts, but by a unique act of faith from which no man is excluded by the absence of natural capacities or of education. Thus in a practical manner the Renaissance rejection of metaphysics, as it was taken up in Protestantism, finally liberated the individual believer from subjection to theological experts. In this way the Renaissance had prepared the way for the lay religion of the Reformation, with its attention to the spiritual dignity of the individual, a dignity that depended only on the humanity all men possess in common.

The same skepticism also encouraged flexibility in dealing with all practical problems. Metaphysical argument could no longer be exploited to support claims for the absolute superiority of one vocation, one form of government, or one kind of social organization over another. What mattered was the satisfaction of concrete human needs, such as the necessity of political order; Calvin seems to have recognized the political implications of Renaissance laicism in a preference for republican government that allied him not only with Zwingli and Bucer but also with the champions of Renaissance Florence and Venice, but the great Reformers were notably undogmatic about the forms of government.[1] Released from the bondage of metaphysics, the arrangement of this world's affairs could now be fully secular and thus be judged simply on the basis of practical results. The same pragmatism can also be observed in Protestant conceptions of ecclesiastical polity, at least where positive Scriptural prescription was lacking. By the same token wealth appeared neither good nor bad in itself, but only in the manner of its use.

At the same time Protestants generally accepted the new anthropology of the Renaissance. It was fundamental to their definition of sin, whose location chiefly in the lower levels of the personality they decisively rejected. Since the personality was for them a unity, they were clear that every part of it had been vitiated. Luther saw the pursuit of "spiritual values" as a serious temptation,[2] and Calvin attributed the localization of sin in the senses to pagan influence.[3] Man, for the Reformers, was the complex unity of Renaissance thought, but now even

---

[1] Cf. *Institutes*, IV, xx, 8.

[2] *Römerbrief, WA*, LVI, 258-59.

[3] *Institutes*, II, ii, 4.

more sharply defined; the core of his being was certainly not his reason, and indeed even his will responded to deeper impulses. The Reformers tried to convey their meaning here, like some Italian humanists, by frequent references to *the heart*, the mysterious center of the personality, which determines man's beliefs and actions alike. And they shared the conviction of the rhetoricians of the Renaissance that the essential problem of communication lay in penetrating this vital core. Like Renaissance oratory, the gospel had to be conveyed into the hearts of the many rather than into the intellects of the few, for it had to transform lives rather than—merely—to change minds. The living word of Christ was not dialectic but rhetoric.[1]

As in the Renaissance this conception of man was combined with an emphasis on life in society; the existence appropriate for the human condition was not solitary contemplation but rather responsible action among other men; thus the Christian commandment of love complemented the Renaissance sense of social obligation.[2] Similarly Protestantism shared the Renaissance vision of life as conflict and change. The Christian life was dynamic; it was marked by progress towards godliness through temptation, which had therefore to be regarded not as an evil from which men should flee but as God's method of disciplining and purifying the soul. Milton's rejection of a cloistered virtue reflected Reformation and Renaissance simultaneously.

The same dynamism was more broadly reflected in a sense of the importance of historical change. The Reformers shared the Renaissance vision of the past as a decline into Gothic darkness from a better age, and also its hope for renewal; like the humanists, indeed, Calvin associated the decadence of his own time with the decline of literary culture.[3] But there was a larger point here. The God of Protestantism was once again the God of history rather than the author of a static system of metaphysical absolutes; and the destiny of man was no longer per-

---

[1] Melanchthon's esteem for rhetoric is well known, and for Calvin see Breen, "John Calvin and the Rhetorical Tradition," *Church History*, XXVI (1957), 14 ff. But Luther's attitude to rhetoric has received less attention, although he discussed it from time to time in the *Tischreden*, for example 193 (called to my attention by Professor Steven Ozment) and 3528. *WA Tr*, I, 85-86; III, 378.

[2] For Luther see the massive documentation in George W. Forell, *Faith Active in Love : An Investigation of the Principles Underlying Luther's Social Ethics* (New York, 1954). There is a good deal to the point for Calvinism in Michael Walzer, *The Revolution of the Saints* (Cambridge, Mass., 1965), esp. ch. 1.

[3] *Institutes*, III, iv, 7, for example.

ceived as conformity to an ultimate and unchanging general order of things, but as the indefinite realization of his spiritual capacities in time, in accordance with the particular circumstances of concrete existence.[1]

But in none of its dimensions does Reformation theology more clearly reflect the rhetorical culture of the Renaissance than in its conception of God himself. The God of Luther, and even more of Calvin, may be seen as a transcendent expression of the Renaissance ideal of the orator, who, as active and personal governor of all things, supremely unites wisdom and virtue with eloquence, and power with a direct love and concern for his human subjects that is manifested in a desire to communicate to them what their welfare requires and to win their inward assent.[2] In fact, as Luther early remarked, God's works are identical with his words;[3] just as he communicates himself in his Word, so his words, whether through the law by which man is enslaved, or by the gospel which sets man free, actively accomplish his purposes for mankind.[4] Furthermore, as Calvin emphasized, God's discourse is not couched in the timeless abstractions of logic. He appeals rather to the imagination than to the intellect; and in addition, like a skilled orator, he speaks to men in a language adapted to their capacities and their needs, taking historical and cultural differences into account and adapting his communication to the times.[5]

As representatives of the underlying tendencies of Renaissance culture, the great Reformers were also forced to confront the problems raised by the profound anxieties implicit in Renaissance culture, anxieties of which they were deeply aware. Calvin, indeed, was prepared to exploit positively "that religious fear by which we ought to be affected" for its value in driving man to rely on God alone, and he employed his own considerable eloquence in a deliberate effort to intensify it.[6] Not the least of his contributions to the needs of the age was, in addition, a system of both external constraints and inter-

---

[1] For the general point in Luther, see John Headley, *Luther's View of Church History* (New Haven, 1963), and the stimulating suggestions of Gerhard Ebeling, *Luther : An Introduction to His Thought*, R.A. Wilson, trans. (Philadelphia, 1970), pp. 87-88, 161-62.

[2] Headley, p. 2; Trinkaus, "Renaissance Problems in Calvin," pp. 68, 72.

[3] *Dictata super Psalterium*, *WA*, III, 152,

[4] Ebeling, esp. pp. 66-67, 119-21.

[5] *Institutes*, II, viii, 10; II, xi, 13; III, xviii, 9, xxiv, 9; IV, viii, 5-7.

[6] *Institutes*, III, ii, 23. On the general point, Walzer, *passim*.

nalized discipline that supplied a practical substitute for the discredited metaphysical structures that had previously been a source of guidance and comfort.

Yet it was Luther, with his doctrine of *sola fide*, who took the essential step toward dissipating the religious anxiety of the Renaissance. The skepticism of the Renaissance had closed off access to God through the understanding, and its conception of man had radically altered the problem of salvation, which could no longer be conceived as the reduction of the soul to a proper order as the source of meritorious works. Luther accepted these contributions of the Renaissance, but he perceived too their radical implications for the spiritual impotence of man. He was able to do so, as he was later to recall, because, he "learned to distinguish between the righteousness of the law and the Gospel." [1] Thus he was able to distinguish also, as the religious thought of the Renaissance had failed to do, between the civilization of men, in which the will may be adequate, and salvation, in which it is powerless. The result was to eliminate the major impediment to a full acceptance of man's dependence on God's love. Completing the insights of the Renaissance, Luther recognized that the full realization of human freedom depended paradoxically on the complete acceptance of the sovereignty of God, for the work of salvation as well as the words of revelation, which in the end proved identical. He saw that any other conception of freedom resulted only in enslaving men to their own anxieties and, by way of relief, to human ordinations. In this way Luther met the religious needs implicit in the new culture of the Renaissance, and in ways largely consistent with its fundamental assumptions.

---

[1] *WA Tr*, V, 210, 5518.

RENAISSANCE AND REFORMATION

BENGT HÄGGLUND

The word Renaissance was originally only a term in the history of art. It signified the new style in architecture and ornamental art that followed upon the Gothic.[1] Until the middle of the nineteenth century this meaning of the word was dominant. According to the modern use of the term Renaissance, it refers to the whole cultural life of an epoch, to a variety of phenomena in the fields of philosophy, literature, and art.[2]

We could discuss whether it is of any importance at all to compare or contrast on one hand the Reformation that can be relatively firmly defined and is concentrated in the field of religion and theology, and on the other that complex and variegated secular current of culture that we call the Renaissance. The lecture of Prof. Bouwsma has shown us that this question can be answered in the affirmative. He has made the attempt to describe not only the humanism north of the Alps, but also the Italian Renaissance as prehistory and context to the Reformation. Even where the real historical connections are few and thin, the confrontation on the structural level can open new perspectives for our understanding of the Reformation. Against the background of the new understanding of world and of man in the Renaissance our conception of the theology of the Reformation can be clarified on many points.

At this point we might add that our picture of the Renaissance in turn can also be clarified and our interpretation can be deepened through the confrontation with the more comprehensive and more clearly explicated ideology of the Reformation. Parts of the Renaissance literature, that formerly were evaluated on a basis of artistic creations, through a comparison with the Reformation and its view of man and world can be better understood in their inner structure and in ideological context and consequences. The interaction between Christianity and culture here as elsewhere might be a fruitful and important theme in the history of ideas.

---

[1] See e.g. ,"Renaissance," *Allgemeine deutsche Real-Encyklopädie* (Leipzig, 1847), XII.

[2] Cf. George Clarke Sellery, *The Renaissance, Its Nature and Origins* (Madison, 1950).

The main thesis of Prof. Bouwsma's lecture is that the Reformation accepted and developed certain fundamental tendencies in the Renaissance and therefore can be considered as its fulfillment and complement.

This conception presupposes that certain tendencies and ideas in the early Renaissance, among the Italian humanists such as Petrarch and Valla, are considered typical of the Renaissance, but later phenomena, such as the Florentine Platonism or the theology of Erasmus, are described as inadequate lines of development. Their religious ideas are not so much genuine fruits of the Renaissance, as rather a sign that the Renaissance was incapable of solving its own problems adequately. Then the Reformation is interpreted as the real fulfillment of the original tendencies of the Renaissance, the real solution of its problems.

Later I will take up the question whether this theory can be considered tenable. First I believe it useful to point out, that it brings into light some facts that are often overlooked elsewhere : 1) that parallels and related ideas really are to be found in the Italian early Renaissance and the Reformation ; 2) that the new scientific ideal that was expressed in rhetoric may have been of greater importance for the Reformation than has been clarified until now in Reformation research. But instead of continuing these two lines of thought that are drawn up and in an interesting way elaborated in Prof. Bouwsma's lecture, I find it more in accordance with my duty as *Korreferent* to point to such facts and circumstances that call in question the main thesis or argue against it.

First, I should like to give some examples to explain how even in those points where we can find a close connection or relationship on the ideological level, the inner structure of the two currents here compared must be considered to be quite different.

The Spanish philosopher Juan Luis Vives, in his renowned work *De anima et vita*, expounded the new understanding of man in a scientific way. The scholastic concept of higher and lower forces of mind was replaced by an empirical presentation of man as a unity out of an affectual center. We have here a clear parallel to the Lutheran concept of *totus homo*, that in itself is founded on Biblical and theological arguments. However, it can also be considered as a new attempt in psychology, with far-reaching consequences. The similarity between Luther and Vives lies in the area of descriptive psychology. Their deeper interpretation of anthropology shows us quite another picture.[1]

---

[1] Cf. Bengt Hägglund, *De homine : Människouppfattningen i äldre luthersk tradition* (Anthropology in the Earlier Lutheran Tradition), (Lund, 1959), pp. 22 ff.

The same Vives has also written a little "Fable about Man," *Fabula de homine.*[1] In it he tells that the Olympic gods were gathered one day to celebrate the birthday of Juno. After the banquet an amphitheater was arranged and Jupiter ordered a play to be performed as a fitting finale to the celebrations. All the gods as invited guests were the spectators. The stage in the center of the theater was the whole earth, and the play, highly appreciated by the divine spectators, was the history of mankind, all what is done on the earth. Man as the main actor of the play made such an impression on the gods that they invited him to get out of the play and take his place among them and look at the play with them. When night came and supper was ready, man was invited to partake with the gods in the meal and sit down at their table.

It may be of little importance that in this fable Vives speaks only of the Olympic gods and says not a word about the God of the Bible. It is only meant as a symbolic frame and as merely a literary form. The most astonishing feature is that the likeness of god in man is expounded so undialectically and without restrictions. Neither in the drama of the history nor in the afterplay of the drama, the nightly table-fellowship with the gods, is anything said about the power of evil, sin, judgment, or reconciliation.

I have chosen this example presupposing that the fable of Vives can be considered typical of the Renaissance view on man. My question is : Does not this fable with its very clear ideological structure reveal a fundamental difference between the Renaissance and the Reformation at decisive points ?

A second example that I should like to use must perhaps be pursued further. It is borrowed from Florentine Platonism, which Prof. Bouwsma describes as a sideline and not a typical development of the Renaissance. I believe that it is justifiable to compare also this later development of Renaissance philosophy—consequent or not related to an earlier stage—with the Reformation. Only under this condition can the following example contribute to the clarifying of our main question.

In his "Oration on the Dignity of Man" Pico della Mirandola has taken up the old question about what constitutes the specific position of man in relation to other created beings.[2] He sees the particularity of man not in his power over creation but in the possibility of his free

---

[1] Reedited in an English translation in the excellent collection, *The Renaissance Philosophy of Man*, Ernst Cassirer, Paul Oskar Kristeller, and John Herman Randall, Jr., ed. (Chicago, 1948).

[2] *Ibid.*, pp. 223 ff.

choice between different forms of life. He can lead a merely vegetative or animal life, but through rational thinking and spiritual life (*vita intellectualis*) he can also draw near to the Godhead. In this freedom lies a responsibility for man, always to be intent on the highest, disdaining earthly things, striving for the nearness to the Godhead. The patterns which he must follow are the cherubim, the seraphim, and the thrones, who represent the highest forms of intelligence, love, and steadfastness of judgment.

The man who will train himself in these forms of life must listen to the wisdom of the ancient fathers. Also the Biblical authors are taken into consideration here, e.g., the Apostle Paul. But the use the author makes of the Biblical examples is very odd. He refers to the passage where Paul is said to have been exalted to the third heaven. What Pico wants to know is what the cherubim said and did on this occasion. As we know, it is impossible to get any information of this kind in the writings of St. Paul himself. But Pico finds that he can be supplemented on this point by the interpretation of Dionysios the Areopagite in his commentary on the mentioned passage.

Another witness among the ancient fathers is the Patriarch Jacob. In a dream he saw a ladder extending from the earth to the highest heaven and the angels ascending and descending on it. As in the case of St. Paul it is not enough for Pico to take the Biblical author as an example, or to interpret what he has really said. The soul of man can not only look at the sight of the angels or hear the voice of God as Jacob did, but he himself can try to ascend and descend on the ladder that leads to heaven. We can be "companions of the angels going up and down on Jacob's ladder." [1] Through the art of discourse and reasoning the soul can be freed from earthly desires and "inspired by the cherubic spirit." By using philosophy as the steps of the ladder it can reach the felicity of theology, "resting at last in the bosom of the Father who is above the ladder." [2]

Pico describes a man who is wholly free also in spiritual things, in relation to his own salvation and his ultimate destiny, so that he can realize a divine form of life through his own striving and will already on earth. The word of the Psalms : "Ye are all angels and Sons of the Most High" (82, 6) that is used, e. g., by Origen with regard to the last restoration of mankind, Pico also used in his tract on the dignity of man.

---

[1] *Ibid.*, p. 230 ("Oration on the Dignity of Man," 11).

[2] *Ibid.*

But he related it to man already in his life on earth, especially to his freedom of choice.[1]

If it is adequate to take Pico as a representative witness, we may say that an optimistic and idealistic idea of freedom might be characteristic for the Renaissance view of man.

It may be unnecessary to show explicitly how deeply the Reformation view of man is separated from this standpoint. However, this difference or rather contrariety is of great importance, since not only a scientific presupposition is in question, but also the inner structure of theology or theological anthropology.

The contrariety between the Renaissance and the Reformation that has now been underlined is not denied in the lecture of Prof. Bouwsma, but is only hinted at in passing when he describes the theology of the Renaissance as "Pelagian." But in the main the relation between the Renaissance and the Reformation is not seen as a contrariety. Prof. Bouwsma underlines instead such lines of thought in the Renaissance that are more easily put in harmony with the Reformation: the rejection of scholastic philosophy by Lorenzo Valla; the hints about salvation only through the mercy of God; the anxiety of life, supposedly characteristic for the Renaissance.

The question is how much weight we must allot to these tendencies. Are they more than single elements in a greater complex of thought, where the optimistic idea of freedom and moralism (these two belong together) are decisive for the inner structure of the whole way of thinking?

An important question in the lecture of Prof. Bouwsma is the relevance of rhetoric for the Renaissance and for the Reformation. Prof. Bouwsma sees the revival of rhetoric as a manifestation of the deepest tendencies in Renaissance culture. Instead of the dialectics of Scholasticism a new scientific ideal was developed. The solution of practical problems and the appeal to the human will and emotions, through the oral or written word, came to the foreground in the discussion of scientific methods. The rules for language-communication, corresponding to the new anthropology, were elaborated with a new interest.

What importance did rhetoric have for the Reformation? It may not be too bold to say that Luther himself, however much he thought and talked about the question of language-communication, was nonetheless little concerned about the scientific rhetoric of his time.

---

[1] *Ibid.*, p. 227 ("Oration on the Dignity of Man," 6).

In spite of that it can be said, on other grounds, that this discipline and the tendencies that lie behind its new elaboration also played an important role for the Reformation.

Prof. Bouwsma sees the influence of rhetoric in three points : 1) it emphasized the important role of preaching and had certain consequences for homiletics; 2) it had its parallel in the Reformation doctrine of the Word of God; 3) it influenced the concept of God.

It is unquestionable that preaching or at least the theory of preaching during the post-Reformation period was influenced by the study of rhetoric. We find it clearly defined already in the methodologies of preaching from that time. But the question is if this consistent use of rhetoric in preaching can be considered as something typical for the Reformation. The new inspiration for preaching that was connected with the message of the Reformer had another source. A very clear expression of the new motivation for the evangelical preaching that lay in the gospel itself is to be found in the preface to Luther's Wartburg-Postille.[1] The only motive and reason for preaching lies in the mandate of the divine Word to proclaim the message of the gospel. So the adequate form of preaching was at first a simple unrhetorical expounding of the gospel story. Only secondarily, for pedagogic motives, was the methodology of preaching elaborated with the support of rhetorical rules.

Melanchthon, who himself wrote a textbook on rhetoric, ascribes only a rather modest role to this discipline. No one can be a good orator only from an adequate knowledge of rhetoric. Many other presuppositions are necessary for that. The rules of rhetoric, however, are useful to learn as a help for the young students to understand the works of classic authors. Melanchthon defines rhetoric as a purely descriptive discipline and compares it with the scientific description of the different styles and characteristics of the works of art.[2]

More important is another point of view. Prof. Bouwsma says in his lecture : "Like Renaissance oratory, the gospel had to be conveyed into the hearts of the many rather than into the reason of the few, for it had to transform lives rather than...merely...to change minds. The living word of Christ was not dialectic but rhetoric."

According to this, rhetoric should have a direct parallel in the very center of the Reformation theology, namely in the communication of

---

[1] *WA*, X, i, 1, 1 ff.

[2] "Elementorum rhetorices libri duo," 1531, *CR*, XIII, 412 ff.

the gospel as a vivifying word. How far this parallel can be drawn is an important question. At least, it must be underlined that there is also a deep difference that hinders us from identifying the rhetorical point of view with the Reformation doctrine about the efficacious Word. I mean, we have to take seriously the distinction made in the theology of that time between the effect of the divine Word by the preaching of the gospel and the rhetorical persuasiveness of human speech. The strong emphasis on the efficacious Word that is a characteristic of the Reformation might have its main source in what the Bible says about the divine Word, that it is "alive and active" (Heb. 4:12). From this point of view it seems to me that the connections between the rhetoric of the Renaissance and the Reformation doctrine of the Word, if there are any, must be considered as secondary and occasional, while the sources of the ideas are quite different.[1]

The transforming of the human will and motives through rhetorical persuasion and the creating of faith through the preaching of the gospel (cf. Rom. 10 :17) can appear as analogous phenomena. But the question is: Are their different sources and different contexts so decisive that the likeness may be held as only a seeming one ?

Finally, some rather general points of view, taken from the wider context of the history of ideas.

It has been questioned why the Reformation had so little influence in Italy, although the ground there was prepared through the Renaissance. Such a question can perhaps never find its adequate answer. But when we, on the whole, ask about the subsequent history and the effects of the two movements, we shall see that the lines of development lead in quite different directions. In Italy there really arose a religious movement, parallel to the Reformation and spiritually related to the Renaissance, namely Sozinianism. In its theological structure this cur-

---

[1] What J. Huizinga has said with reference to the Calvinistic Reformation and the Renaissance can be transferred with other arguments to the relation between the Lutheran Reformation and the Renaissance : "... dass Inhalt und Richtung von Renaissance und Reformation nur sehr teilweise parallell liefen. ... Die strenge Frömmigkeit, der puritanische Sinn und der heftige Aktionsdrang der Reformierten gegenüber dem ruheverlangenden und manchmal frivolen Indifferentismus der Humanisten machten Reformation und Renaissance viel eher zu Gegensätzen als zu verwandten Äusserungen ein und desselben Geistes." "Das Problem der Renaissance" in *Wege der Kulturgeschichte* (1930), p. 117, quoted by E.M. Janssen, *Jacob Burckhardt und die Renaissance* : *Jacob Burckhardt-Studien* (te Assen bij, 1970), I, 245. His examples, it must be added, are not applicable to the Lutheran Reformation, but his conclusions might be.

rent is far distant from the Reformation, though there are some outer likenesses. In the following centuries the spirit of the Renaissance survives in the humanism of the sixteenth and seventeenth centuries, in the new philosophy of the seventeenth century and then in the Enlightenment. The Reformation for its part has its continuation—perhaps not always ideologically adequate but fundamentally of the same spirit—in the evangelical churches, in the seventeenth century school theology and in Pietism.

May this difference in their later development be an indication that the sources of the Renaissance and the Reformation are also different and that they are separated from each other in a decisive way, if not always in their outer appearance, much more so in their inner structure ?

CONSCIENCE AND AUTHORITY IN LUTHER

BERNHARD LOHSE

A comprehensive treatment of the theme, "Conscience and Authority in Luther," would demand, first, a detailed discussion of conscience, secondly, of authority, and, finally, of the relationship between both. In basing the following expositions on this tripartite division, it must be pointed out immediately that attention will be given in the case of each of these three problems predominantly to those aspects which stand in relation to the over-all theme of the Congress, "Luther and the Beginnings of the Modern Age." Only the most important lines can be traced. In the question concerning authority we shall confine ourselves essentially to Luther's attitude toward the church's authority.

The claim that Luther brought about the end of the Middle Ages and the beginning of the Modern Age has frequently been made by referring to his new conception of conscience. K. Holl called Luther's religion a "religion of conscience" and called special attention to "personal freedom" as well as "personal decision." [1] Beyond this, Luther is said to have elevated "the ethical...to the only valid standard of viewing the world." [2] In his examination of Luther's doctrine concerning conscience, E. Hirsch explicitly took over this definition and defended it against the criticism that had been voiced.[3] In opposition to this, Th. Siegfried,

---

[1] Karl Holl, "Was verstand Luther unter Religion?" *Gesammelte Aufsätze zur Kirchengeschichte* (7th ed. Tübingen, 1948), I (Luther), 35. "Luther's religion is a religion of conscience in the most comprehensive sense of the term." *Ibid.*, 37. "Luther emphasizes all the more strongly that side of religion that - precisely as a religion of conscience - addresses itself to personal freedom and personal decision."

[2] *Ibid.*, I, 41.

[3] Emanuel Hirsch, *Lutherstudien* (Gütersloh, 1954), I, 134, n. 2. "I know of nothing objectionable about Holl's... characterization of Luther's religion as a religion of conscience. Holl's thesis proves itself true in ever new ways on the basis of Luther's own statements concerning conscience." Hirsch's investigation, which also contains an excellent overview of the pre-Luther conception of conscience, is subject to criticism in that, over against Holl, the anthropocentric orientation is made even stronger and the relation of conscience to the Word is de-emphasized. The one-sidedness of Hirsch's interpretation of Luther is especially evident in a statement such as this : "The true end of all discussion concerning

among others, as early as 1930 pointed out that Holl's interpretation of
Luther had moved too closely in the direction of Immanuel Kant [1]
although Siegfried, too, thinks that "with his concept of conscience"
Luther stands "at the decisive turning point from the Middle Ages to
the 'autonomous thinking' " of the Modern Age.[2]

Holl is probably right to the extent that Luther is practically the
"discoverer of conscience." [3] This means that more than any earlier
thinker or theologian Luther viewed man under the aspect of conscience.
Luther means to say that it is impossible to exchange the human existence.[4] However, Luther is not concerned about conscience in the sense
of an individualistic isolation of man.[5] Beyond this, E. Wolf has emphatically maintained that the conscience in man is not something like a
constant substantive core since, if that were the case, Luther's conception of man's sinfulness would be ignored.[6] Hence it dare not be overlooked that Luther does not regard man's conscience as autonomous
but sees it always in relation to something else.

In view of our theme further thought must be given to the fact that
this opposite something is not any kind of authority for Luther. It
would be completely improper to speak of a correlation between conscience and the church's authority. But also the assertion of a confrontation between conscience and Scriptural authority would not yet really
strike Luther's view. He is concerned about the confrontation between
man and God, and when he speaks so pointedly of the conscience he is

---

religious matters (lies in) is subjectivity." *Ibid.*, 210 f. On the contrary, Hirsch stresses the
significance of the Holy Spirit in connection with the gift of peace of conscience, *ibid.*, I,
154.

[1] Theodor Siegfried, *Luther und Kant; Ein geistesgeschichtlicher Vergleich im
Anschluss an den Gewissensbegriff* (Giessen, 1930), p. 23.

[2] *Ibid.*, p. 34.

[3] Rudolf Hermann, *Luthers Theologie. Gesammelte und nachgelassene Werke* (Göttingen, 1967), I, 219, n. 2.

[4] Gerhard Ebeling, "Theologische Erwägungen über das Gewissen," *Wort und Glaube*
(2nd ed.; Tübingen, 1962), p. 432. See also Heinrich Bornkamm, "Äusserer und innerer
Mensch bei Luther und den Spiritualisten", *Imago Dei, Beiträge zur theologischen Anthro-
pologie, Gustav Krüger zum siebzigsten Geburtstage am 29. Juni 1932 dargebracht; im
Auftrage der Theologischen Fakultät Giessen hrsg. von Heinrich Bornkamm* (Giessen, 1932),
pp. 85-109.

[5] Ebeling, *Wort und Glaube*, p. 432.

[6] Ernst Wolf, "Vom Problem des Gewissens in reformatorischer Sicht", *Peregrinatio.
Studien zur reformatorischen Theologie und zum Kirchenproblem* (2nd ed., Munich, 1962),
p. 88.

thinking of man as responsible in the presence of God. The problem of
the mutual relationship between conscience and the church's authority
does not come into view until one sees clearly that God encounters man
in His Word and that this Word reaches man in no other way than
through the medium of human words, that is, Scripture as well as
church. [1]

This fact involves the conclusion that in the case of Luther one can
only speak discreetly of a concept of conscience or a concept of authority. Since Luther has deepened and expanded the understanding of
conscience in an extraordinary way, the conscience and, consequently,
also authority can no longer be inserted into an anthropological design. Rather, conscience is ultimately concerned with man himself.[2] It
is by no means a self-contradiction for Luther to say, on one page, that
the conscience is something greater than heaven and earth,[3] and to
establish, on another page, that the teachings of men, however attractive, collapse and with them the conscience that rests on them; for only
the Word is eternal.[4]

I

In our consideration of conscience it may be useful to look briefly at
the early Luther and consider the most important aspects of his new
formulation of the understanding of conscience.

---

[1] The study of Rupert E. Davies, *The Problem of Authority in the Continental Reformers : A Study in Luther, Zwingli, and Calvin* (London, 1946), does not sufficiently take
these connections into consideration and therefore distorts Luther's stance toward authority.

[2] This is emphasized, among others, by Wolf, *Peregrinatio*, p. 102; Otto Hermann
Pesch, *Theologie der Rechtfertigung bei Martin Luther und Thomas von Aquin : Versuch
eines systematisch-theologischen Dialogs* (Mainz, 1967), p. 36. Günter Jacob, *Der Gewissensbegriff in der Theologie Luthers* (Tübingen, 1929), pp. 6 and 8, correctly states that Luther
sees conscience in "existential correlations" like *lex-conscientia, mors-conscientia, Satan-
conscientia, and Verbum (Christus)-conscientia.*

[3] See, for example, *WA*, XLIV, 546, 30-31 (Lectures on Genesis, 1535-1545). *LW*, VII,
332, "Conscience is something greater than heaven and earth. It is killed by sin and
quickened through the Word of Christ."

[4] *WA*, X, iii, 172, 19-24 (Sermon, 1522). "The teachings of men, no matter how beautiful, will collapse as will also the conscience resting on them. There is no help or escape.
But the Word of God is eternal and must stand forever. No devil, etc., can demolish it.
This is the foundation that must be provided for the consciences, in order that they may
for ever be founded upon it, rest on it and maintain themselves."

Since the days of high scholasticism a distinction had been made on the basis of earlier linguistic usage between *synteresis* and *conscientia* in connection with what we call conscience.[1] In general, *synteresis* was regarded as an ability of the soul, not entirely corrupted by the fall, to incline toward the good, whereas *conscientia* makes practical application of the principles of *synteresis*. Whether, following Thomas and Duns, *synteresis* is primarily associated with reason or, following Bonaventure, with the will, or whether it is regarded as a *habitus*, as Thomas did, or as a *potentia*, as Biel did,[2] makes little difference. In any case the basic design remained the same.

It is true that in the late Middle Ages the trials (*Anfechtungen*) experienced by the mystics could no longer be fitted into the design created by high scholasticism. It was especially the orientation of the idea of conscience to the Law which led to extreme tensions with men like Eckhart, Tauler, and Gerson,[3] who was particularly important for Luther. These tensions were, however, not resolved by a basically new conception of conscience. On the contrary, they threw the problems of the scholastic conception into bold relief.

Luther accepted the scholastic distinction between *synteresis* and *conscientia* and although he no longer used the term *synteresis* in later years, he did not reject what it was meant to express.[4] The fact that a man senses both in his reason and in his conscience [5] that he is not what

---

[1] For the scholastic understanding of *synteresis* and *conscientia* see, in addition to E. Hirsch, especially Heinrich Appel, *Die Lehre der Scholastiker von der Synteresis* (Rostock, 1891); Heinrich Appel, "Die Synteresis in der mittelalterlichen Mystik", *Zeitschrift für Kirchengeschichte*, XIII (28 January 1893), 535-44; Ernst Wolf furnishes a concise overview, s.v. "Gewissen", *RGG* II, col. 1550-1557; see also Yrjö J.E. Alanen, "Das Gewissen bei Luther", *Annales Academiae Scientiarum Fennicae*, B XXIX (1934), 2.

[2] Hirsch, p. 48; Heiko A. Oberman, *Spätscholastik und Reformation; Der Herbst der mittelalterichen Theologie*, (Zürich, 1965), I, 64-65.

[3] Hirsch, pp. 84 and 155, n. 3.

[4] Lennart Pinomaa, *Der existenzielle Charakter der Theologie Luthers* (Helsinki, 1940), pp. 46-47, affirmed that Luther in the process of his lectures on Romans, 1515/16, moved from a cautious recognition of *synteresis* to a flat rejection. Pinomaa said the reason was that *synteresis* bore a Pelagian stamp. Wolf, pp. 86-87, n. 12, had aligned himself with this view. In opposition, and rightly so, Hirsch, p. 121; also Bernhard Lohse, *Ratio und Fides. Eine Untersuchung über die ratio in der Theologie Luthers* (Göttingen, 1958), pp. 46-47, n. 6.

[5] According to Luther there is a certain parallelism between reason and conscience; cf. p. 166, n. 2. Yet conscience is the larger concept. Siegfried, p. 36, correctly states: " '*Conscientia*' is broader than experience. It is related to limits which are not located in experience itself and yet determine the experience of *conscientia*." - At this place we have translated the concept "*synteresis*" with "conscience"; see also Alanen, p. 30.

he should be applies to every one, according to Luther.[1] The desire for
the good is inextinguishable in man.[2] It is self-evident that beyond this
Luther, in his early years as well as later, knows and shares the customary usage, namely that because of certain actions a person reproves
himself in his conscience or, on the other hand, has a good conscience.[3]

Nevertheless, it is noteworthy that already in Luther's first lectures
on the Psalms the essential approaches to a new view of conscience are
discernible. E. Hirsch has shown "that for Luther the conscience is the
origin or place of the strongest emotions and emotional manifestations."
This is given expression in the manifold statements that, for example,
the conscience is disturbed, is afraid, is timid, trembles or quakes or is
desperate.[4] The enormous concentration of theological statements on
the theme of judgment and Gospel have the result that in a hitherto
unknown measure man is directed to his sinfulness. And the conscience
is the place where man becomes aware of his sinfulness and his implication in guilt, and where at the same time man must accuse himself.[5]

Luther arrived at this new understanding of conscience not only
exegetically but also on the basis of his own trials. The statements of the
old Luther concerning the trials before his reformatory break-through as

---

[1] *WA*, LV, II 1, 113, 4-7 (= *WA* III, 94, 17-19, Schol., Ps. 10: 5). "Because no one is so
evil but that he feels the murmur and prodding of reason, according to the saying, 'Reason
always turns away toward the best things.' And that interpretation is very attractive."

[2] *WA*, III, 238, 11-13 (Schol., Ps. 41: 8). "There is such a natural desire in human
nature, because the prodding and desire for the good is inextinguishable in man, though
impeded in many."

[3] So, for example, *WA*, LVI, 23, 24-24, 11 (marginal gloss, Rom. 2 :15). "Any man's
conscience (as long as it is not erring or neglected by too much contempt) bites and mur-
murs when he has done wrong and is quiet when he has done well. Thence also Cicero :
'The conscience of a well-lived life is the most delightful recollection.' This is why, on the
contrary, reproof comes from those thoughts, so that they might know what to do and not
do, i.e., the law."

[4] Hirsch, p. 130.

[5] *WA*, III, 499, 9-15 (Schol., Ps. 73 :5). "All of these things however (namely v. 5 : 'And
they did not know, as in the exit at the upper level'), are done best tropologically, if they
are done : So that a man may become ignorant and set up his signs for signs (that is, his
sins) and go out from his own estimation from above, from his pride, or at the upper level,
so that he may seem to himself to be the chief sinner, just as they regard themselves as the
chief saints, which I leave to be done from the preceding, because this can easily happen.
That a man may set his own sins before him in his conscience and accuse himself concerning the things they have done in his heart, all those evils which are written in this
psalm." On this passage see also Werner Jetter, *Die Taufe beim jungen Luther. Eine
Untersuchung über das Werden der reformatorischen Sakraments - und Taufanschauung*
(Tübingen, 1954), p. 234.

well as concerning the inadequacy of the counsels given him ¹ reproduce
Luther's later insights in view of his sharp critique of scholasticism. Yet
as far as the distress of conscience as such is concerned, Luther's own
experiences are here given substantive expression just the same.

Viewed formally, Luther's new exegesis as well as his personal trials
lead to the result that he no longer delimits *synteresis* and *conscientia*
against each other,² but combines them and now sees in conscience the
place where man learns what and who God is.³ Thus conscience becomes
a basic concept in Luther's theological anthropology. If in the period
before Luther conscience was not really understood in a religious sense,
already in his lectures on Romans (1515/1516) he says that it is the
conscience which shatters man in the presence of God or gives him hon-
or.⁴ A little later Luther labels conscience, in a way similar to the heart,
the innermost part of man.⁵

Hence conscience is not, at least not primarily, an organ of ethical
consciousness which rules on the right or wrong of man's action, but it
is the "bearer of man's relationship to God." ⁶ In his conscience man
experiences his culpable inadequacy before God, recognizes God's punish-

---

¹ Of the many sources we mention only a few. Otto Scheel, *Dokumente zu Luthers
Entwicklung* (2nd ed.; Tübingen, 1929), p. 92, 11-13. Cf. *LW*, XII, 304 (= *WA*, XL, ii,
317, 2-4, Enarr., Ps. 51, 1532). "But they have persuaded themselves thus : If your
conscience bothers you, put on the cowl, fast, and go to St. James, and by these things
they wished to please God." Scheel, p. 55, 7-11, (*WA*, XXXIV, I, 35, 14-36; Sermon, 4 1531)
" Thou shalt love God altogether' (Matth. 22: 37). But I and others have risked our body
and life, have been serious about it, have given no thought to wife, goods, and honor.
And there were others who tried, but what happened ? I remained in a terrified and
despondent conscience, and it was the same with others. They worked hard, but nothing
came of it." See also Scheel, pp. 182, 20-21; 53, 30-32; 124, 21-23; 131, 16-17; 50, 2. *WA*,
XL, iii, 630, 1-2. "Therefore I cannot be an idle witness as to what a bad conscience is
and what this executioner, the Law, can do in the conscience." See also Bernhard Lohse,
"Die Privatbeichte bei Luther," *Kerygma und Dogma*, XIV (1968), 207-28.

² Hirsch, p. 127.

³ Ebeling, "Elementare Besinnung auf verantwortliches Reden von Gott", *Wort und
Glaube*, p. 367.

⁴ *WA*, LVI, 526, 31-32 (Schol., Rom. 15: 20): "It is the conscience which either shatters
man before God or gives him honor." Cf. already *WA*, III, 231, 14-15 (Schol., Ps. 40,2).
"It is in the conscience alone that the soul is at peace or disturbed, because of grace or
because of guilt."

⁵ *WA*, V, 525, 11-13 ("Operationes in Psalmos," 1519-21) : "What, then, is our lantern
which enlightens with this light of the Word ? Without a doubt it is our heart, and it
makes no difference whether you call it conscience or intellect."

⁶ Hirsch, pp. 127-28.

ment, and is therefore attacked.[1] In this connection ultimately it makes
no difference whether Luther says that this attack comes on the basis
of the knowledge of the Law which is written in the hearts of all men,[2]
or whether he says that God Himself "tickles" the conscience,[3] and thus
causes man distress. The concentration of the anthropological statements on conscience *coram Deo* even leads Luther to reshape the traditional doctrine concerning purgatory and to maintain that hell itself
may now be experienced in trial (*Anfechtung*).[4] Since man in his conscience is exposed to the judging and punishing God, it must be said that
for Luther man does not have a conscience but is conscience.[5]

As radical as Luther's new comprehension of the attacked conscience
is, so far-reaching is also the transformation of what Luther understands
a good conscience to be. Apart from the fact that the old Luther can also
speak of a good conscience in the idiomatic sense, and if one understands conscience in a strictly theological sense, it must be said that
Luther identified a good conscience with faith. For the first time this
equation is found in its full rigor in the Heidelberg Disputation of 1518;
here it becomes evident at once that Luther understands a good conscience to be the proper confidence in God.[6] In ever new formulations

---

[1] *WA*, X, i, 2, 171, 2-5 (Advent Postil, 1522): "As long as these two are in the heart,
awareness of sin and recognition of God's punishment, the conscience must constantly be
sad, timid, and frightened, and worry every moment that God is standing behind the
person with the club."

[2] See, for example, *WA*, LVII, i, 27, 14-18 (marginal gloss, Rom. 2 :15) : "The sense
of this, that their conscience and their thoughts accuse or excuse them, is that they
clearly show and demonstrate that they know the work of the Law, even though they
might not have it written in codices or have heard it with their ears. If they did not know
it, they could not have been accused by the conscience for doing evil or quieted for doing
well."

[3] *WA*, XIV, 152, 9-10. (Sermon on Genesis, 1523/24): "There God tickles the conscience
of Adam and Eve."

[4] On this see, for example, the obviously autobiographical report, *WA*, I, 557, 33-558,
18; *LW*, XXXI, 129 ("Explanations of the Ninety-Five Theses", 1518), especially the
discussion of the experience of eternal punishment, *WA*, I, 558, 2-3, 13-15; *LW*, XXXI,
129-30.

[5] Ebeling, p. 440.

[6] *WA*, I, 372, 34-42 (Heidelberg Disputation, 1518). *LW*, XXXI, 67 : "Nevertheless,
faith in Christ is a good conscience, as Peter says : 'As an appeal to God for good conscience' [I Pet. 3 :21], that means that it thoroughly confides in God. If therefore a work
without faith were not a mortal sin, it would follow that Paul would greatly concern himself with a venial sin, which is false, since no one can live without venial sin. Therefore,
everything that does not proceed from faith is a mortal and damnable sin, because it is

Luther gives expression to this thought. So he says, for example, that the conscience is liberated under the rule of Christ,[1] or that the kingdom of Christ is a kingdom of good consciences,[2] or that deliverance from evil conscience is achieved only when one obtains a gracious God.[3] In order to reach this goal conscience must be completely severed from the Law with which it is by nature associated.[4] Only the *extra nos* leads to this deliverance. In his late lectures on Galatians Luther says : "Our theology is certain because it places us outside ourselves : I may not rely on my conscience, my personal feeling, my work, but on the divine promise, the truth which cannot deceive." [5]

So it is the strict distinction between the *coram Deo* and the *coram hominibus* that leads to Luther's new conception of conscience. At this instance Luther's understanding of conscience agrees with all of the central themes of his reformatory theology, namely with the doctrine of justification, the distinction between Law and Gospel, the doctrine of the two kingdoms, or the distinction between the two governments of of God.

In our present context these relations to the other problems in Luther's theology cannot be examined. However, we must still note several aspects in Luther's understanding of conscience. In the first place, the

---

also contrary to conscience, the conscience, I say, of faith in Christ. For he does not believe that he pleases God in order thereby to merit something, and nevertheless he acts in such lack of faith and according to his conscience."

[1] *WA*, VII, 241, 1-2 (Sermon on the Day of the Three Kings, 1521).

[2] *WA*, VII, 759, 26-28 ("Ad librum... Ambrosii Catharini," 1521) : "Faith in Christ and the kingdom of good consciences, which Christ calls the kingdom of God, the kingdom of the heavens, the kingdom of truth."

[3] *WA*, X, I, 2, 171, 17-24 (Advent Postil, 1522) : "But how does one get rid of a bad conscience and obtain a gracious God ? Answer :... whoever desires to have a good conscience and to find a gracious God must not begin with works..., but he must despair of himself in all works and lay hold of God in Christ, grasp the Gospel and believe what it promises."

[4] *WA*, XXV, 249, 37-40 (Lectures on Isaiah, 1532-34): "But as far as heaven is distant from the earth, so far must we separate the Law from conscience. For in the conscience the Law can do nothing but terrify, increase sin, and kill. Therefore the realm of conscience pertains to grace alone."

[5] *WA*, XL, i, 589, 8-10 (Lectures on Galatians, 1531) : "Ideo nostra theologia est certa, quia ponit nos extra nos : non debeo niti conscientia mea, sensuali persona, opere, sed in promissione divina, veritate, quae non potest fallere." Only from the perspective of the freedom of conscience understood in this way is the well-known statement intelligible : *WA Br*, 2, no. 424, 84-85. "Sin boldly, but rely more strongly on Christ and rejoice in Him, who is the victor over sin, death, and the world."

deepening and sharpening in the definition of conscience in natural man make it possible for Luther to pass the most rigorous judgments on conscience. Similar to the reason of natural man, so also conscience can be called a *mala bestia* by Luther, because it has the result that man stands in opposition to himself and always sinks into more severe trials.[1] Again, as in the case of reason, it can be said also of conscience that it is killed by sin and is made alive again through the Word of Christ.[2] These assertions make it impossible to see anything in conscience that can ultimately maintain itself in the midst of experiencing judgment and grace. On the contrary, they call attention to the rupture that exists between the natural man and the pardoned man, without permitting us to understand this rupture in a pietistic sense as a one-time act of conversion.

Furthermore, it is astonishing that in spite of these harsh statements about conscience Luther can still say occasionally that the good conscience, which the Christian obtains in faith, is important for his works, yes even for his certainty about his own call. Even though such utterances are comparatively rare in Luther,[3] they nevertheless make clear that the rejection of work righteousness and the conquest of a frightened conscience have nothing to do with indifference toward the works which

---

[1] *WA*, XLIV, 545, 16-17 (Lectures on Genesis, 1535-45). *LW*, VII, 331 : "Conscience is an evil beast which makes a man take a stand against himself." On Luther's sharp judgments concerning reason see Lohse, *Ratio und Fides*, pp. 70-71, 90.

[2] *WA*, XLIV, 546, 30-31; *LW*, VII, 332 : "Conscience is something greater than heaven and earth. It is killed by sin and quickened through the Word of Christ." For corresponding statements on conscience see *WA*, XL, i, 362-63; *LW*, XXVI, 228 (Galatians Commentary, 1535) : "But faith slaughters reason and kills the beast that the whole world and all the creatures cannot kill." Further sources in Lohse, *Ratio und Fides*, p. 90, n. 6.

[3] *WA*, VI, 205, 9-13 (Concerning Good Works, 1520). *LW*, XLIV, 24 : "Now that is not faith, nor is it a good conscience toward God; therefore, their works are pointless and their life and goodness all amount to nothing. This is the reason that when I exalt faith and reject such works done without faith they accuse me of forbidding good works. The fact of the matter is that I want very much to teach the real good works which spring from faith."

The disputation on Luke 7 :7 (1535) is especially clear. *WA*, XXXIX, i, 131, 41-42, Thesis 57 : "That also good works make our calling and election sure, because they are a witness of true faith." Also, *WA*, XXXIX, i, 292, 10-12 ("Zirkulardisputation de veste nuptiali," 1537) : "It is true that works certify to us and testify before men and brothers and even to ourselves that we truly believe and are children of God in hope and heirs of eternal life." *WA*, XXXIX, II, 248, 13 (Promotionsdisputation Hieronymus Nopp... 1543). "We are commanded to make our calling sure through good works."

are also assigned to the Christian.[1] Luther can even go so far as to speak of a good conscience in view of the last judgment, a conscience which may be had by one who has faithfully and honestly performed his service of proclamation.[2]

Again, throughout his life Luther was aware of the linguistic usage that a man must be concerned about having a good conscience in the secular realm and also that essentially he is in a position to live up to the demands made on him in this area.[3] Although we cannot develop this thought further, we must at least mention it.

Finally, beyond the personal realm conscience is of special significance also for the entire area of political responsibility. However, this complex too we cannot explore. Nevertheless, we want to emphasize that talk about the "unpolitical Luther" in no sense does justice to the practical attitudes of the Reformer. [4] Luther expressed himself for the sake of his conscience not only when he dealt with questions of the right of resistance,[5] but also in countless cases he appealed to his conscience when by word and deed he intervened in various affairs and addressed himself to princes in exactly the same way as to the common man.[6] For the total area of conscience and authority also these questions themselves would be significant.

---

[1] On this see especially Ole Modalsli, *Das Gericht nach den Werken*; *Ein Beitrag zu Luthers Lehre vom Gesetz* (Göttingen, 1963).

[2] *WA*, XL, ii, 154, 17-22 (Commentary on Galatians, 1535). *LW*, XXVII, 120 : " 'On that day, when God judges the secrets of men (Rom. 2 :16), the testimony of your conscience will stand either for you or against you : against you if you have your boast in others; for you if you have it in yourself, that is, if your conscience bears testimony to you that you have carried out the ministry of the Word properly and faithfully, with a concern only for the glory of God and the salvation of souls, in other words, that you have done your duty rightly." See also *WA*, VII, 232, 1 f. ("Quaestio, utrum opera faciant ad justificationem," 1520), Thesis 13. "Faith diminishes conscience in sins and increases conscience in merits."

[3] *WA*, XXXVI, 363, 10-16 (Sermon, 1532). "Behold, every Christian should also have such a reputation and boldness to live in relation to every one and to practice and manifest his love in such a way that no one could bring an accusation against him... That is a good conscience for people or against people."

[4] This has been emphatically noted by Kurt Aland, "Martin Luther als Staatsbürger," *Kirchengeschichtliche Entwürfe; Alte Kirche, Reformation und Luthertum, Pietismus und Erweckungsbewegung* (Gütersloh, 1960), pp. 420-51, especially p. 450.

[5] See, for example, Luther's remark on the federation plan of Philip of Hesse, in a letter to Elector John, 18 November 1526, *WA Br* V, No. 1496, 9-10. "For in our conscience we can neither approve nor advise such an alliance."

[6] On this see Aland, p. 427. Also Hermann Dörries, "Das beirrte Gewissen als Grenze

Since we are here restricting ourselves to the relationship between conscience and the church's authority, we shall now, in summary, discuss the definition of freedom of conscience which Luther furnished in his essay On Monastic Vows (1521) : [1]

> Christian or evangelical freedom, then, is a freedom of conscience which liberates the conscience from works. Not that no works are done, but no faith is put in them. For conscience is not the power to do works, but to judge them. The proper work of conscience (as Paul says in Romans 2:15-20), is to accuse or excuse, to make guilty or guiltless, uncertain or certain.

This definition states that the conscience is extremely important for justification. Where man seeks self-justification on his own and in the process succumbs to pride or despair, then the conscience of the justified man is liberated from slavery under the Law. Therefore, to the extent that it is bound to Christ,[2] his conscience can distinguish between condemnation and man's pardon and thus makes faith certain.[3] Like the human will, so also conscience is bound either to the devil or to God.[4]

---

des Rechts : Eine Juristenpredigt Luthers," *Wort und Stunde* (Göttingen, 1970), III, 271-326.

[1] *WA*, VIII, 606, 30-35; cf. *LW*, XLIV, 298 ("Judgment on Monastic Vows," 1521): "Est itaque libertas Christiana seu Evangelica libertas conscientiae, qua solvitur conscientia ab operibus, non ut nulla fiant, sed ut in nulla confidat. Conscientia enim non est virtus operandi, sed virtus iudicandi, quae iudicat de operibus. Opus eius proprium est (ut Paulus Roma. 2 ait) accusare vel excusare, reum vel absolutum, pavidum vel securum constituere."

[2] *WA*, VIII, 609, 40-41; *LW*, XLIV, 303-4 : "The conscience belongs to Christ and Christ to the conscience." In a substantively similar manner Luther expresses himself already in his lectures on Romans, *WA*, LVI, 204, 24-25 (Schol., Rom. 5 :12) : "God is the defender, the heart is the accuser."

[3] Luther repeatedly stated that it was his real task to make consciences certain. *WA*, VIII, 668, 26; *LW*, XLIV, 399 ("Judgment on Monastic Vows," 1521). Luther had written this document to "raise up consciences to stand before God with confidence and make them safe and sure." *WA*, XVIII, 749, 20-23 ("De Servo Arbitrio", 1525): "I believe you (namely, Erasmus) that you regard the certainty of Holy Scripture as of no consequence, and therefore such arbitrary interpretation would be quite acceptable to you. But for us who labor to make the consciences firm nothing can be more troublesome, nothing more harmful, nothing more destructive than this dexterity."

[4] See, for example, *WA*, XV, 426, 27-29 (Sermon, 1524) : "The heart and conscience must have a word, either good or bad. Thus the conscience, either good or bad, trusts either in God or the opposite. There is no middle ground, where the conscience would have neither God nor the devil."

II

Turning now to Luther's critique of the church's authority, we must stress, first of all, that Luther gained his new conception of conscience during the first years of his Wittenberg labors without being aware of an opposition to ecclesiastical authority and without using his understanding of conscience to attack the authority of the church in any way. Hence for the complex, "Luther on Conscience and Authority", this true, as has already been observed for numerous other aspects of his new reformatory theology. In this connection the controverted question about the time of Luther's reformatory break-through is of little importance, for at the beginning of the indulgence controversy it might appear that Luther's conception of conscience need not necessarily have led him into opposition to Rome.

The young Luther, it is true, often sharply criticized certain theological developments of the last centuries before the Reformation. Also, it seems, that in his early years Luther expressed himself comparatively seldom on the question of the church's authority. Besides this, one must affirm, that in general Luther is stirred by questions completely different from those having to do with the church's authority. But even up to about 1517/1518 his extant statements on the church's authority do not as yet indicate the impending rupture.

In his first lectures on the Psalms Luther emphasizes somewhat that God has not bound the spirit of the Law to the letter, on which heretics rely, but to the superiors in their offices and service; otherwise everyone would be his own master.[1] Or he warns against heretics who have their own understanding of Scripture and in that way wrongfully arrogate authority to themselves.[2] He is convinced that Peter was the first among the apostles and churches. He criticizes the Bohemians for

---

[1] *WA*, III, 579, 1-7 (Schol., Ps. 77:25). "God did not put the Spirit of the Law in letters written on paper, in which the heretics put their trust, but in men placed over offices and ministries, so that they are held responsible. Otherwise, what would be easier for the devil than to seduce him who rejects the ministry of a man and counts on being his own master in the Scriptures? One word badly understood can bring confusion into the whole Scripture."

[2] *WA*, IV, 436:33-37 (Marginal gloss, Ps. 139:6). "This is the most destructive kind of deception, namely to stretch the Holy Scriptures through improper glosses and turn them into a lie, so that because of such great authority the lie becomes believable. For thus all heretics rest not only on their reason (although they start from there and at first set up what their own reason suggests), but also on the Scriptures; in such a way, however, that they stretch the Scriptures to conform to the figments of their reason."

espousing divergent teachings about the sacraments and the Papacy.[1]
Also in his lectures on Romans he occasionally defends the authority of
the church as it subsisted in the Roman church at that time.[2] Here too
he turns against heretical presumption. In a sermon of 1516 he stated
that Christ transferred his entire authority to one man, namely Peter;
otherwise there would be no perfect *ordo* and every one could, like the
heretics, claim he himself had the Holy Spirit.[3] Finally, in the *Decem
Praecepta* of 1518 there is a sentence which still sounds fully Catholic,
that the church cannot err.[4] One can say with certainty that until the
onset of the indulgence controversy Luther regarded "faith in Christ
and faith in authority" as "self-evidently" still "completely in each
other." [5] At the same time it must be stressed that on the basis of his
new theology of the Word Luther understands the church not in institutional but in functional terms.[6]

Since Luther had already promoted his new theology for several
years, it seems at first glance coincidental that the indulgence controversy led to a confrontation between him and ecclesiastical authority. For a while Luther still thought that the pope was essentially on
his side. Luther expressed this opinion in the letter to the pope which he
affixed to the "Resolutions Concerning the Theses on Indulgences" of
1518. In this letter Luther subjects himself to the verdict of the pope

---

[1] *WA*, IV, 169, 25-26 (Marginal gloss, Ps. 103 : 17) : "Is (this passage) perhaps thinking
of Saint Peter as the head of the apostles and the churches ?" *WA*, IV, 345, 24-25 (Schol.,
Ps. 118: 79)... "So also with the Bohemians concerning the sacraments and the rule of
the Roman church." See also Bernhard Lohse, "Luther und Huss," *Luther-Zeitschrift
der Luthergesellschaft*, XXXVI, (1965), 108-22.

[2] *WA*, LVI, 423, 13-14 (Schol., Rom. 10 :14) : "Thus therefore the church's authority
was established, as the Roman church still holds it : They preach securely who preach
the Gospel without other vices." Note also the context of the passage.

[3] *WA*, I, 69, 11-16 (Sermon on 1 August 1516) : " 'Whatever you shall bind on earth,
etc.' (Matth. 18 :18). Unless Christ had given all His power to a man, there would not
have been a perfect church because there could have been no order, since anybody might
wish to say that he was touched by the Spirit. This is what the heretics did, and thus
anybody might set up his own rule and there would be as many churches as heads. Thus
He wants to exercise no authority except through a man and given to a man, so that He
might gather all into one."

[4] *WA*, I, 444, 17-18 (Ten Commandments, 1518). "The church cannot err."

[5] Rudolf Mau, *Der Gedanke der Heilsnotwendigkeit bei Luther* (Berlin, 1969), p. 54, in
connection with the lectures on Romans.

[6] See also Mau, p. 55. For the early period see, for example, *WA*, IV, 81, 12-13 (Schol.,
Ps. 91 : 7) : "The church as the work and creature of Christ does not publicly appear to be
anything, but its entire structure is inward, before God, invisible."

and states that he would acknowledge the pope's voice as the voice of Christ.[1] But when Luther says in the same letter that he could not recant,[2] it is evident at this point that he does not yet see how much the authority of the church and his own decision have diverged. Essentially even at that time the two positions were no longer reconcilable.

In the discussions of the following years Luther again and again appealed to his conscience and emphasized at the same time that he was concerned about properly instructing consciences. For example, in the fall of 1518 Luther humbly begged Cardinal Cajetan to deal gently with him, to have sympathy with his conscience, and to provide him with a better explanation of the controversial issues than he had up to this time received for he had the witness of his conscience and he could not deviate from it.[3] At the Leipzig Debate in the summer of 1519 the central issue was the problem of the church's authority.[4] Here Luther stated publicly for the first time that pope and councils may err and that several of Hus' articles were genuinely evangelical.[5]

The criticism, which Luther leveled at the church's authority in Leipzig and subsequently, was basically limited to the question whether the church had the authority to establish new articles of faith. The acrimony of the debate in the next years did not always show clearly that Luther criticized the church's authority only in this precisely

---

[1] WA, I, 529, 22-26 : "Therefore, most holy Father, I lay myself at the feet of your Blessedness with all that I am and have. Give me life, kill me, call me, recall me, approve, disapprove, as you please : I shall acknowledge your voice as the voice of Christ dwelling and speaking in you. If I have deserved death, I shall not refuse to die."

[2] WA, I, 529, 3 : "I cannot recant." The letter to the pope from which this and the previous citation is taken may probably be dated shortly before 30 May 1518. Cf. WA Br, I, No. 78.

[3] WA, II, 16, 7-12; LW, XXXI, 274-75 ("Proceedings at Augsburg," 1518) : "(...) I humbly beg your most reverend highness to deal leniently with me, to have compassion with my conscience, to show me how I may understand this doctrine differently, and not to compel me to revoke those things which I must believe according to the testimony of my conscience. As long as these Scripture passages stand, I cannot do otherwise, for I know that one must obey God rather than men [Acts 5 :29]." Cf. also a few lines farther : "I do not want to be compelled to affirm something contrary to my conscience..."

[4] Leif Grane, "Die Anfänge von Luther's Auseinandersetzung mit dem Thomismus," Theologische Literaturzeitung, XCV (April 1970), col. 241-50, 248. In col. 246 Grane correctly points out "that Luther did not want to destroy the church. But one thing he wanted very definitely : he wanted to do away with scholasticism and bring about a thorough-going reform of learned studies."

[5] See, above all, WA, II, 279, 11-24.

limited way.[1] Just in this respect Luther proved himself to be a conservative Reformer. His appeal to conscience in this matter was significant for showing that the Word alone is vis-a-vis to conscience, not human commandments or teachings.

Over against these, conscience is free, and the church may not violate this freedom by decisions contradicting the Gospel. Otherwise the church's authority would become tyranny,[2] since she would exceed the power commited to her. By his critique Luther does not intend to say that ecclesiastical directives were all too numerous or in some instances too oppressive. Rather, he is concerned about the freedom of conscience before God.[3] Precisely because of this Luther did not for some time initiate any practical reforms. Significantly in *The Babylonian Captivity of the Church* Luther indeed criticizes the withholding of the cup, but then declares that he did not want to demand a forcible change in this matter. He only wanted to instruct consciences so that they might know that violence had been done to them.[4]

---

[1] See, for example, *WA*, VI, 322, 1-22; *LW*, XXXIX, 101-2 ("On the Papacy in Rome," 1520): "I fight for only two things: First, I will not tolerate it that men establish new articles of faith... Second, I shall accept whatever the pope establishes and does, on condition that I judge it first on the basis of Holy Scripture. For my part he must remain under Christ and let himself be judged by Holy Scripture... If these two things are granted, I will let the pope be; indeed, I will help to elevate him as high as they please. If they are not granted, then to me he shall be neither pope nor Christian. Whoever cannot do otherwise may make an idol of him. But I will not worship him."

[2] *WA*, VI, 536, 7-9; *LW*, XXXVI, 70 ("The Babylonian Captivity," 1520): "Therefore I say : Neither pope nor bishop nor any other man has the right to impose a single syllable of law upon a Christian man without his consent." *WA*, VI, 537, 12-14; *LW*, XXXVI, 72 : "I lift my voice simply on behalf of liberty and conscience, and I confidently cry : No law, whether of men or of angels, may rightfully be imposed upon Christians without their consent, for we are free of all laws." *WA*, VI, 537, 19-20; *LW*, XXXVI, 72 : "Nevertheless, since but few know this glory of baptism and the blessedness of Christian liberty..." Hence, for Luther Christian liberty is based on baptism, more specifically, on the promise imparted in baptism.

[3] *WA*, VII, 670, 26-30; *LW*, XXXIX, 202 ("Answer to the Hyperchristian Book... Emser," 1521): "I only desire to have the conscience free and to have all Christians make the sign of the cross against a faith which believes that the pope is right in his rule. For such a faith destroys faith in Christ and drowns the whole world in nothing but sin and destruction."

[4] *WA*, VI, 507, 21-25; *LW*, XXXVI, 28 ("The Babylonian Captivity," 1520). "Therefore I do not urge that both kinds be seized upon by force, as if we were bound to this form by a rigorous command, but I instruct men's consciences so that they may endure the Roman tyranny, knowing well that they have been forcibly deprived of their rightful

We cannot now pursue the continued development in Luther's criticism of the church's authority, a criticism that he based in essence on conscience. As is known, this criticism reached its climax in Luther's famous answer at Worms in 1521 where in addition to the Scriptures he appeals to his conscience "captive to God's Word." [1] However, it may be useful, to discuss some of the thoughts expressed in the disputation *De potestate concilii* of 1536, because here Luther dealt with the question about the church's authority in a larger context and in greater detail than elsewhere.

Here Luther first singles out the unique position of the apostles and prophets who have the highest authority after Christ, whereas all others are only their successors or disciples. The specific authority of the apostles is based on the fulfilled promise of the Holy Spirit given to them. For that reason they are called the foundation of the church. They gave the church her articles of faith. Of course, it does not follow from this that their successors have the same power. On the contrary, everything that they teach or prescribe must be measured by the authority of the apostles. [2]

However, if the successors forsake the foundation of the apostles, they are heretics or antichrists. Even bishops and councils may err, and

---

share in the sacrament because of their own sin. This only do I desire - that no one should justify the tyranny of Rome... "A few lines farther Luther expresses the wish that Christian liberty in this area might be restored through a general council.

[1] *WA*, VII, 838, 2-9; cf. *LW*, XXXII, 112 ("Luther at the Diet of Worms"): "Since therefore Your Serene Majesty and Your Lordships desire a simple answer, I shall give one that has neither horns nor teeth, in this way : Unless I shall have been convicted by the testimonies of the Scriptures or by clear reason (for I believe neither the pope nor the councils alone, since it is a matter of record that they have often erred and also contradicted themselves), I am bound by the Scriptures cited by me and my conscience is captive to the words of God. I neither can nor wish to recant anything, since it is neither safe nor honest to act contrary to conscience." See Bernhard Lohse, "Luthers Antwort in Worms," *Mitteilungen der Luthergesellschaft*, XXIX (1958), 124-34.

[2] *WA*, XXXIX, i, 184,4-185,7 : "1. After Christ no authority can be equated with the apostles and prophets. 2. All other successors must be regarded only as their disciples. 3. The apostles (not just as a group, but also as individuals) had the promise of the Holy Spirit. 4. Therefore they alone are called the foundation of the church as the ones who must present articles of faith. 5. No successors as individuals had the promise of the Holy Spirit. 6. Hence it does not follow that since the apostles could do this or that, therefore their successors could do the same. 7. But whatever they want to teach or establish, they must follow and bring to the authority of the apostles." On this disputation as well as the entire complex of the authority of doctrine see the detailed treatment in Karl Gerhard Steck, *Lehre und Kirche bei Luther* (Munich, 1963), pp. 62-122; especially pp. 76 ff.

that even in their official capacity. If they do not err, this is due not to
their inherent authority but by accident or thanks to a holy man or the
church. There is no special promise that the Holy Spirit would bind
Himself to an assembly of bishops or of a council. Whoever teaches
otherwise falls into spiritual pride.[1]

Next, Luther enters into the churchly character of assemblies of
bishops and councils. He concedes that such assemblies represent the
total church. But for that reason they are not yet the church herself;
they only exhibit the church, in somewhat the same manner as a person
is depicted in a portrait. If beyond this it should happen that such assemblies are in fact the true church, this is accidental and not because of
the council as such. A council is the true church only *per accidens*. One
individual may contradict an entire council if he has better reasons than
those given by the council.[2]

What, then, is the task of a council? Since in Luther's view the apostles possessed a unique authority which is not transferable to any of
their successors, the council is charged with abiding by the teaching of
the apostles. Expressed in another way, a council should provide an

---

[1] *WA*, XXXIX, i, 185, 23-186, 13: "11. But if the successors do not follow or give
heed to the foundation of the apostles, they are heretics or Antichrists and will be destro-
yed as being outside the foundation. 12. Therefore the assembled bishops or the council
can err, just like other men, in public as well as in private. 13. If they do not err, this is
an accident, or by the authority of some saint among them, or of the church, but not by
authority of their assembly... 15. For the Holy Spirit is not bound by any promise to
an assembly of bishops or of a council, and they cannot prove this. 16. Accordingly they
boast arrogantly and falsely, not to say blasphemously, that they are legitimately assembled in the Holy Spirit."

[2] *WA*, XXXIX, i, 186, 24-187, 28 : "19. This they say rightly, that they represent
the universal church, for they are not necessarily the church, but more often only represent the church. 20. And if they only represent the church, they are the church the
way a man portrayed is a man, that is, only in a representative fashion. 21. But if they
are something more (that is, the true church), this happens by accident (as was said),
not by virtue of the representative church. 22. The histories bear witness that the councils were more often only the representative church, but rarely the true church. 23. Yea,
a council is always the representative church, speaking by itself, but by accident it is the
true church. 24. No one therefore is held to accept the decrees of the representative church,
that is, the councils, unless they judge and speak according to the writings of the apostles,
which happens by accident. 25. All other things are matters of only the representative
church, or a pictured church, and can be promoted if they are not ungodly. 26. And they
themselves say that one man can contradict a whole council, if he would have better reason or Scripture. 27. They say this, but they are lying, since they strongly deny and condemn this by their actions."

example of confessing. But even here no council possesses infallibility. One who appeals for the infallibility of a council to Matth. 18:20, where Jesus promised to be in the midst of two or three gathered in His name, mistakes the invocation of the name of Jesus for an assembly in His name. Hence the question whether a council is really assembled in Jesus' name is decided on the basis of what such a council says and determines.[1]

In this connection Luther also discusses the well-known statement of Augustine, that he would not believe the Gospel of Christ unless the authority of the church would induce him to do so. Luther declares that this statement can be understood only within its context. At this place Augustine was dealing with Manichaeans who claim that the Holy Spirit was promised to the apostles but imparted only to them (the Manichaeans), who for that reason set their own church above that of the apostles. Hence Augustine meant to say that he does not believe the Manichaeans because he finds nothing of the Gospel in their midst, and that he believes the apostles because they have received the Holy Spirit. Accordingly Augustine accents the authority of the church because she has the Word. Thus, according to Luther, Augustine's statement can be understood only if one realizes that the Manichaeans questioned the authority of the apostles. There may be a degree of wilfulness in Luther's interpretation, yet he is undoubtedly right in saying that Augustine's statement does not automatically cover the church's claims to authority in the Late Middle Ages.[2]

To round off this section we quote Luther's definition of the church

---

[1] *WA*, XXXIX, i, 188, 16-190, 12, See especially 189, 11-13: "[Christ] commands you to remain in the apostolic office. A council must be an example of confession, not a power to establish new things." 189, 30-190, 1: "They (that is, the supporters of conciliar authority) say this: We are assembled in the name of Christ. But it is not so. To cite the name of Christ is not to assemble in his name. If they are assembled in Christ's name, then this will be the sign, that they act in accordance with Christ, not contrary to the Gospel." On Luther's attitude toward the council see Christa Tecklenburg Johns, *Luthers Konzilsidee in ihrer historischen Bedingtheit und ihrem reformatorischen Neuansatz* (Berlin, 1966), especially pp. 179-198.

[2] *WA*, XXXIX, i, 191, 1-22; especially lines 9-13. "There Augustine answers: 'I do not believe you, because I find nothing about the Gospel in you, and because I believe the apostles who received the Holy Spirit, I believe you least of all.' Thus he points to the text concerning Pentecost. He believes the apostles, who were the church, not the Manichaeans. I give more weight to the authority of the church, because it has the Word, than you."

from this disputation: The true church is not that "which succeeds the apostles but which confesses that Christ is the Son of God, that He suffered and was crucified for our sins." With his characteristic sharpness Luther continues by saying that the pope was unwilling to make that confession and for that reason was not the true church.[1]

By way of summary it may be said with regard to Luther's critique of the church's authority, as understood at that time, that it is based in essence also on his new conception of conscience. No ecclesiastical power may be permitted to insert itself in the confrontation between God and man, as Luther saw it. For the assailed conscience there is liberation only by God Himself, i.e., through His Word. If a human authority were to intervene at this point, it would both arbitrarily reshape the person's trial and deny the person God's consolation.

III

To gain a proper grasp of Luther's conception of conscience as well as of authority, we must yet discuss how conscience is bound to the authority of the Word. It will be necessary, first of all, to treat the question whether there is subjectivism in Luther.

As is known, Roman Catholics have repeatedly raised the charge against Luther that he was taking his stand alone against the total tradition of the church and already for that reason could not be right. Already at the Diet of Worms, after Luther had given his famous answer "without horns and teeth," the Trier official, Dr. von der Ecken, retorted to Luther that he should abandon his conscience, as he was obligated to do, since he was in error.[2] To the present day to some extent Catholic Luther

---

[1] *WA*, XXXIX, i, 191, 28-192, 4. "Sed haec est vera definitio Ecclesiae, non quae succedit Apostolis, sed quae confitetur, quod Christus sit filius Dei, passus, crucifixus pro peccatis nostris. Hoc papa confiteri non vult. Ergo nec est vera Ecclesia. Haec definitio sumpta est ab effectu." Luther betrays a pronounced onesidedness in exegesis at this point especially in the following sentence, where he deals with the controversy between Peter and Paul at Antioch (Gal. 2). *WA*, XXXIX, i, 194, 28: "Peter did not sin in teaching but in pretending."

[2] *WA*, VII, 839, 33-34; *LW*, XXXII, 130 (Dr. Ecken to Luther): "Lay aside your conscience, Martin; you must lay it aside because it is in error."

research has charged Luther with subjectivism, most emphatically recently in the writings of Joseph Lortz [1] and Ernst W. Zeeden.[2] Admittedly Luther does in fact adopt a stance for which there is practically no model in church history. For example, statements that God alone desires to be in the conscience and have His Word rule alone [3] seem to call forth the charge of subjectivism. Again and again Luther stressed that only the divine Word itself without any human authority must convince man and give him certainty.[4] In this respect Luther is theoretically not too far removed from the spiritualists of the Refor-

---

[1] Joseph Lortz, *Die Reformation in Deutschland* (5th ed., Freiburg, 1965), *passim.* Against various criticisms of his claim that Luther was subjective, Lortz defended himself in his essay, "Reformatorisch und Katholisch beim jungen Luther (1518/19)," *Humanitas-Christianitas* : *Festschrift Walther v. Loewenich zum 65. Geburtstag*, Karlmann Beyschlag, Gottfried Maron and Eberhard Wölfel, ed. (Witten, 1968), p. (47-62) 52, n. 21. Here Lortz states that he by no means wanted to deny that Luther had recognized "objective values." "I was not suggesting any malicious or narrow stunting." Nor does Lortz deny Luther his humility which is said to have "complemented his high self-consciousness." "This is not what I had in mind with 'Ego-relationship', but that extraordinarily frequent positive reference to his own conscience and its conviction, in which the Reformer is captive and liberated." In these words Lortz has thoroughly captured the central point of the difference between Luther and Rome. We would only add that Luther understood not only the conscience but also authority in a different way.

[2] Ernst Walter Zeeden, *Martin Luther und die Reformation im Urteil des deutschen Luthertums*; *Studien zum Selbstverständnis des lutherischen Protestantismus von Luthers Tode bis zum Beginn der Goethezeit* (Freiburg, 1950), I, 13. Zeeden says, for example : "The authority of the conscience had taken the place of the authority of the church (that is, for Luther)... This conscience impelled Luther to prefer his own understanding of Scripture to that of the church and to proclaim it as the pure, clear Gospel. Thus his conscience became one of the chief principles from which the Reformation developed." On Zeeden's book see the critical review by Ernst Wolf, "Martin Luther und die Prinzipien des Protestantismus in katholischer Sicht," *Theologische Literaturzeitung*, LXXVI (1951), col. 271-276.

[3] *WA*, VIII, 151, 35-152, 2 ("Von der Beicht...," 1521).

[4] *WA*, X, I, 1, 130, 14-16 ("Church Postil," 1522) : "The Word by itself, without any respect of the person, must suffice for the heart, enclose and grasp man, so that he will at once feel himself caught in it, how true and correct it is." *WA*, X, i, 1, 131, 2-3 ("Church Postil," 1522) : "For it (i.e., faith) stands on the bare Word and despises all men." *WA*, X, II, 23, 4-9; *LW*, XXVI, 248 ("Receiving Both Kinds in the Sacrament," 1522) : "For you must be Christ's disciple, not Luther's. It is not enough that you say : Luther, Peter, or Paul has said this; but you yourself in your own conscience must feel Christ himself. You must experience unshakably that it is God's Word, even though the whole world should dispute it. As long as you do not have this feeling, just so long you have certainly not yet tasted of God's Word."

mation age.[1] However, he differs from them in the concept of how faith is mediated to the individual.

The matter that has been termed subjectivism is in fact so revolutionary that it could all too easily be misunderstood; even in Luther's own church it has frequently not been grasped and realized correctly. The certainty and the assertions in Luther's reformatory labors were colossal. Luther could say that he did not stand alone in opposition to traditional teaching, but that truth was on his side.[2] Or he maintained that he had two insuperable witnesses for his cause, namely the Scriptures and his conscience.[3] It cannot be denied that Luther came forth with an incomparable claim, a claim that necessarily led to a dividing of the spirits. In addition, Luther basically granted every one else the same right that he claimed for himself. Every one must learn in his conscience to distinguish the spirits and prophecies.[4]

It is true, Luther is here basically concerned neither with individual freedom nor with a principle that is most profoundly critical of authority. He is concerned with the fact that there can be no substitute for a man's personal faith. To speak of subjectivism in this connection would be inappropriate, above all because the subject can be understood only in the light of the object, in fact derives its whole being from the latter. It does not seem adequate to speak here of objective values which Luther

---

[1] Steck, p. 121.

[2] See, for example, *WA*, I, 611, 8-13; *LW*, XXXI, 221 ("Explanations of the Disputation Concerning the Value of Indulgences," 1518): "Does not the pope err along with the whole church, which is of the same opinion (namely, with regard to the merits of the saints)? Or are you the only one and the first one to have the right opinion? My first answer is, I am not the only one: the truth is on my side, as many others, namely those who have doubted and still doubt the validity of indulgences. They do not sin because of this doubt. Since remissions are only for punishments, a person will be saved whether or not he believes in them and whether he obtains them or not." On this thought see the section in Hirsch, pp. 172-220. On p. 174 Hirsch rightly says: "A churchly court that would strike down an honest expression of disagreement simply by virtue of its authority is, by that very fact, already convicted for him as being antichristian, and whoever supports or follows it heaps guilt on his conscience. Truth and conscience stand in a living essential relationship, to which only an inner process of being convicted and convinced is conformable."

[3] *WA*, XXX, ii, 673, 15-16 ("*De loco iustificationis*," 1530): "I have two most reliable and invincible witnesses, namely Scripture and conscience, which is experience."

[4] *WA*, XIV, 647, 17-19 ("Lectures on Deuteronomy," 1523/24): "Everyone's own conscience must be guarded. Therefore the right of judging spirits and prophecies is necessary for every one."

is said still to have acknowledged, because in this way one would fail to do justice to the starting point of Luther's conception of conscience and authority. What conscience is can ultimately be experienced only in its confrontation with the truth, as truth, in turn, must demonstrate itself as truth to the conscience of the individual. Luther's appeal at Worms to his conscience held captive to the Word of God [1] did not only substitute a new authority for another, but by means of the radical distinction between divine and human authority, authority itself is conceived of in a new way.

In our context we can only briefly refer to the fact that Luther's understanding of the authority of the divine Word did not imply the authority of the Bible as a whole or of individual passages in a biblicistic sense.[2] Although he does occasionally give voice to such an understanding, ultimately he thinks of Christ in connection with the Word, that is, God's gracious promise to man. This promise has unconditional authority. Therefore it must be said that because of the authority of the Word Luther came into conflict with the authority of the church in his time.

But precisely the fact that Luther's critique was a limited one, in the sense mentioned above, involves that he ascribes supreme authority to the church in so far as she proclaims the Word. The rejection of the authority claimed by pope and council can be correctly understood only if it is viewed in connection with the affirmation of churchly authority in the reformatory sense. Only the principal aspects involved here can be mentioned.[3]

First, it is significant that according to Luther the holy church is by no means without sin. However, Luther can qualify this to mean that this sinfulness refers to life, whereas another rule applies to doctrine as proclamation of forgiveness. In his late writing, "Wider Hans Worst," 1541, Luther could say that a preacher, if he is a true preacher, must not

---

[1] See p. 173, note 1.

[2] On Luther's understanding of Scripture see, above all, Gerhard Ebeling, *Evangelische Evangelienauslegung; Eine Untersuchung zu Luthers Hermeneutik* (2nd ed., Darmstadt, 1962); Harald Østergaard-Nielsen, *Scriptura sacra et viva vox : Eine Lutherstudie* (Munich, 1957); Ruben Josefson, "Christus und die Heilige Schrift," *Lutherforschung Heute; Referate und Berichte des 1. Internationalen Lutherforschungskongresses, Aarhus, 18.-23. August 1956*, Vilmos Vajta, ed. (Berlin, 1958), pp. 57-63; Jaroslav Pelikan, *Luther the Expositor - Introduction to the Reformer's Exegetical Writings. Luther's Works, Companion Volume* (St. Louis, 1959).

[3] On this problem see the comprehensive investigation by Steck.

ask for forgiveness for his proclamation but rather say, "*Hec dixit Dominus*." "In this sermon I have been an apostle and prophet of Jesus Christ. Here it is unnecessary, even bad, to pray for forgiveness of sins, as if one had not taught truly, for it is God's word, and not my word, and God ought not and cannot forgive it, but only confirm, praise, and crown it, saying 'You have taught truly, for I have spoken through you and the word is mine.' " [1] Yes, to the extent that the church lives and speaks in the Word and faith of Christ, Luther regards her as holy and righteous; but if she acts and speaks without Christ, she errs and sins. [2]

Furthermore, in addition to this thought, attention must be called to the authority which the decisions of the ancient church in the doctrine of the Trinity and in Christology had for Luther. Here, too, it must be said by way of qualification that Luther does not accept these decisions because they were made by the church's authority, but because he was convinced that these decisions correctly interpreted and reproduced the statements of Scripture in view of the problems that then needed to be resolved. As for the degree of obligation of these decisions, Luther is no less committed than any Catholic theologian of his time. Both the doctrine of the Trinity and Christology are of fundamental significance for his theology. [3]

Finally, it must also be borne in mind that according to his own words Luther has no thought of rejecting all the holy teachers of the church. He says : "I do not reject them. But everyone, indeed, knows that at times they have erred, as men will; therefore, I am ready to trust them only when they give me evidence for their opinions from Scripture, which has never erred." [4]

In answer to the Catholic objection that Scripture was also of human origin, Luther could point out that the words of the apostles were commanded by God and confirmed and proved by great miracles, something

---

[1] *WA*, LI, 516, 15-517, 16; cf. *LW*, XLI, 216 ("Against Hanswurst"); the citation is *WA*, LI, 517, 9-15.

[2] *WA*, XXX, iii, 342, 13-16; *LW*, XXXIV, 76 ("Commentary on the Alleged Imperial Edict," 1531).

[3] See Jan Koopmans, *Das altkirchliche Dogma in der Reformation; aus dem Holländischen von H. Quistorp* (Munich, 1955). On the doctrine of the Trinity which, with a view to Luther, has not yet been investigated in a large context, see, most recently, the remarks in Klaus Schwarzwäller, *Theologia crucis - Luthers Lehre von Prädestination nach De servo arbitrio, 1525* (Munich, 1970), pp. 201-12.

[4] *WA*, VII, 315, 29-32; *LW*, XXXII, 11 ("Defense and Explanation of all the Articles," 1521).

that could not be said of any human teaching.[1] It is true, it is not so much specific individual reasons which Luther adduces for the authority of the Scriptures, but rather the consciousness which was uncritically shared by him and most of his contemporaries that ultimately no one but God Himself speaks in the Scriptures, even though they might contain also a variety of human elements. Yet the distinctive character of Luther's view of Scripture lies in the fact that Luther regarded as decisive the proclaimed Word which liberates conscience and in this way makes it certain.[2]

Of the host of problems that could be discussed in connection with the binding of conscience to the authority of the Word we shall, in conclusion, touch briefly on the question whether one may speak of freedom of conscience in Luther in the sense that no compulsion may and dare be exercised in questions of faith.[3] One could think that freedom of conscience in the modern sense would follow logically from Luther's new understanding of conscience and his restrictions on the church's authority. There are in fact many expressions in Luther according to which there must be no coercion of any kind in matters of faith.[4] They are,

---

[1] *WA*, X, ii, 91, 5-16; *LW*, XXXV, 152 ("Avoiding the Doctrines of Men," 1522).

[2] Gustav Wingren, "Kritische Erwägungen zum Begriff der Lehrautorität in der lutherischen Kirche," *Kerygma und Dogma*, X (1964), 246-56, has concisely worked out Luther's specific concept of authority in contrast to that of Orthodoxy and its understanding of Scripture and Confession as *norma normans* and *norma normata*.

[3] See Heinrich Hoffmann, "Reformation und Gewissensfreiheit," *Archiv für Reformationsgeschichte*, XXXVII (1940), 170-88; Heinrich Bornkamm, "Das Problem der Toleranz im 16. Jahrhundert," *Das Jahrhundert der Reformation - Gestalten und Kräfte* (Göttingen, 1961), pp. 262-91.

[4] See, for example, *WA*, X, iii, 18, 10-12 (Sermon, 1522) : "I will preach it, say it, write it. But I will not force or coerce any one, because faith wants to be drawn willingly and without pressure." *WA*, XI, 264, 16-20 ("Von weltlicher Obrigkeit," 1523) : "Since, then, it is a matter for everyone's conscience how he believes or does not believe, and since this takes nothing away from the government, let the government be satisfied and look after its own affairs, and permit people to believe this way or that, as they can and will, and coerce no one. For faith is a voluntary matter to which no one can be forced." *WA*, XV, 291, 1. ("Letter to the Saxon Princes about the Rebellious Spirit," 1524): "Let the spirits collide with each other." *WA Br*, III, No. 950 (Letter to Elector John, 30 November 1525). Evangelical preachers should be installed only with the consent of the "people." *WA*, XVII, ii, 123-24. (Lenten Postil, 1525), especially 125, 2. "We must not extirpate or destroy them (i.e., the heretics and false teachers)." *WA Tr*, II, No. 2325a, 7-10 : "We must get to the point where everyone is permitted to believe as he can justify it in his conscience before God. But if they permit this to us, we must also let them follow their conscience." It is true that here Luther is probably thinking only of evangelical and traditional estates. See Hoffmann, p. 184.

indeed, found above all in his early years. Even at a later time Luther continued to insist that faith cannot be commanded and therefore no one can be forced to accept or reject a specific faith. Nevertheless, Luther subsequently wished to see the public propagation of heretical teaching prohibited. The decisive cause for this change in attitude is to be found in his experiences with the so-called *Schwaermer* and Anabaptists, and especially the rebellious peasants. Luther thought that the rejection of certain governmental offices or duties, a rejection espoused by many Anabaptists, was equivalent to a call to revolution. In 1531 Luther even agreed with Melanchthon's opinion, which demanded the death penalty for stubborn Anabaptists.[1]

Accordingly, one cannot speak of actual freedom of conscience in connection with Luther. Beyond this, it must be asserted that Luther, who repeatedly appealed so emphatically to his conscience, did not grant the same right to others. In a letter to Elector John, 9 February 1526, Luther states with a view to reformatory measures that an "instructed conscience" will not tolerate any "abomination." Here Luther indeed insists that conscience must be instructed, but he does not at all count on the possibility that one might arrive at divergent decisions. Futhermore, he denies several canons the right to appeal to their consciences, since they had declined a disputation on the basis of the Holy Scriptures.[2] But even in cases where others appealed to Scripture in decisions dictated by their conscience, Luther raised objections. In the Eucharistic controversy Luther could accuse his opponent, Carlstadt, that he had no conscience,[3] or, Luther was convinced, Carlstadt's conscience was "uneasy" or "uncertain."[4] Luther could not imagine that binding the conscience to the Word could lead to anything but full unanimity.

Coming back, finally, to the question posed at the beginning, in what respect Luther's new conception of conscience and authority is involved

---

[1] See Bornkamm, p. 272.

[2] *WA Br*, IV, No. 978, 12-41 (Letter to Elector John, 9 February 1526). See also *WA Br*, III, No. 946 (Letter to Spalatin, 11 November 1525), 28-29: "Our princes do not compel to faith and the Gospel, but prohibit abominations..."; 33-35: "We are speaking of public curses and blasphemies by which they blaspheme our God. This (I say) we must prohibit if we can."

[3] *WA*, XVIII, 150, 24-25 ("Against the Heavenly Prophets," part 2, 1525); *LW*, XL, 160.

[4] *WA*, XVIII, 161, 18-19 ("Against the Heavenly Prophets," part 2, 1525); *LW*, XL, 171. See also Alanen, p. 8.

with the beginnings of the Modern Age, it must be remembered that Luther's concept, as is inevitable, was timebound in several essential points. This fact must be soberly recognized.[1]

First of all, the self-evident way in which Luther presupposed the authority of Scripture as given and valid was possible in the sixteenth century but can no longer be re-affirmed since the Enlightenment. But precisely because in the sixteenth century the divine authority of Scripture was still accepted without question practically everywhere in Europe, Luther's appeal to Scripture, especially the Word of God encountered in it, and his critique of the church's authority could have such a powerful effect.

But as the correlate of conscience was immediately viewed in a way different from Luther's, the understanding of conscience also had to undergo a change. Here, too, Luther's concept could not simply be maintained, but was changed by a certain inevitability in the direction of subjectivism.

One may therefore hesitate to give an affirmative answer to the question whether Luther inaugurated the beginning of the Modern Age. However, this much may be affirmed that Luther's attitude toward the problem of "conscience and authority" signals the end of the Middle Ages,[2] because Luther cast doubt on the church's authority more strenuously than the men before him. The fact that his conscience was "captive to God's Word" has made unavoidably clear for all time that an appeal to conscience is possible only on the basis of an ultimate obligation.

---

[1] On this, with specific reference to the questions of conscience, see Hirsch, especially pp. 217-18; Steck, pp. 225-26.

[2] This has recently been denied, among others, by Erich Hassinger, *Das Werden des neuzeitlichen Europa, 1300-1600* (2nd ed., Braunschweig, 1966), p. 134, with reference to Luther's answer at Worms.

Translated by the Rev. Prof. Herbert J.A. Bouman, D.D.

CONSCIENCE AND AUTHORITY IN LUTHER'S
EXPLANATION OF THE FOURTH COMMANDMENT

JOS E. VERCRUYSSE, S. J.

In our minor essay we should like to follow a path somewhat different from that of the major essay, although our remarks received their impetus from what the essay said about the special significance of conscience for the entire area of political responsibility. In our opinion some supplementary thoughts on the relationship between conscience and *human* authority would not be out of place. Since even this area is still too broad, a further limitation suggests itself. We therefore propose to sketch this relationship on the basis of Luther's explanations of the fourth commandment in the Decalog. In this way we hope to contribute to the study of the relationship between conscience and authority and at the same time call attention to a complex of texts which receives too little attention, for example, in the comments on the problematics of the two-kingdom doctrine [1] and yet contains important material for a proper attitude over against authority.

There remains to recall that Luther in his pastoral and catechetical sermons and publications repeatedly dealt with the ten commandments, starting with the "Decem Praecepta Wittenbergensi praedicata populo," a revision of sermons from 1516-1517 published in July 1518, and including the "Einfältige Weise zu beten für einen guten Freund" (1535) and the "Annotationes in aliquot capita Matthaei" (1538).[2] Did not the

---

[1] See E. Kinder, "Luthers Ableitung der geistlichen und weltlichen 'Oberkeit' aus dem 4. Gebot" in *Für Kirche und Recht*: Festschrift Johannes Heckel (Köln, 1959), pp. 270-86. Also in *Reich Gottes und Welt* (Darmstadt, 1969), pp. 221-41.

[2] We rely especially on: "Eine Kurze Erklärung der Zehn Gebote," 1518, *WA*, I, 250-56 (cited as "Erklärung"); "Instructio pro confessione peccatorum," 1518, *WA*, I, 258-65 ("Instructio"); "Decem Praecepta Wittenbergensi praedicata populo," 1518, *WA*, I, 398-521 ("DPW"); "Eine kurze Unterweisung, wie man beichten soll," 1519, *WA*, II, 59-65; "Von den Guten Werken," 1520, *WA*, VI, 202-76 ("VGW"); "Eine kurze Form der 10 Gebote," 1520, *WA*, VII, 204-29 ("Form"); "Ein Betbüchlein der 10 Gebote...," 1522, *WA*, X, ii, 375-482; *LW*, XLIII, 11 ff.; "Predigt über 4.-6. Gebot," 28 February 1523, *WA*, XI, 39-41; "Ad Gasparis Schatzgeyri Minoritae plicas responsio per J. Briesmannum pro Lutherano libello de votis monasticis epistola," 1523, *WA*, XI,

preacher have to preach on the Decalog four times every year [1] and was this not a fixed part of the Catechism? But the Reformer frequently touched on the fourth commandment also in his comments on monastic vows [2] and on marriage,[3] especially in connection with the required parental consent for the marriage. Thus Luther's comments on this commandment do not belong to the mere *allotria* or *curiosa* of his theology but are related to the essentials of his thought. Since Luther in the course of his life often dealt with this commandment, these texts also permit us to document the development of his thought.

I

We ask first who exercises human authority and government, and whom, according to the fourth commandment, one must honor and obey. In Luther's explanations the scope of authority is broader than simply "physical father and mother."[4] It is a matter of "obedience and service to all who have been placed to govern us." [5] This government is subdivided into the office of parents, church ˌand civil government, and rule of the household.

To this we offer only two observations. First, from the beginning the parental office occupies a central position; it is the cornerstone of every human authority and thus its explanation, "It is certain that

---

284-91 ("Briesmannum"); "Predigten über das 2. Buch Mose," 1525, *WA*, XVI, 485-519 ("Pr. 2. M."); "Evangelium, 8 Sonntag n. Trinitatis, Mt. 7, 15-21," 1526, *WA*, X, i, 2, 332-40; "Predigt über Mt. 2, 13," 1528, *WA*, XXVII, 5-8; "Katechismuspredigten," 1528, *WA*, XXX, i, 2-122; *LW*, II, 135 ff. ("KPr. I, II or III"); "Deudsch (Grosser) Katechismus," 1529, *WA*, XXX, i, 125-238 ("GK"); "Der kleine Katechismus," 1529, *WA*, XXX, i, 243-425; "Eine einfältige Weise zu beten für einen guten Freund," 1535, *WA*, XXXVIII, 358-75; *LW*, XLIII, 193 ff. ; "Annotationes in aliquot capita Matthaei," 1538, *WA*, XXXVIII, 447-667 ("Annotationes").

[1] See *WA*, XXVIII, 510 9 : "Cum ergo quater auditis in anno redire 10 praecepta..."; also *WA*, XXVIII, 595 10.

[2] See, e.g., "De votis monasticis iudicium," *WA*, VIII, 573-76 ("Widmungsbrief") and 623-29 ("Adversari vota caritati"); *LW*, XLIV, 326 f.

[3] See, e.g., "Das Eltern die Kinder zur Ehe nicht zwingen noch hyndern... sollen," *WA*, XV, 163-69; *LW*, XLV, 385 ff.; "Eine Predigt vom Ehestand," *WA*, XVII, i, 12-29, *passim*.

[4] "VGW," *WA*, VI, 250 33; LW, XLIV, 80 ff.

[5] "VGW," *WA*, VI, 250 23; *LW*, XLIV, 80. Also : *WA*, VI, 236 32; *LW*, XLIV, 63. 'Form," *WA*, VII, 206 4 : "... wie man sich halten soll gegen alle Ubirkayt, wilch an Gottis statt sitzen"; "Pr. 2. M.," *WA*, XVI, 486 14 : "... wie man sich halten soll gegen alle Obirckeit..."

authority of parents is greater than all authority which is under God." [1]
This priority of rank is given expression by means of the greater attention which Luther accords the relationships in the more intimate family
circle, as he does, for example, in the "Decem Praecepta Wittenbergensi
praedicata populo," or in the first place which is assigned to the "physical father and mother" in his "Treatise on Good Works," where Luther
gives theological value especially to the hierarchy of good works.[2] From
the time of the "Sermons on Exodus," especially in the version of
Aurifaber, we find a strong emphasis on the office of father as the source
of the whole political and social structure and as the model for every
power on earth. We meet with the same view also in the three "Catechism Sermons" [3] and in the Large Catechism, "Out of the authority of
parents all other authority is derived and developed." [4]

In the second place, we should like to call attention to a significant
shift within this order of powers. Next to father and mother the church's
authority, hierarchy, and the commandments of the church take prece-
dence over other forms of government, according to the earliest explanations. In the "Treatise on Good Works" (1520) the "spiritual mother,
the holy Christian church, the spiritual authority" explicitly occupies
the second place.[5] The only important difference between the explanation of the fourth commandment in the "Prayer Booklet" (1522) [6] and
in the "Short Form of the Ten Commandments" (1520), which is related
to "A Short Form of Confession" (1519), the "Short Explanation of the
Ten Commandments," and the "Instruction for the Confession of
Sins" (1518), lies in omitting mention at the second place of the obedience toward the commandments of the church and the reverence toward the priesthood.[7] In the later writings the churchly government is

---

[1] "Briesmannum", *WA*, XI, 289 21. See also: "Predigt 1523," *WA*, XI, 40 2:
"Non est maior potestas in terris quam, quam parentes in liberos habent, ut curent
corpus et erudiant animam."

[2] Cf. "VGW," *WA*, VI, 250 22-32; *LW*, XLIV, 81.

[3] "KPr I," *WA*, XXX, i, 6 36: "Ex domo venit Civitas, Regio, Regnum & omnium
istorum origo est paternitas," *WA*, XXX, i, 35 3 and 23; *WA*, XXX, i, 69 2. Also:
"Pr. 2. M.," *WA*, XVI, 500 16: "... denn da ist das erste Regiment, davon ein ursprung
haben alle ander Regiment und herschafft."

[4] "GK," *WA*, XXX, i, 125 20. Theo. G. Tappert, ed., *Book of Concord* (Philadelphia:
Muhlenberg Press, 1959), Art. I, 141. Abbr. as *L.C.*

[5] "VGW," *WA*, VI, 255 18; *LW*, XLIV, 87.

[6] "Betbüchlein," *WA*, X, ii, 382 15-25.

[7] "Form," *WA*, VII, 209 14-25. "Die Übertretung... widder das vierdt: Wer die
gebott der Christlichen kirchen nit haltet mit fasten, feyren &. Wer priesterstand uneret,
nachredt und beleydigt.", l. 19-20.

barely mentioned in a positive way in the expositions of the fourth commandment. Thus in the Large Catechism Luther is very reserved with reference to the church's authority. It is mentioned only hesitantly in the last place. Luther distinguishes the true spiritual fathers, "who govern and guide us by the Word of God." [1] and about whom he does not want to say much "because I am also one of them," [2] from the spiritual fathers in the papacy "who applied this title to themselves but performed no fatherly office." [3]

To this point we have briefly marked off the area in which we meet authority. We have pointed to the growing hierarchization in Luther's presentation of the authorities of which the parental office is the heart, and from which in a subsidiary way, the rule of the household and of the country proceed. Although in connection with the fourth commandment there is continued reference to the rule of the church—especially in a negative way as the attacked papal church and the monastic institution —it no longer occupies the second place as it once did. There is here a trace and a confirmation of the claim in the previous essay that, in Luther's view, no earthly element may intrude in the confrontation between God and man. [4] This applies particularly to the spiritual power where God rules *without intermediary* through faith and where the church manifests herself. This divine rule really belongs to the first table. Hence we face the question of the relationship between conscience and churchly authority, as Prof. Lohse raised the question in his essay.

II

Keeping this sketch in mind, we now ask : *How is man to conduct himself in respect to this authority, according to the fourth commandment ?* How does the Reformer describe the proper, conscientious attitude of man toward this human government ? From this point of view we ask about conscience and authority according to Luther.

"Honor "in God's commandment, "Honor thy father and thy mother," the "magnificent verb"[5] or the "sublime word,"[6] expresses the

---

1 "GK," *WA*, XXX, i, 155 6; *L.C.*, art. I, 158.

2 "KPr III," *WA*, XXX, i, 71 9; *LW*, LI, 149.

3 "GK," *WA*, XXX, i, 155 5; *L.C.*, art. I, 158.

4 See Lohse's essay.

5 "Pr. 2. M.," '*WA*, XVI, 487 10.

6 "KPr III," *WA*, XXX, i, 67 2; *LW*, LI, 146.

complete depth of the attitude toward government and so illuminates also the essence of authority.

When we compare the various texts, we discover that the word *honorare* has never undergone essential change in Luther's explanations of the fourth commandment. In the "Instruction for the Confession of Sins" (1518) Luther wrote :

> Honor goes beyond love and also includes honor and reverence. Besides, the Lord wants, that we should think here of the practice and the reality of honor, as is clear in the Gospel. The Lord has put parents and superiors into his place and has commanded that they be regarded as his representatives.[1]

In the Large Catechism he writes, It is "a much greater thing to honor than to love. Honor includes not only love but also deference, humility, and modesty, directed (so to speak) toward a majesty hidden within them."[2]

For Luther this honoring by no means consists "only in greeting or bowing, but rather in doing or not doing according to their will or need." [3] More important, however, this *honorare* points up the special position of the fourth commandment in the Decalog, for this commandment points both to the first table, which presents our obligations to God, and to the second table, which is concerned with our neighbor. Simultaneously it deals with our spiritual and our secular relationship. *Honorare* gives expression to both the divine and the social dimension of every authority.

In the first place, "honor" means more than "love." The love to fellowmen speaks about essential human equality [4] and about willing service to the neighbor.[5] This is the concern of the six subsequent com-

---

[1] "Instructio," *WA*, I, 258 19-22.

[2] "GK," *WA*, XXX, i, 147 27ff; *L.C.*, art. I, 106.

[3] "Erklärung," *WA*, I, 251 3-4. Cf. also "Instructio," *WA*, 258 20; "... opus et veritatem honoris... "; "DPW," *WA*, I, 447 19 ff. Here is an implicit reference to Mt. 15, 5 and Mark 7, 10-11 : "Hoc praeceptum Iudaei foecerunt irritum per traditiones suas, sicut et omnia alia, Quia honorem hunc exponebant solum in verbis et signis, irritatores facti verborum legis"; "VGW," *WA*, VI, 250 33 : "... wilche ehre nit darinnen stets allein, das man sich mit geberden ertzeigt, sondern... "; "Pr. 2. M.," *WA*, XVI, 495 7-8 : "Tu, inquit, honora, Tu i.e. cum omni eo quod es, ratione, voluntate, manu, non solum pileo, Tu, non solum manus, sed corpus et anima." "KPr III," *WA*, XXX, i, 67 6-7 : "Honorare autem non solum fit corpore, mit bücken, hut abziehen, sed ehrlich von yhn halten, ut corde &"; *LW*, LI, 146.

[4] See : "Pr.2.M.," *WA*, XVI, 492 2 : "Nam honorare est plus quam diligere, in hoc enim aequalitas solum est, in illo agnoscitur eciam principatus."

[5] "DPW," *WA*, I, 447 31 : "... quia charitas solummodo diligit prompta servire proximo... " Also : *WA*, I, 448 14-15.

mandments. Under the heading "Adversari vota caritati" (vows are against love) in "de Votis Monasticis Iudicium" the second table is divided into *obedientia parentum* and *charitas proximi* (obedience to parents and love to the neighbor).[1] Thus, the fourth commandment obviously addresses itself also to our relationships to our fellow man, as these relationships possibly confront us as *government*. "In illo agnoscitur eciam principatus" (In it also sovereignty is recognized).[2] For that reason honor is more than mere love. It is "reverence united with love,"[3] or it means "to esteem them highly in the heart for God's sake."[4] Since, as the Reformer emphasizes again and again, we are all equals in the sight of God as far as our *person* is concerned, the basis for the superiority expressed in the *office* is found in God and in His Word. *Honorare* contains an immediate reference to this basis and thus to the first table. This thought is often expressed in the explanations of the Decalog. In the third series of "Sermons on the Catechism" we read : "He has put father and mother next to himself and uses the word with which one honors him."[5] We are to honor the government because here God is present in a special way.

In the older documents, as in "The Ten Commandments Preached to the People in Wittenberg"[6] and in the "Instruction for the Confession of Sins"[7] and in the two related writings, "A Short Form of the Ten Commandments"[8] and the "Prayer Booklet,"[9] the rulers are called *vicarii Dei*. Thus we read in "The Ten Commandments":

---

[1] "De votis monasticis," *WA*, VIII, 623-29, *passim*; *LW*, XLIV, 326 ff.

[2] "Pr.2.M.," *WA*, XVI, 494 3. See note 4, p. 188.

[3] "VGW," *WA*, VI, 251 6; *LW*, XLIV, 81. Also *WA*, VI, 251 15 : "... sondern mit der ersten (Furcht), die mit liebe und zuvorsicht gemischt ist." "Instructio," *WA*, I, 258 19; "DPW," *WA*, I, 447 30; "Pr.2.M.," *WA*, XVI, 494 2; "KPr I," *WA*, XXX, i, 6 7; "GK," *WA*, XXX, i, 147 27; *L.C.*, art. I, 105.

[4] "KPr I," *WA*, XXX, i, 6 34. Also "KPr II," *WA*, XXX, i, 67 7, 12, and 19; 68 6; 72 10. "DPW," *WA*, I, 448 13 : "... magnificam opinionem in corde habere."

[5] "KPr III," *WA*, XXX, i, 67 2; *LW*, LI, 146. Also "Pr.2.M.,"*WA*, XVI, 488 1 "Honor soli deo debetur, tamen hic iubet eciam exhiberi parentibus, principibus eciam debetur honor."

[6] "DPW," *WA*, I, 448 33 ("vicaria... [1. 35] in isto ut in alio, scilicet regentibus, qui sunt sedes, officina, altare, propitiatorium eius"); 456 24-31; 459 10 ;460 5; 461 4 ("locum tenentes"); 461 13 ("vicarii").

[7] "Instructio," *WA*, I, 258 21.

[8] "Form," *WA*, VII, 206 4 : "an gottis statt sitzen..."

[9] "Betbüchlein," *WA*, X, ii, 378 18; *LW*, XLIII, 15.

> This commandment is placed immediately after the commandments of the
> first table because it speaks of those who are the representatives of God.
> Hence, just as God must be reverenced with honor and fear, so also his re-
> presentative.[1]

In the later texts the accent rests more strongly on the positive command of God *extra me*, as it confronts me in the Decalog. In the commandment I know what God commands me, for there are "no good
works...except those which God has commanded." [2] This ever-recurring
thought has an explicit anti-papal and anti-monastic slant, against
every form of "lengthy, invented works of men, such as pilgrimages,
building churches, seeking indulgences, and the like." [3] From the Word
of God God's commandment is recognized and confirmed by Christ in
Matth. 15 :4.[4] The Word of God gives authority *ab extra* to parents and
every government, to people who of themselves are nothing. So Luther
writes in his letter to Briesmann : "Not because the parent as a man
commands and ordains, but because God in his commandment has
established the parent's commandment and demands obedience." [5] In
contrast, the monastic authority has been invented by men and is "an
authority and obedience without the Word of God." [6]

It is hardly surprising to find in the Large Catechism again much that
appeared already in the earlier writings about the question of the basis
for this obedience. To honor the parents means to esteem and prize them
as the most precious treasure on earth, [7] "for God sets father and
mother apart and "places them next to himself." [8] 'God has exalted
this estate of parents above all others; indeed, he has appointed it to
be his representative on earth.' [9] This "honor includes...deference, hu-

---

[1] "DPW," *WA*, I, 447 32-448 3.

[2] "VGW," *WA*, VI, 204 13; *LW*, XLIV, 23.

[3] "VGW, VI, 264 8-9; *LW*, XLIV, 98. See also "Predigten 1528," *WA*, XXVII, 6 33, "electicia opera et sine dei mandato."

[4] "Annotationes," *WA*, XXXVIII, 584 36ff.

[5] "Briesmannum," *WA*, XI, 289 13f.

[6] *Ibid.*, *WA*, XI, 289 19. Also r. 31 : "Deum ipsum cum suo praecepto negando." Also "Pr.2.M.," *WA*, XVI, 491 3 : "Hic filius oculos aperiat, non in carnem patris, quae nihil est, sed in verbum dei. O magna gloria patris propter hoc verbum. Auro ornan- tur reliquiae sanctorum, sed hic pater ornatus est verbo dei." "Predigten 1528," *WA*, XXVII, 6 21-7 26 (*passim*), e.g., 7 20 : "Et est homo sanctus (Joseph) propter opus in obedientia factum... Non propter opus, sed quia commissum." KPr III," *WA*, XXX, i, 96 8 : "non propter meam dignitatem, sed propter praeceptum"; *LW*, LI, 170.

[7] "GK," *WA*, XXX, i, 148 8; *L.C.*, art. I, 109.

[8] "GK," *WA*, XXX, i, 147 26; *L.C.*, art. I, 105.

[9] "GK," *WA*, XXX, i, 150 26; *L.C.*, art. I, 126.

mility, and modesty, directed (so to speak) toward a majesty hidden within them." [1] Children are to be taught "to revere their parents as God's representatives" [2] and "not to think of their persons, whatever they are, but of the will of God, who has created and ordained them to be our parents." [3] Here too, in an anti-monastic sortie against the monastic obedience invented by men; the superior quality of God's commandment and of obedience to parents and divinely ordained government is explicitly emphasized : "What God commands must be much nobler than anything we ourselves may devise." [4] Through the Word and the commandment, God Himself is, as it were, the guarantor of authority. The Word is the positive guarantee that God has commanded this reverence and this obedience and has thereby equipped men *ab extra* with government. In the Large Catechism this *ab extra*-character is fittingly illuminated in the discussion about baptism. There Luther compares the relationship between water and Word in baptism with the elevation of the person through the commandment.

> But because the commandment is added, "You shall honor father and mother," I see another man, adorned and clothed with the majesty and glory of God. The commandment, I say, is the golden chain about his neck, yes, the crown on his head, which shows me how and why I should honor this particular flesh and blood.[5]

In the external application (first use of the law) obedience can and should under certain circumstances—as in the Old Testament—be extracted by force, where the child or subject refuses to obey[6]. But the salutary, spiritual application of the law (second use) springs from a believing heart. It discloses the inability to fulfill the law and thus impels to reliance on God who provides the internal freedom for obedience. Obedience—if it is really Christian obedience—presupposes faith, the proper conscience, "where man experiences what and who God is"[7], and "the proper confidence toward God." [8] "As their conscience stands and believes in relation to God, so are the works which proceed from it."[9]

---

[1] "GK," *WA*, XXX, i, 147 28; *L.C.*, art. I, 106.

[2] "GK," *WA*, XXX, i, 147 34; *L.C.*, art. I, 108.

[3] "GK," *WA*, XXX, i, 148 2; *L.C.*, art. I, 108.

[4] "GK," *WA*, XXX, i, 148 27; *L.C.*, art. I, 113. Cf. *WA*, XXX, i, 149 17-31; 153 11-28; *L.C.*, art., I 116f; 144ff.

[5] "GK," *WA*, XXX, i, 214 25-29; *L.C.*, art. IV, 20.

[6] "Predigten 1523," *WA*, XI, 40 9.

[7] See Lohse's essay.

[8] *Ibid.*

[9] "VGW," *WA*, VI, 205 8; *LW*, XLIV, 24.

Faith is the chief work without which other works cannot be pleasing to God.[1] But this presupposes the prior transformation of man through grace : "Si...quidam obediunt, fit ex nova spiritus gratia..." ("if there are those who obey, this arises from the new grace of the Spirit").[2] In the third series of "Sermons on the Cathechism" the primacy of the first commandment is expressly stated. There Luther states that one should not keep the fourth commandment for the sake of the parents, but "propter 1. praeceptum, quod mandat : Time Deum etc." ("for the sake of the first commandment which commands, 'Fear God' ").[3] This applies equally to all other commandment and is already present in all of Luther's explanations of the Decalog. The emphasis on obedience for God's sake stands under the primacy of the first commandment. Even government itself dare never become an idol.

The *ab extra* of authority and the *ab intra* of obedience are important for the relationship between conscience and authority. Human authority appears in God's shadow ; it is essentially ordained and instituted by God. It is like a *sacramentum*, where the believing man meets God mediately. We must not blur the fact that for Luther the authority of "fathers by blood, fathers of a household, and fathers of a nation" [4] thus takes on an explicit divine weight. Only the specifically churchly authority has increasingly been lessened in his theology and finds less and less positive expression in the explanations of the fourth commandment. Because the proper service of the church through preaching of the Word and administration of the sacraments belongs directly to the relation with God, it is treated in connection with the first table. The purely ecclesiastical and human traditions which the church proposes to us in the church's laws and ordinances and which belong in the fourth commandment are quite secondary. They are to be observed insofar as they do not conflict with the lofty first commandment.[5] Because conscience has a decidedly theological significance for

---

[1] See e.g., "VGW," *WA*, VI, 206 15.

[2] "Pr.2.M.," *WA*, XVI, 498 7. See also "KPr I, "*WA*, XXX, i, 6 26 : "nullus puer considerat... nisi spiritus sanctus suggerat."

[3] "KPr III," *WA*, XXX, i, 67 13; *LW*, LI, 146. Also "KPr III, "*WA*, XXX, i, 77 17 : "Ad unumquodque praeceptum scribe : time et confide deo." Also *WA*, XXX, i, 68 2; 69 15; 72 3 and 10; 76 10; 81 4; 85 7 : "Iam wollen wir alle praecepta zusamen fugen ynn ein krentzlein, das letzte ynn das erste. Ubique haec duo invenies, ut timeas deum et fidas deo."

[4] "GK," *WA*, XXX, i, 155 3-4; *L.C.*, art. I, 158.

[5] "Annotationes," *WA*, XXXVIII, 584 22ff.

Luther and deals with our position in the presence of God, it is clear that obedience to an order established by God is a strict obligation of conscience. A right conscience demands obedience.

III

And yet, precisely in the just mentioned primacy of the first commandment there is also the counterweight against every evasion of one's own responsibility in favor of an unlimited, absolute obedience. It is true, obedience is for Luther an essential and capital virtue; but in no sense an absolute one. We shall mention only two limitations.

First, most of the explanations of the fourth commandment present a diptych, where alongside the duties involved in the obedience of subjects there is also a more or less detailed treatment of the considerateness of parents and every government for their children and subjects.[1] The governor, too, must in faith place himself under God and His commandments; he is not excluded from the fourth commandment.[2] The position of this office is appropriately defined in the Large Catechism : God does not

> assign them this honor (that is, power and authority to govern) merely to receive homage. Parents should consider that they owe obedience to God, and that, above all, they should earnestly and faithfully discharge the duties of their office. [3]

The government dare not set itself up as an idol. It, too, is under God. It, too, has its obligation of conscience, even though it may be at a different place and with different responsibilities over against men.

Secondly, in case of a conflict the obeyer's observance of the fourth commandment is conditioned by obedience to the first commandment. In the explanation of the Decalogue the *Clausula Petri*, "we must obey God rather than men," Acts 5 :29,[4] has a pendant in the similar state-

---

[1] See e.g., in summary, in "VGW," *WA*, VI, 264 16ff. : "Tzum Zwentzigsten...";
LW, XLIV, 99. Also "GK," *WA*, XXX, i, 156-57.

[2] "KPr III," *WA*, XXX, i, 74 5-6 : "Ideo vos parentes bene discite vos non esse exclusos ex hoc 4. praecepto." "KPr III," *WA*, XXX, i, 73 4 : "Et quicunque tandem hoc nomen (pater) gerit, videat, ut suum paternum officium exequatur."

[3] "GK," *WA*, XXX, i, 156 10-14; *L.C.*, art. I, 168.

[4] See H. Dörries, "Gottesgehorsam und Menschengehorsam bei Luther. Ein Beitrag zur Geschichte des Apostelworts Acta 5.29," *ARG*, XXXIX (1942), 47-84. Also in *Wort und Stunde* (Göttingen, 1970), III, 109-94.

ment, give honor " so long as it is not contrary to the first three commandments," [1] This reservation is found, even though quite incidentally in various explanations, most detailed in the "Treatise on Good Works"[2] and in the "Annotations on Some Chapters of Matthew." [3] From this it follows that the refusal to obey can never be the rule or norm. It is the exception which one must be ready to justify by taking "a firm hold of...the First Table." [4] Because of the negligence and sinfulness of every government it is clear from both of the cited documents that the scope of the application of the exceptions can be very broad; it refers not only to that which is commanded contrary to the first commandment but, as the illustrations demonstrate, it refers to everything that contradicts the Decalogue.[5] Every one, father, son, master and subject, stands under the same commandment. "Si contra deum vult pater, ut obediam & dicam : pater, eundem habemus deum cui uterque subditur, in aliis ergo tibi sum subiectus..." ("If the father wants me to obey him in opposition to God, I shall say, Father, we have the same God to whom we are both subject. Therefore I am subject to you in other things").[6]

We have presented only an outline. However, in our opinion, it represents a necessary supplement to the main essay. This study of Luther's explanations of the fourth commandment, which needs to be elaborated further in view of what the Reformer has said in other contexts about this commandment, casts light on Luther's possible answer to the question of the relation among conscience, authority, and obedience, as understood today.[7]

---

[1] "VGW," WA, VI, 251 2; LW, XLIV, 81.

[2] "VGW," WA, VI, 253 1-5; LW, XLIV, 82-83, WA, VI, 255 18-261 22 passim; LW, XLIV, 84-89. WA, VI, 265 15-21; LW, XLIV, 91.

[3] "Annotationes," in Mt. 8, 21-22 : WA, XXXVIII, 470 12-471 4; in Mt. 10, 35 : WA, XXXVIII, 511 1-512 10; in Mt. 15, 1-4 : WA, XXXVIII, 581 21-589 3, especially 584 7-21 and 587 34-588 15.

[4] "VGW," WA, VI, 257 1; LW, XLIV, 89.

[5] E.g., "VGW," WA, VI, 265 15-26; LW, XLIV, 100; and "Annotationes," WA, XXXVIII, 588 7-15.

[6] "Pr.2.M.," WA, XVI, 496 1-2. Also "Fastenpostille," WA, XVII, ii, 67 13-18; "KPr II," WA, XXX, i, 33 34 : "Quicquid illi dicunt, scito deo placere, nisi sit contra Deum, tum enim creavit te, ut prius honores eius verbum et opus."

[7] This short essay has been worked out in a larger study : Jos E. Vercruysse, "Autorität und Gehorsam in Luthers Erklärungen des vierten Gebotes", Gregorianum 54 (Rome, 1973), 448-476.

COLLOQUIUM

"From 'Aristotle' to 'Reason': The Topical Index of the Weimar Edition as a Tool for Luther Scholarship."

1. Prior to the beginning of the Congress, all participants received copies of the working models of proposed index articles entitled *Probeartikel zum Sachregister der Weimarer Lutherausgabe (Abt. Schriften)*. These model articles were prepared under the auspices of the commission responsible for the editing of Luther's works ("Kommission zur Herausgabe der Werke Martin Luthers"). They were written by researchers at the Institute for Late Medieval and Reformation Studies at the University of Tübingen under the direction of Prof. Heiko A. Oberman. The model articles, which appeared both in the *Archiv für Begriffsgeschichte* (XIV/2, 1970, pp. 172-265 and XV/1, 1971, pp. 7-93) and separately in one volume (Bonn : Bouvier, 1971), include SOL by W. Bohleber, RATIO by K.H. zur Mühlen, ERUDIO by H. Jürgens, and ARISTOTELES by G. Rokita.

The main body of each article is prefaced by an introduction which serves two purposes. First, it gives an outline of the article and, secondly, it calls attention to bibliographical material, semantic matters, and historical background which will help the reader use the article effectively. In the main body of the article, the occurrences of the entry word within Luther's works are ordered primarily according to systematic criteria, although the chronological sequence of the texts is adhered to under systematic headings. These model articles were intentionally printed in the most expanded format possible in order to provide the material for intensive discussion on the length and structure of the articles.

2. In opening the colloquium, Prof. H.A. Oberman recounted briefly the history of the topical index and described the academic and administrative framework of which the project is a part. S. Hendrix then explained the operational procedures employed in compiling the index. After this, brief critical reviews of the RATIO article were presented by Prof. B.A. Gerrish and Prof. B. Lohse.

B.A. Gerrish devoted most of his attention to the question of what kind of information the topical index intended to provide. If the purpose of an index article is to provide access to Luther's thought through a systematic ordering of the material, then the purely semantic treatment of a word (as e.g. in the second part of the RATIO article) should be distinguished from this and confined to the introduction of the article along with an appropriate list of references. In this way the length of an article could be considerably reduced. The length could be further reduced if a Luther text were quoted verbatim only when it illustrates a significant conceptual distinction. All other occurrences of the word could be identified simply by reference to their location in Luther's works.

Gerrish next observed that Luther used different words to describe the same thing (e.g. *ratio humana, sensus humanus, lumen naturae* et al.). As a result, the word family treated in an index article might not completely cover a concept which is also identified or signified by other words. This problem should be cared for by the use of cross references within the index. Gerrish asked why a computer could not be used in the preparatory stages of the index (cf. *infra*, 3 d). With the above comments in mind, Gerrish concluded that an article like the RATIO article would fulfill the expectations which he as a Luther scholar has of a topical index to the Weimar Edition.

Like Gerrish, B. Lohse favored limiting the semantic discussion of an entry word to the introduction to each article. The introduction should also provide an overview of the most important references to an entry word, e.g. those places where Luther offers a definition of the word or treats the concept in detail. Furthermore, cross references within an article should point out those passages in the Weimar Edition where the entry word is discussed at length, but which, due to the outline of the article according to systematic criteria, are referred to only piecemeal at different points in the article. (E.g. in the RATIO article reference should be made to *WA* 39 I; 175-177.) It is desirable to quote as much context as possible around the occurrence of an entry word. Nevertheless, in view of the length of the index, Lohse asked whether it would not suffice in many cases simply to cite the occurrences of an entry word when at least one or more texts are quoted in full.

3. These two evaluations were followed by a period of general discussion. The most important matters raised were: a) the distinction between the topical index and a concordance; b) the relationship of German and Latin entry words to one another; c) financial and d) technical problems involved; e) further planning.

a) Two possible alternatives to the topical index as presently conceived were suggested: either a concordance which would encompass all the occurrences of an entry word, or a theological wordbook limited to the most important concepts of Luther. A concordance would be especially useful for translators of Luther (e.g. for the American Edition). A complete concordance would also rule out any distortion due to a subjective selection of texts.

In reply to this, it was emphasized that such a concordance would have to include all occurrences of every word of Luther in order to be "complete". Since 67 volumes of the Weimar Edition at ca. 600 pages per volume are involved, such a concordance would be virtually impossible to compile, much less to use. It was pointed out, however, that all relevant occurrences of each important entry word are carefully compiled and will be available on index cards in the archive at the Institute in Tübingen. The published index will of necessity include only a limited number of the most significant texts and references selected from the archive. (The selection criteria and structure of the index will be up for discussion at the next Luther Congress.) Nevertheless, the entire archive will be available to scholars and a duplicate archive could perhaps be located in the U.S.A.

In this connection Prof. H. Bluhm reminded the audience of the *Index verborum* of all the German works of Luther being prepared under his direction. It is already complete for the years 1516 -1524 and publication should begin around 1981.

b) The question was raised how German entry words would relate to their Latin equivalents (e.g. *Sonne* and *Vernunft* to *sol* and *ratio* in the present articles). Would it not be possible to include German and Latin words in the same article and discuss nuances of meaning and usage in an excursus or in the introduction to the article? In reply it was explained that the current consensus is that generally the German and Latin words must be dealt with in separate articles in order to do justice to the semantic peculiarities of each language and the unique place of each word in the historical and linguistic tradition. However, cross referencing will certainly be used in the index to indicate the relationship between a Latin word and its German equivalent (and vice versa) and to avoid needless duplication.

c) At several points during the discussion the concern was voiced how it would be possible realistically to complete a thorough index in the foreseeable future with the financial resources available. According to one suggestion, it might be more feasible to provide indices only for individual volumes of the Weimar Edition. The response to this emphasized that all the organization and working procedures up to this point have been directed towards the goal of supplying an index to the complete Weimar Edition. In any case, an index providing access to the totality of Luther's thought and writings is much more desirable and useful. The financial problems involved would be solved by publishing only a selected portion of the accumulated material and leaving the remainder available in the archive.

d) Since some 40,000 pages of Luther's writings are involved in this mammoth project, it is imperative to examine the possibility of using all the modern technological resources available. In particular, the question was raised whether the employment of electronic data processing equipment might not accelerate the work considerably. It was necessary, therefore, to explain why a computer had so far not been used in the compilation of the index.

The groundwork for the index had been completed for approximately one-third of Luther's works before technological developments reached the point where the employment of computers could even be considered. More important, however, was the problem of feeding the proper information correctly into the computer—which still poses a dilemma for much electronic data processing. In order to transfer the ca. 40,000 pages of the Weimar Edition onto punchcards or tape, one would have to transcribe not only the text of the Weimar Edition itself, but also countless interpretive symbols and references. In addition, every entry word would have to be rewritten in the basic form (case, tense, etc.) according to which it would be sorted. This transcription process would introduce an unmanageable source of human error.

In contrast to this, the photocopy procedure presently employed allows the text of the Weimar Edition to be reproduced on index cards without the necessity of any manual transcription. Besides the lesser time expenditure involved, it offers—over the computer—the advantage of absolute textual reliability, which is especially important for an instrument designed to aid historical research.

This advantage was unanimously recognized by the participants in the discussion.

(Instead of a computer, however, other electronic equipment could perhaps be used to eliminate the time consuming process of manually sorting index cards. Currently under study, therefore, is the possibility of using an automatic sorter, which could mechanically sort the index cards after the entry word has been written on each card in OCR *-letters.)

e) The target date for completing the archive with all index cards is 1981. At that time the production of the published index can begin.

---

* Orthographical Character Recognition.

SEMINAR REPORTS *

Luther and Nominalism

Chairman : Leif Grane, University of Copenhagen
Discussion Leaders : Bengt Hägglund ; University of Lund ; Jane Douglass, School of Theology at Claremont

The following texts were discussed in the seminar :
1) Luther's exegesis of Psalm 113, 1 (*WA*, IV, 261 f.) ;
2) Scholion on Rom. 4, 7 (*WA*, LVI, 268-287) ;
3) "Disputatio contra scholasticam theologiam," thesis 46-49 (*WA*, I, 226) ;
4) Some theses from the disputation on John 1 :14 (*WA*, XXXIX, i, 4 f.)

Some texts from Gabriel Biel's *Collectorium* and from the *Quaestiones super libros sententiarum* by Pierre d'Ailly, a short general bibliography, special references to the secondary literature concerning each of the texts to be discussed, and four contributions to the general discussion of the subject "Luther and Nominalism" (Grane, Hägglund, Iserloh, and Oberman) were sent to the participants of the seminar.

The text from the "Dictata" to Psalm 113 has often been discussed in the more recent literature. Luther there used the terminology of the doctrine of *facere quod in se est*. That raises the question : Is Luther there still convinced of the truth of this doctrine, or is he just trying to explain his own theology by it ? Through the discussions we came to agreement at least on the following points :

1) As Luther without the slightest reservation uses the doctrine of *facere quod in se est*, there can be no doubt that he at the moment has no consciousness of being in opposition to the school on this particular point, but that does not necessarily lead to the conclusion that he meant what this doctrine would express.

2) It is necessary to keep in mind that the interpretation of the psalm verse in question does not depend on the mentioning of the *facere quod*

---

* The seminar reports appear here as formulated by the seminar secretaries and approved by the chairmen.

in se est, but that this doctrine is only being intoduced by Luther as an affirmation of the exegesis already made. The *facere quod in se est* must be understood against the background of :

a) The *adventus Christi* is not given on merit, but exclusively on the *promissio* through which God has made Himself our debtor. That counts as well for *adventus in carnem* and *spiritualis adventus* as for the second *adventus*.

b) The difference between Luther's use of the *facere quod in se est* and the meaning of this doctrine, as, for instance, expressed by Gabriel Biel, can be illustrated through the different form they give to the traditional parable of the king and criminal, as James Preus has pointed out. Whereas Biel let a coin of *lead* be exchanged for the promised gold coin, the criminal has in Luther nothing whatsoever, except the promise of the king. In late medieval preaching, it was mentioned, the lead coin also was lacking, but so was the promise.

Discussing the different interpretations in the recent literature, we found it difficult to maintain the thought of merit in Luther, who is very clearly holding the doctrine of *bonitas* as an exclusively divine quality. But there was no agreement on the question, if the *promissio*, as expressed in this text, is still influenced by the Ockhamistic *pactum*-theology or if it is really the end of the medieval conception of grace. The *facere quod in se est*, it seems, does not mean any longer that man can obtain grace through it, but means that man only in the situation of *petitio* is open for the *promissio, capax doni*. Therefore, as far as a solution can be reached, it must at least involve the conclusion that Luther is using the doctrine mentioned exclusively for his own purposes, which are irreconcilable with the ideas on which the doctrine builds. Therefore, there should be no reason to find in this and similar texts any kind of *noch nicht überwundene Reste*.

The discussion of the scholion on Rom. 4, 7 did not lead to any general agreement. After a short discussion of the *simul iustus et iniustus*-thesis at the beginning of the scholion we tried to make out how this thesis is related to the different scholastic doctrines of sin and grace, especially the Thomistic and Ockhamistic doctrines. Whereas some of the participants were convinced that Luther's attack on the doctrine of the immediate disappearance of original sin also excludes the doctrine of Thomas Aquinas, one of the participants was of a different opinion. To put it briefly, the question debated is this : Does Luther's *simul* and the consequence thereof, the denial of the disappearance of original sin in one moment, only concern his Ockhamistic schoolmasters, or does it involve every doctrine of habitual grace, that is also, for instance, the Thomist ?

The next point discussed was the attack on the doctrines of *diligere Deum super omnia ex viribus suis* and of the two modes of fulfilling the law. Here it was clear that the doctrines Luther has in mind are those to be found in some of the followers of Ockham, as, for instance, in Gabriel Biel. Since Luther sees this attack as a consequence of the attack on the immediate disappearance of original sin, then the question arises if he has been of the opinion that the theology *ad modum Aristotelis in ethicorum*, as he says, *must* have this consequence. If that was what he would say, then we shall have to observe very precisely the connection between his criticisms of theological principles and the material content of his attacks on scholastic theology, which he sees as necessary consequences. Should it, on the other side, be that the material criticism also can be understood without observing its relation to the principles of theology, which the *simul*-thesis leads to, then it might be possible to isolate the attack on Ockhamism and leave open, whether also, for instance, classical scholasticism could be meant. In the last instance the whole question of Luther's attack becomes less important and seems only to be of value for the understanding of Luther's relation to his own school. On the other side, if the first opinion should correspond better to the texts, then his criticism is much deeper and of much importance if we want to understand the beginnings, not only of Luther, but of reformation theology.

At last we discussed the corollarium, where Luther opposes the definition of *iustitia* in Scripture (*sola reputatione Dei*) to the definition of the philosophers (*qualitas animae*). The questions which arise here can be put in this way : Should Luther's distinction here be understood as an understandable opposition to Ockhamism only so that we should not take the *categories*, which he uses, too seriously, but try to look behind them ? Then one might be able to see that Luther only tries to take sin and justice seriously, just as scholasticism in its classical period did, and then some sort of harmony between Thomism and Luther might arise, against the sinister background of Ockhamism. Some, however, would perhaps rather put the question this way : Is the way in which Luther opposes the two definitions, for him not one way among others, but the only possible way ? If that is the case, then we should realize that expression and content both are of the same necessity. That means : The wording of the two ways is already identical with the content. If so, is it still true that he makes himself clear in his opposition to Ockhamism ? Is he doing it in a way, which leads him away not only from Ockhamism, but from scholasticism as a whole ?

LUTHER AND ERASMUS

Chairman : Lewis W. Spitz, Stanford University
Discussion Leaders : John Payne, Bradley University; Roland Bainton, Yale University; Gottfried Krodel, Valparaiso University; Gunnar Wertelius, Edsbruk, Sweden; William Bouwsma, Harvard University; Jared Wicks, University of Chicago

Preamble contributed by Roland H. Bainton, the Nestor of Reformation studies in America : The Erasmian seminar has been conducted in an Erasmian spirit. No more offensive four letter words have been used than dear and love. But if nothing worse has been said, there may have been groanings unutterable. The young men show such competence that the old can say : "Now let us depart in peace for Erasmus will survive without us ! "

The six sessions were led by *periti* with special knowledge and publishing prowess on the topic selected for each meeting of the seminar. Pointing up specific topics from the nearly infinite subject matter helped the seminar gain in focus and provided for a certain progression in the discussions.

In the first session, led by Roland H. Bainton, who has, of course, published distinguished biographies of both Luther and Erasmus, attention was directed to a general comparison of the two great figures of the Reformation, their biographical, psychological, intellectual development, and religious similarities, shared experiences, and differences. The discussion raised in a preliminary way questions such as predestination rather than free will as the central issue in their famous exchange, the extent to which each held man's nature to be vitiated by the fall, cooperation and reward, *potentia absoluta* and *ordinata*, the importance of the consensus of the church for Erasmus, the relative importance of Origen, Chrysostom and other fathers for Erasmus, and the question of natural reason as understood by Luther, as well as the matter of Neoplatonism and mysticism's influence on Erasmus.

In the second session Gottfried Krodel guided the discussion through a comparison of the *Philosophia Christi* and the *Theologia crucis*, focussing attention upon three major points, 1. the theological structure of the two men's thought, 2. their conception of God involving such problems as the *potentia absoluta* and the *mysterium*, 3. the task of the Christian theologian, the concepts of the cross, sacramentum, and exemplum. A spirited discussion developed over the definition of "theologian." Père Georges G. Chantraine contributed a learned discourse on the idea of "mysterium" and the "ineffable" in Erasmus' thought about God, which conceptions Robert Bertram and Ed Schroeder compared with the *deus absconditus* dimension in Luther's view of God in the *theologia crucis*. Gunnar Wertelius developed the polarities in Luther's theology such as law and gospel, sin and grace, and his view of salvation and the good, a way of thought not congenial to the anthropological optimism of Erasmus. This contrast was challenged by other participants, Père Chantraine holding, for example, that in his understanding of flesh and spirit Erasmus was close to St. Paul, while John Payne and others maintained that with law Erasmus meant ceremonial law and therefore differed from Luther's view of law as accusatory and as demanding not only compliance but fulfillment. Erasmus' understanding of *justitia* also entered the discussion of the *theologia crucis* issue. It was suggested that Erasmus wanted God to exercise a single justice understandable to man in contrast to Luther's *justitia duplex*. The relation of Erasmus to the scholastic tradition elicited from John Payne the opinion that possibly Jean Gerson's may have been his preferred school.

The third session, shorter in length, led by Robert G. Kleinhans, focussed attention directly upon the presuppositions and arguments of the *De libero arbitrio* and the *De servo arbitrio* with some comments on the *Hyperaspistes*. The interpretations of Harry McSorley and E. Gordon Rupp were discussed in relation to the text.

In the fourth session John Payne led the discussion of Luther and Erasmus on the sacraments. Father Jared Wicks emphasized that Luther stressed the sacramental life. A significant part of the discussion, however, centered on the place of the sacraments in the thought of Erasmus, concluding that for him the sacraments were "more for him who is weak than for the strong." The ecclesiological implications of the sacramental theology of Erasmus were spelled out. The intriguing question of Erasmus' favoring a second baptism for adults and his possible spiritual paternity for Anabaptism was raised.

With the fifth meeting of the seminar led by James Tracy the discussion turned toward a broader subject, Erasmian humanism and Protestantism. The discussion leader structured the conversation of the *confabulatores* around two major subjects : 1. Erasmus' influence in particular within the various Protestant traditions and 2. the

Ausgänge of humanism in European culture. It was agreed that certain Erasmian themes were particularly important for the later Protestant tradition : 1. his opposition to clerical tyranny (which came to a focus during the years 1518-1521, as in the important letter to Paul Volz). Thus the *Paraphrases* contrasted the simplicity of the gospel with the splendor of the church; 2. his ironicism which was important not only immediately at the colloquy of Augsburg but lived on in the Arminian tradition in the Netherlands; 3. his spiritualism, stressing interiority at the expense of external practices. Was he close to Zwingli, to Anabaptists ? ; 4. his radical interpretation of the New Testament text and contribution to Biblical studies. A particularly enriching aspect of this session proved to be a bibliographical discussion which brought to light a particularly interesting array of articles and books not generally known in the seminar. Ancillary subjects covered were the tradition of patristic studies and the social implications and applications of Erasmus' religious teachings and humanism.

The sixth and final meeting of the seminar with Jared Wicks, S.J., serving as discussion leader was devoted to the question of Luther, Erasmus, and Catholicism. He developed the question of the understanding of the *De servo arbitrio* in the light of the work of Harry McSorley and Otto Pesch, and the implications of the work of Wilfred Joest in the ontology of the person in Luther's theology. An extensive discussion followed on the continuity or discontinuity between the *De servo arbitrio* and the official Lutheran position presented in the Augsburg Confession and the colloquy of August, 1530, where the principals were Melanchthon and Eck. The examination of the large Galatians commentary, Robert Bertram suggested, may elucidate the matter of continuity between the positions of the *De servo arbitrio* and the Luther of the 1530s.

LUTHER AND THE COUNCIL OF TRENT

Chairman : Otto Hermann Pesch, Albertus-Magnus Akademie
Discussion Leader : Ulrich Kühn, Leipzig

I. OBJECTIVES OF THE SEMINAR

According to the pre-planning of the chairman and discussion leader the task of the seminar was understood as a systematic-theological one. Accordingly the seminar did not discuss purely historical questions about the attitude of Luther to the impending council and the stance of the Lutherans toward the council. It occupied itself with the doctrinal formulations of the council in confrontation with Luther's theology.

Since a limitation of the theme was necessary and since, moreover, for the first time at a Luther Research Congress the theme "Luther and Trent" was being treated, the seminar turned to the central point of Tridentine doctrine and discussed questions pertaining to the decree on justification.

The main question was : Which assertions of the decree on justification are still today (1971) so controversial, that because of them the split between the churches is and must remain justified theologically. "Still today"—that means in the light of the historical understandings of Trent and Luther's theology on the one hand, and in the light of the hermeneutical insights into Lutheran and Roman Catholic systematic theology on the other hand.

II. The Seminar's Methodology

The bases of the discussion were the canons of the decree on justification in connection with their pertinent chapters. These were compared with corresponding pronouncements by Luther. At times these were represented by a characteristic Luther text, which pulled together in preeminent fashion the representative thoughts of Luther, without however thereby excluding other Luther texts from the discussion. The seminar was conscious of the methodological problematic of comparing an official pronouncement by a council with a scientific theological statement. However it could not urge a decisive reservation, if in some measure the task of the seminar was to be accomplished.

Every session had three stages : 1. interpretation of the Tridentine canon; 2. interpretation of Luther texts, respectively a Luther test; 3. comparison between the two pronouncements. Every session which took up a new aspect of the theme was introduced by a written statement by one of the participants, which a) presented the problem of interpreting the particular canon, b) clarified the substance of the problem, and c) set up theses for discussion and conclusions about the comparison.

The seminar dealt with the problem of freedom (canons 4-7), the concepts "justification" and "grace" (canons 10-11), and the problem of faith and the certainty of salvation (canons 12-14). The program included the doctrines of Christ as Law-giver and of merit; these could not be treated for lack of time. Other important themes were not even put on the agenda because of the time element. The session on the final day dealt with questions of the proclamation of justification in our day together with the actuality of both the Lutheran and the Tridentine formulations.

III. Progress, Results, Open Questions

Sixteen participants, including the chairman, were enrolled in the seminar; on the final day the number of participants totalled twenty. The seminar did not repeat in a *coup de main* either the Council of Trent or the plenary session of the Lutheran World Federation in Helsinki in 1963. Hence it cannot offer any suggestions for new canons or proposals for some kind of a Formula of Concord. The value of the seminar lay in probing beyond mere lectures on theological niceties which do not do more than give information about problems and spiritual viewpoints. In this respect tendencies of the questions and differences of opinion were evident, but there were no formulations on which all were agreed. Such tendencies were :

1. The Roman Catholic participants in accord with the practice of their church urged a formal, strict interpretation of the Tridentine texts in so far as their dogmatic obligation played a role in the discussion. They insisted that the Council did not condemn Luther in a formal, judicial sense, although in the canons the fathers wanted to strike at Lutheran concepts. However, it is still basically a question and still to be investigated, whether the Council really condemned Luther's teachings. Many participants were of the opinion that Luther's doctrine has actually been countered in the canons. Others were of the conviction that the council fathers did not understand the expressions, which Luther employed, in their proper sense. It was admitted that the Tridentine formulations of Luther's teachings in no wise pulled together *everything* that Luther said in various ways about the question.

2. In the course of the debate the interpretation gained ground that, on the one hand, the Council wanted to speak biblically and by no means wanted to define a specific, scholastic conception of being justified and its implications (the pattern of the three theological virtues and others). On the other hand the Tridentine fathers could think predominantly only in scholastic categories. Hence they were not capable of comprehending more about Luther's new statements than was contained in those categories, especially in the realm of the *causa* and *habitus* doctrine. That a concept such as *fiducia* (canon 12) or the certainty of salvation of those who believe (canon 13) could be equated

with justifying faith could therefore for the Tridentine fathers seem absurd.

3. Also with these suppositions one cannot assume that between the two positions there need be forever an exclusive either-or. Nevertheless, such a possibility can be open to discussion, only if each position emerges from its own self-understanding as a closed interpretation and articulation of the Christian message of salvation that has arisen out of specific, historical conditions and is drawn from them. With that the conviction prevailed that *today* Roman Catholic doctrine can no longer circumvent the expressions which Luther's understanding of justification introduced in the Christian knowledge of faith.

4. Finally, the seminar turned to the question which is mutual to Roman Catholic and Protestant theology, namely, in which way can the dogmatical formulations of the sixteenth century be transferred to the present. The question of the criteria to which such a "transfer" must be subjected was the decisive question. On the one hand, the kernel of the New Testament was pointed to as the decisive criterion. On the other hand, it was discussed in what way the change in the historical situation might be decisive for the articulation of the Christian message.

LUTHER AND CALVIN

Chairman : Brian Gerrish, University of Chicago
Discussion Leaders : Basil Hall, University of Manchester; Edward Dowey, Princeton Theological Seminary

It was decided to approach the subject of the seminar through three selected themes rather than by concentration on a single theme. We avoided moving directly to the most commonly discussed area of disagreement between the Lutheran and Reformed communions, viz., the doctrine of the Lord's Supper, although this subject was discussed at some length in the course of the seminar's considerations of ministry and ordination. Somewhat surprisingly, in view of the nature of the Congress and our location, the voice of Calvin was heard more loudly than that of Luther in the earlier sessions of the seminar. That is, the attention was focused on questions of Calvin interpretation rather than on differences between Luther and Calvin. But by the final day there was a genuine *Auseinandersetzung* concerning some of the alleged theological differences between Luther and Calvin.

The first theme, "The Role of Law in the Theologies of Luther and Calvin," was introduced by Edward Dowey of Princeton Theological

Seminary. Mr. Dowey's thesis was that in their explicit *definitions* of law the two reformers were in basic agreement, but that in the way in which they apprehended the whole complex of ideas associated with the word law a divergence must be noted. The negative connotations of the law for Luther prevented him from placing under the rubric of law many of his utterances which Calvin would have placed under the *usus tertius legis*.

This thesis stimulated a vigorous discussion, but it also elicited general consent. The suggestion was made, however, that the discussion had been carried on in too abstractly a theological fashion, and that consideration must be given not only to what Calvin said but also to how he behaved.

The group was thereby prepared for the second theme, "The Reformers and Their Historical Environment," introduced by Basil Hall of Manchester University. Mr. Hall argued that by reason of the peculiar situation in Geneva Calvin was drawn into civic activities in which he might not ordinarily have been engaged. Luther, on the other hand, faced with a much larger, more complex situation, not just one city, played a less active role in social affairs. The extent to which Luther and his associates were involved in social concerns was debated by members of the seminar. Further, in response to Mr. Hall's emphasis on the pragmatic character of many of Calvin's decisions in the realm of civic affairs, it was argued that Calvin regarded his political and economic policies as embodiments of the theological principle of love which he regarded as the sum of the law. Mr. Hall nevertheless maintained that he could find no direct, or even indirect, road from Calvin's theological positions to some of his activities in the political and economic sphere.

The third theme, "Ministry and Ordination in Luther and Calvin," was introduced by Hellmut Lieberg from Braunschweig, who summed up his findings in a series of five theses. The two areas of greatest contrast were : 1. in Calvin the idea of the external means of salvation is qualified by the divine transcendence and freedom (thesis 1); 2. the priesthood of all believers is not the way in which Calvin grounds the Christian ministry, whereas Luther has two ways of grounding the Christian ministry, in the institution of Christ and in the priesthood of all believers. The first of these contrasts evoked a lively debate centered on the doctrine of God and the nature of the incarnation and the sacraments. Concerning the second contrast, on ministry and priesthood, an initial disagreement was qualified by the recognition that the one line in Luther's thinking (viz., the divine institution) was the more prominent. One further area of disagreement concerned the sacramental quality of ordination in Luther.

REFORMATION AND SOCIETY

Chairman : Robert M. Kingdon, University of Wisconsin
Discussion Leader : George Forell, University of Iowa

The seminar on the Reformation and society has examined the connections between religion and society, particularly between religion and government, in the period of the Reformation. We began by considering some general theories which seek to explain some of these connections. First we considered the theory advanced by Guy Swanson, which claims to find in antecedent changes in the political structures of European states causes for the decisions made by these states either to adopt one version or another of the Protestant Reformation or to remain loyal to Roman Catholicism. Then we considered certain Marxist theories, which seek to find in class struggles over the control of the means of production causes for these same decisions. Then we considered a less general theory advanced by Bernd Moeller, which seeks to explain the religious decisions of the free cities in the Germanic empire by examination of the political and ecclesiastical traditions of these communities.

After discussing these theories at some length, we turned to four case studies of the connections between religion and politics in specific states. The four we selected for this more intensive examination were the city-states of Nuremberg and Geneva and the larger territorial states of Bohemia and the Habsburg holdings in Austria.

Our first conclusion is that general theories of explanation, in the present state of historical knowledge, do not seem very useful. The Swanson thesis is not only flawed by many gross errors of fact, but is also stated in such simplistic terms that it would be difficult even to refine it. Certain Marxist theories are somewhat more useful, but they need to be amplified. Even a middle-range theory which seeks only to explain limited categories of these phenomena, such as the Moeller thesis, contains some problems. Some of us suspect, for example, that Moeller may give undue importance to the individualistic thrust of Luther's thought. Some of us doubt that it is even possible to develop any general theory of explanation for these phenomena. All of us think that it is probably more fruitful at present to concentrate on mono-

graphic studies which explore in detail the connections between not
only religion and politics, but also between religion and other social
phenomena in specific states over relatively short periods of time.

One of the reasons these general theories are defective is that they
often fail to take into adequate account the fact that relations between
religion and politics include a great deal of mutual interaction. A
political phenomenon which one observer argues is a cause of a religious
development may, in fact, be its effect. Thus republican government in
Geneva may be the result rather than the cause of the Calvinist Reformation. Or the interactions between political and religious developments
may be so close that it is impossible to distinguish causes and effects.
Or one side of the political-religious equation may be much more interesting and better documented than the other. In our seminar, for
example, we found it more fruitful to examine the social and political
consequences of Luther's teaching in very specific ways, than to search
for the possible social and political origins of that teaching. We found
it particularly interesting to explore the development of Luther's
teachings on freedom, captivity, governmental authority, and calling.
We suspect that they affected such developments as the Peasants' War,
the Schmalkaldic wars, and the collapse of Protestantism in Austria,
and in turn were often modified by those events.

We have some suggestions for further research which are methodological. We would like to see some more intensive work on relevant
series of correspondence, collections of pamphlets (*Flugschriften*), visi-
tation reports, records of legal proceedings and similar archival materials. We recognize that these materials must often be examined with
highly refined critical techniques.

We also have some suggestions for further research which are topical.
We would like to see more work on the role of laymen in the Reformation,
in its reception, its institutionalization, and its propagation. We endorse
and encourage intensive studies not only of individual laymen but also
of significant groups of laymen who contributed in vital ways to Reformation developments. We would also like to see more work on the role
of law and of lawyers in the Reformation. Some of us are convinced that
principles of Roman and feudal law had a profound and often unap-
preciated effect on the thinking of many of the most prominent Protestant reformers. We also feel that the Reformers were dependent in many
very important ways upon professional lawyers for the implementation
of the Reformation, ways which are still not fully understood and
appreciated by the scholarly community.

In summary, we think that much remains to be done in these and other ways to advance our understanding of the Reformation and society. The task deserves the attention not only of experts in Luther studies but of students of other aspects of the Reformation as well. It deserves the energy not only of church historians but of several varieties of secular historians.

LUTHER AND PATRISTICS

Chairman : Bernhard Lohse, University of Hamburg
Discussion Leader : Jaroslav Pelikan, Yale University

The seminar addressed itself to the patristic references in five documents that spanned Luther's career :

1) The Heidelberg Disputation (1518);

2) The paragraphs on the three hypostases in the Godhead in part three of the "Great" Confession on the Sacrament of the Altar (1528);

3) Luther's preface to the pseudonymous books against the idolatry of the Arians ascribed to St. Athanasius (1532);

4) Luther's anti-Schwenckfeldian disputation on the Godhead and humanity of Christ (1540);

5) Luther's autobiographical preface to his collected Latin works (1545), as a kind of inclusive parenthesis bracketing the other four.

The seminar profited greatly from the fact that Professor Lohse had invited European members of the seminar to prepare themselves to provide detailed introductions to several of the documents. It may or may not be significant that none of the documents from Luther's pen to which the Church of the Augsburg Confession commits itself in the Book of Concord were selected for examination.

Professor Lohse himself introduced the autobiograpical statement of 1545. The discussion centered on the extent to which two factors determined Luther's position. One factor was the residual Augustinian element in late medieval theology generally and among the Hermits of St. Augustine in particular. The second factor was Luther's own direct and deliberate first-hand study of St. Augustine's writings. A consensus emerged that Luther's autobiographical statement does not exclude the possibility that he had had contact with *De spiritu et littera* before that reading of it in which he stumbled by accident upon the Augustinian insight that he personally found so congenial and reassuring.

Dr. Heiko Jürgens introduced the patristic quotations in the Heidelberg Disputation with a careful essay. A number of important points came out of the paper and the subsequent discussion. (1) Luther cites the fathers of the church as a kind of counterweight to support his rejection of the authority of the schoolmen. (2) Luther sees the authority of the fathers as derived; the fathers are authoritative when their view supports a given teaching in the Sacred Scriptures. (3) The fathers are part of the fabric of Luther's organic proof, which draws on the Sacred Scriptures, the fathers, and "reason." The question of Luther's dependence on chrestomathies and florilegia was raised by the obvious fact that some of his quotations in the Heidelberg Disputation are ultimately derived from Peter Lombard's *Sentences*.

A statement by Père Reinoud Weijenborg initiated the discussion of the paragraphs in Luther's personal confession of faith at the end of the "Great" Confession on the Sacrament of the Altar. A number of insights developed from the discussion. (1) In Luther the teaching about the Holy Trinity is typically related to the atonement and to soteriology in general. (2) There is some ambiguity on the degree to which it is the fathers or later theologians that inform Luther's terminology. (3) In any case, Luther clearly stands in the Western Catholic tradition, and he is determined to assert his adherence to the traditional Catholic faith and in the great essentials to maintain his position in the Latin-Roman tradition.

Professor Lohse introduced the discussion on the preface to the pseudo-Athanasian books against Arian idolatry. The discussion indicated a general feeling that while the traditional teaching about the Trinity is not central to Luther's theology, it is nevertheless a basic and indispensable constituent of his theology. Like his predecessors among the schoolmen and the fathers, Luther was acutely aware of the limitations of the traditional terminology. For Luther part of the problem lay that in engaging in the theological enterprise at his particular place in time and in geography he was compelled to translate the vocables that he had inherited and on occasion to attempt to devise new terminology.

Dr. Holsten Fagerberg provided an able introduction to the disputation on the Godhead and humanity of Christ. This disputation turned out in the discussion to be crucial for the view of the fathers that the mature Luther entertained. It is true that Luther misunderstood and in the heat of his polemic distorted details of Schwenckfeld's position; the latter is not in any case easily reducible to a consistent formulation. Luther held a high view of the creedal formulae that he found in the church's worship, especially the *Symbolum Quicunque vult* and *Te Deum laudamus.* He did not regard the fathers as being above criticism. Later generations, he held, must forgive the fathers, but at the same time later generations should not imitate the weaknesses of the fathers on issues where the church subsequently achieved clarity.

The seminar observed that, as far as one may generalize from this limited sampling, the role of the fathers increases in the course of Luther's theological career. Again, as Luther's understanding of the Sacred Scriptures grows, he operates with notably greater freedom and confidence in his use of his patristic authorities.

The seminar discussions disclosed that among the areas that might fruitfully have been investigated were such matters as Luther's use of the fathers in the Leipzig Debate, in the Marburg Colloquy, and in his liturgical work; some of the technical problems connected with the sources of Luther's patrological information; inquiries into the influence of individual fathers on Luther; and further clarification of the role of the fathers in Luther's handling of the Sacred Scriptures and tradition.

TEXT SEMINAR ON THE DICTATA

Chairman : Reinhard Schwarz, University of Tübingen
Discussion Leader : Steven E. Ozment, Yale University

The "Text Seminar on the *Dictata*" compared Luther's commentary on Psalm 50 with commentaries by Augustine, Nicholas of Lyra, Paul of Burgos, Matthew Doering, Johannes Reuchlin, and Faber Stapulensis. The following conclusions resulted.

First, the seminar noted parallels in Luther's terminology and thought with Franciscan (and late nominalist) covenant theology, especially at the crucial point of relating "accusare seipsum" and "iustificare Deum." [1] There was disagreement on the degree to which the priority of confession to justification was simply logical and not also, at least in part, conditional. This of course remains a hotly debated issue in Luther scholarship.

On the whole, it was clear to the seminar that Luther had broken already at decisive points with the medieval exegetical and theological traditions. Especially striking over against the exegetical tradition was

---

[1] Cf. *Luthers Werke in Auswahl* : *Der junge Luther*, ed. Erich Vogelsang (Berlin, 1955), V, 70 11-12, 73 30, 120 4-8, 15-27, 123 23-29.

Luther's interpretation of vs. 6 ("Tibi soli peccavi") by way of Romans 3:4. The exegesis of this verse occupies the bulk of the *scholia*—an inordinate preoccupation by comparison with the exegetical tradition. Further, Luther associates the *agnitio et confessio peccati* with *peccatum originale* rather than with *peccata actualia* in glossing this verse.[1] By contrast, the exegetical tradition had waited until verse 7 ("Ecce enim in iniquitatibus conceptus sum") before bringing up the topic of original sin. Since the latter was considered to have been dispatched in baptism, the confession of sin in the medieval sacrament of penance always involved actual sins. A medieval theologian might well have considered Luther's interpretation a misunderstanding. However, Luther's novelty here may rather be indicative of a very profound conception of sin and a willingness to modify the content of traditional vocabulary. The young Luther, as the student of the *Dictata* soon discovers, says very different things with a very traditional theological terminology.

It was clear to the seminar that Luther was struck by the way union with God was accompanied by the discovery of distance from God. To be "conformed" with God meant to agree with God's judgment of oneself as sinful. According to the psalmist, confession of sin and beauty before God are simultaneous. Luther glosses vss. 6-7 : "He who is most beautiful to God is the basest of men in his own eyes, and, vice versa, he who is most unsightly to himself is most beautiful to God."[2] Indeed, confession of sin is said to justify God (in his words) and, in turn, oneself.[3] A "simul" emerges between *accusare seipsum* and *deum iustificare*.[4] Further, the righteous are described as being "always" sinful, those who are "always" to be accused.[5] Also, Luther distinguishes between righteousness *coram Deo* and *coram hominibus*.[6] The sin of which the psalmist speaks is neither legal nor simply moral in nature; it is sin "before God": "Tibi soli peccavi."

The seminar regarded these as forward-looking thoughts, surely in transition from the *caritas* soteriology and *synteresis* anthropology of medieval theology.

---

[1] *Ibid.*, V, 70 15ff.
[2] *Ibid.*, V, 122 21-23.
[3] *Ibid.*, V, 123 35-124 1.
[4] *Ibid.*, V, 124 15-19.
[5] *Ibid.*, V, 122 15-17, 123 20-22, 125 19-22.
[6] *Ibid.*, V, 125 31-35.

Problems of Translation

Chairman : Robert H. Fischer, Lutheran School of Theology at Chicago
Discussion Leader : Paul David Pahl, Highgate, South Australia

Nine persons constituted the seminar on problems of translation.
The members, none of whom was a professional philologist, were bound
together by a common interest in the accurate understanding of sixteenth
century texts. Our program therefore was basically a cooperative en-
deavor of amateurs, exploring the following excerpted texts :
From Latin :
  1. *Bondage of the Will* (*De Servo Arbitrio*) ;
  2. *Preface to Luther's Latin Writings*, 1545.
From German :
  3. Luther's Correspondence : a session in which Dr. Gottfried Krodel,
translator of the three volumes of selected letters for the American
Edition of *Luther's Works*, came into the seminar as a guest leader and
illustrated problems in the realms of (a) grammar and syntax, (b) lexico-
graphy and idiomatic expression, and (c) cultural context.
  4. Melanchthon's *Heubtartickel* of 1558, compared with the Latin *Loci*
of 1559.
  5. Thomas Müntzer's translation of Psalm 19, and his interpretation
of it in a letter to Christoph Meinhard.
  6. Justus Jonas' translation of Luther's *Ninety-five Theses*.

In several cases we compared German and Latin versions of the
passages, and occasionally also the current English translations.

There were two other features of the seminar : (1) a brief discussion,
led by Hilton Oswald of Concordia Publishing House and Helmut
Lehmann of Fortress Press, on publishers' editorial difficulties in
Luther-translations, and (2) a joint effort to draft a bibliography
(particularly for amateurs) on "Aids for Luther-Translation."

Luther and Karlstadt

Chairman : Heiko A. Oberman, University of Tübingen
Discussion Leaders : Ulrich Bubenheimer, University of Tübingen,
Kensuke Tomimoto, Tokushima University

In order not to overlook the historical development of Karlstadt's
thought, the "Luther and Karlstadt" seminar looked at documents in
several stages of both men's development. We focused on four issues.

1. *The Character of Karlstadt's Early Augustinianism*

After comparing Karlstadt's theses of April 1517, and Luther's theses of September 1517, we concluded that although both men taught a *sola gratia*, Karlstadt's *simul bonus et malus* tended to be more ethically oriented and more indebted to Augustine than Luther's *simul iustus et peccator*. It was agreed that differences that became clear later on are not necessarily to be found in the early period.

2. *How Early Did Karlstadt Adopt S o l a S c r i p t u r a ?*

There was agreement that Barge overstated the case in arguing that in the *Apologeticae Conclusiones* of May 1518, Karlstadt preceded Luther in discovering the sole authority of Scripture. Karlstadt already clearly realized that the new theology would require a major rethinking of the problem of Scriptural authority, and increasingly emphasized the primacy of Scripture on the basis of a redefinition of the *sensus literalis* (theses 23ff), but he was not yet ready to place Scripture in direct opposition to the Pope. He did however deny the inerrancy of general councils. There was disagreement over whether the term *sola scriptura* should be applied to such a position, especially in light of Brian Tierney's application of the term to the medieval canonists, upon whom, it has been recently shown, Karlstadt was partially dependent.

3. *Wittenberg Movement*

Did Karlstadt execute the common Wittenberg program or initiate a new movement? Although there was a common theological front at many points (eg. *sola scriptura*, the rejection of works-righteousness, etc.), nevertheless Karlstadt differed from Luther in that he placed, perhaps because of a juridical mind-set, a great emphasis on the normative role of law in the Christian life (see his *Von Abtuhung der Bilder*). We could not reach a consensus on whether the difference in the time-table was due to strategic or theological factors.

4. *Between Luther and Müntzer*

Lacking the apocalyptic immediacy of Müntzer, Karlstadt was interested in reordering life. Karlstadt rejected the use of coercion in establishing his theological program. His emphasis on the Spirit was somewhat counterbalanced by the continuing role of the letter of Scripture. While questioning the use of the class structure as the decisive interpretative category, we recorded that further exploration along the lines suggested by the work of Gerhard Fuchs would be desirable.

5. *Special Presentations*

Special presentations were made by Heiko A. Oberman, Ronald J. Sider, Ulrich Bubenheimer, Calvin Pater, Johannes Wallmann, James S. Preus, and George H. Williams.

H.A. Oberman initiated the discussion with the interpretation of some central propositions from Karlstadt's anti-scholastic theses of April 1517. Whereas the differences with Luther are in no way unequivocal, but rather must be conjectured in a few places from knowledge of the later development of Karlstadt's theology (see section I, above), the parallels and agreements with Luther's *Disputatio contra scholasticam theologiam* (Sept. 1517) predominate. Oberman is of the opinion that in light of the statements under consideration from Karlstadt as well as from Luther, the old formulation of the question—Is Luther dependent on Karlstadt (so H. Barge) or Karlstadt on Luther (so K. Müller)?—is not very fruitful. Oberman suggests that we think rather of the circle of Wittenberg colleagues as the intellectual community in which there arose through mutual interchange and reciprocal stimulation a "Wittenberg University Theology" in which the individual members of the Wittenberg circle participated together. That does not preclude seeing Luther as the central figure of this circle. But it would be questionable to presuppose Luther's course as the only one in the development of the new Reformation theology. In view of the subsequent progressive estrangement between Karlstadt and Luther, Oberman wonders whether Karlstadt does not start from an earlier stage of Luther's theology which Luther himself had transcended.

Ronald J. Sider discussed the problem of Scriptural and papal authority in the young Karlstadt. On the basis of both the *Apologeticae Conclusiones* (May 1518, theses 12ff) and subsequent letters and publications, he argued, *pace* Barge, who totally ignored thesis 15, that not until 1520 was Karlstadt willing unequivocally to adopt *sola scriptura* if that involved declaring that popes had or could err. In 1518, he preferred to think in terms of a harmony between Scripture on the one hand and the teaching of the fathers, the popes, the liturgy, etc. on the other.

U. Bubenheimer advocated the view that Karlstadt's ecclesiology in 1518 did not go beyond the canonist tradition and pointed to the explicit union of theology and jurisprudence which Karlstadt had effected in the *Apologeticae Conclusiones* (especially thesis 37). Bubenheimer posed the question whether Karlstadt's occasional predilection for juridical thought forms even after his rejection of canon law (1520) could have had an influence on his later so-called legalistic attitude. Karlstadt's central argument in *Von Abtuhung der Bilder* is the appeal to the divine law. In light of the condition of ecclesiastical life, he advocated a legalism of a juridical character which demands the uncompromising realization of the divine law which is identical with the entire Scripture (*vetus and nova lex*).

C. Pater finds in *Von Abtuhung der Bilder* not only a differentiation from Luther but also a guarded rejection of the Zwickau Prophets (see Lietzmann's edition, p. 15).

J. Wallmann raised the question whether a reversal in the Wittenberg Movement should be dated with Luther's Invocavit sermons. Wallmann refers to Karlstadt's complaint in *Von Abtuhung der Bilder* that in spite of the resolution of the council apropos images, there had still been no implementation (see Lietzmann's edition, pp. 20, 23). He relates this complaint to the almost simultaneous change in the Wittenberg council in which, under the new burgomaster (the former electoral councillor Christian Beyer) the painter Lukas Cranach and the goldsmith Christian Düring were elected to the council; as friends of images, they endeavored to oppose the implementation of the prohibition of images. Thus Luther was not recalled in February, 1522 by the same council which a month before enacted the Wittenberg order which was hostile toward images. Although Luther's preaching could only have dampened the Wittenberg disturbances, nevertheless one must consider whether a reversal in the politics of the Wittenberg council already accomplished before Luther's return did not merely become final through his preaching.

J.S. Preus expressed a positive attitude toward G. Fuchs' Marxist interpretation of Karlstadt according to which there was only a limited degree of difference between Karlstadt's radical middle-class Reformation and Luther's moderate middle-class Reformation, whereas both opposed the violence to which Müntzer would resort in carrying out his revolutionary program among the peasant and proto-proletarian classes. Fuchs' unqualified recognition of religious motivations in the Reformers is a refreshing revision of earlier Marxist interpretation. But by assessing Karlstadt's significance in the restricted and still imprecise context of class struggle and judging Karlstadt "apolitical", because he

did not join the rebellion, Fuchs underestimates the political significance (both secular and for church polity) of Karlstadt's role at Wittenberg and Orlamünde.

G.H. Williams commented on the typology of the Reformation
presented in his book, *The Radical Reformation* (1962). Whereas for
the years between the outbreak of Wittenberg radicality and his
settlement as professor in Basel, Karlstadt had been set forth in that
book as a "Lutheran Spiritualist" and at the Third Congress for Luther
Research in Jarvenpaa, as a "Revolutionary Spiritualist," Williams
acknowledged that Karlstadt during the *Wirren* was very much dependent upon magisterial sanction for the reforms in which he was briefly
engaged, and that he was a figure subject, indeed, to numerous trans-
formations and that accordingly he should, throughout the course of
his life, be classified successively in different typological categories, as
is indeed true of several others who passed in and out of the radical
phase.

Throughout the seminar, we felt it necessary to avoid the facile use of
terms such as spiritualism, legalism and biblicism. There were fifteen
participants in this seminar.